Praise for Michael Kalanty's

How To Bake *MORE* Bread

"Any serious bread baker will appreciate the deep knowledge Michael Kalanty brings to baking with natural fermentation. If you follow his meticulous instructions, little can go wrong. This is an expert guide, for baking students and aficionados alike."

MARIA SPECK, award-winning author of
Ancient Grains for Modern Meals and *Simply Ancient Grains*

"Michael Kalanty de-mystifies wild yeast fermentation with clear and expert guidance, inspiring all dedicated bread lovers. The well-tested formulas and delicious breads will be welcomed additions to any baker's repertoire. Including mine."

MARY KARLIN, author of *Artisan Cheese Making at Home*
and *Mastering Fermentation*

"Michael Kalanty is a terrific teacher, making the difficult suddenly accessible with a skillfully organized approach and delivery. In *How To Bake MORE Bread*, he deftly takes us into the world of naturally leavened, sourdough breads. And there's now no reason for anyone to ever doubt that they too can bake these extraordinary breads."

PETER REINHART, James Beard Award-winning author of
Bread Revolution, Artisan Breads Every Day,
and *Whole Grain Breads*

for Vaughn

A loaf of bread,

the Walrus said,

is what we chiefly need.

and made from wild yeast, you'll see*

is very good indeed.

Now, if you're ready, Oysters dear,

we can begin to feed.

from "The Walrus and the Carpenter" by
Lewis Carroll, *Through the Looking Glass*

*author's riff

Contents

The Breads

Foreword

There is something fantastically rewarding about baking bread that is leavened with wild yeast. Our devotion is fueled by the diversity of complex flavors and satisfying textures that these organisms lend to breads.

Using wild yeast to leaven bread is one of the oldest forms of baking—the first records of raised bread date back to ancient Egypt. The technique was discovered by accident, as many great culinary innovations are. Imagine the shock and delight of the first baker who pulled a fluffy sourdough from the oven instead of the flatbread that was typically produced. An obsession was born; its proliferation throughout the world was powered by both palate and necessity. Today, nearly every culture makes some form of sourdough and each variety reflects the history and products of that region.

Sourdough techniques have been refined over thousands of years. However, working with natural yeast starters can still seem complicated and intimidating.

Wild yeast floats in the air and occurs naturally in the flour we buy, but it must be harnessed and nurtured before it can contribute to a great loaf of bread. Bread baking is governed by microbes and chemical reactions, much of which originates in the ecosystem of a sour starter. Although maintaining a sour culture requires some understanding of these processes, success hinges equally on our skills as caretakers for tiny living organisms.

It's no wonder that Michael Kalanty has devoted an entire book to working with wild yeast. If this is your first book by Michael, you will soon discover why his approach to bread resonates with aspiring professionals and avid home bakers alike. And if you have read *How To Bake Bread*, you are now holding a copy of his second book for a reason.

In *How To Bake MORE Bread,* Michael expands his taxonomy of bread families to tackle the notorious subject of wild yeast doughs. His classification system helps make sense of the vast number of wild yeast breads and how the nuanced characteristics of each dough inform the entire baking process. He begins by teaching us how to capture roving spores of yeast. Then he guides us through the ins and outs of wild yeast starters, fermentation, shaping, proofing, and the final bake. We're given tools to evaluate doughs at each phase and make confident decisions about what techniques to use when we develop our own recipes.

Michael is a baker, but foremost, he's a teacher. A passionate student of bread, he has traversed the globe to study different recipes and techniques and is particularly knowledgeable about flavor and palate development. Ultimately, Michael measures his own success by the success of his students, and now his readers. His no-nonsense approach to designing the content of his classes is similar to how a scientist designs a solid experiment. The techniques and recipes he shares have been carefully distilled and tested so they are easy to replicate outside the classroom. At the same time, he also understands that *how* information is shared is equally as important as the content itself—he transforms book pages into a hands-on experience where we are able to touch our dough and taste our bread.

Nathan

Former chief technology officer of Microsoft, Nathan Myhrvold is founder of The Cooking Lab in Bellevue, Washington. He created and oversees *Modernist Cuisine*, a team of scientists, research and development chefs, and a full editorial department—all dedicated to advancing the state of culinary arts through the creative application of scientific knowledge and experimental techniques. He is coauthor of the James Beard award-winning *Modernist Cuisine: The Art and Science of Cooking* and *Modernist Cuisine at Home*, and author of *The Photography of Modernist Cuisine.*

De-Mystifying the Whole Process

Wild Yeast is found naturally on flour and all grains. When the flour gets wet, the yeast comes to life. First order of business for the yeast—find a food source and start eating.

The starch and sugars in the flour are the perfect food for the yeast. They eat it, digest it, and burp out bubbles of CO_2 to show their gratitude. Then they start to multiply.

It all happens by itself, and it happens all the time. It was happening over 5,000 years ago, which is the date historians cite for the first leavened breads.

Just about anyone can start a Wild Yeast Starter. The obstacle, it seems, is the wealth of information and resources about sour starters and sourdough breads. Having too much information can sometimes be confusing or even contradictory.

Starting a Wild Yeast Starter is simple, especially once you construct a filing system in your brain with separate drawers for how you think about this vast topic. Here's a quick summary of how the compartments of this book are arranged.

There are three chapters about the Wild Yeast Starter: ***Starting Out, Keeping it Alive,*** and ***Using It.*** Each chapter begins with useful background information, answering the most frequent questions for that topic. The chapter ends with the procedures, given with day-by-day details.

The useful ***Background Information*** section includes facts, details, and the reasons behind the process. This is the *cognitive* aspect of learning and will appeal to the detail-oriented part of your brain.

The **How To:** section includes the technical aspects of collecting wild yeast, what kind of flour to use, and where to store your Starter. This is the *psychomotor* part of learning. This information helps your hands understand a Wild Yeast Starter as an ingredient, something you touch, something you taste and smell.

What's Your Learning Style?

If you learn more comfortably by reading information before setting to work in the bakery, the background information gives you everything you'll need. Read this before you get your hands in the flour and water and you'll be more confident.

If you learn better by jumping into the flour and water, you can skip over the background information. Dive into the Day-by-Day procedures and then read the background information while your Starter is fermenting.

The two fit together like pieces of a puzzle. You can pick up either one first.

Wild Yeast—
Starting Out

- **How To: Collect Wild Yeast Cells and build a safe environment for them, using Flour and Water.**

Wild Yeast is found on the skins of fruits, vegetables, and whole grains. A quick way to isolate and capture the wild yeast is to put one of these ingredients in a container of water. For example, immerse a cup of red grapes in water for a few days. When the fruit is strained and discarded, you are left with water teeming with thousands of wild yeast cells.

Like most living organisms, the yeast cells need a temperate environment, water, oxygen, and a reliable food source to establish a colony. On a daily basis, you add fresh flour and water to the strained yeast water to nourish it.

Continue to add fresh flour and water daily, until you obtain a usable volume. For the formulas in this book, about two quarts of Starter mixture is the target volume.

To maintain this volume, without building more than you can use, you need to remove and use (or discard) some of the Starter before you feed it again with fresh flour and water. That's it.

At the end, you'll have a bubbling, active Yeast Colony.

The whole process takes about 9 to 10 days. This includes 3 days to collect enough wild yeast cells. At the end your Wild Yeast Starter displays consistent bubbling activity a few hours after it is fed. This is the visual sign you've successfully developed a strong colony of yeast cells.

The colony won't have a strong aroma or flavor profile just yet. You'll need another week to develop your Starter's flavor. The details of that stage are in Section 2, *Wild Yeast—Keeping It Alive.*

Section 1 is on pages 11 to 29.

Wild Yeast—Keeping It Alive

In this section, you'll establish a standard feeding regimen of fresh flour and water, along with a routine feeding schedule. Once you have a feeding program in place, your Starter can live indefinitely.

Now we can take a detailed look at the other microbes in your Starter. Bacteria have been in the Starter from the beginning of the process, busy setting up their own colonies. It's the Bacteria that are primarily responsible for the flavor profile of your Starter.

At the end of Stage II, your Starter will have a distinctive flavor, one that is unique to your local environment. At that point, the Starter is usually called a *Culture*.

Section 2 is on pages 31 to 50.

Wild Yeast— Using It

Section 3 shows you:

- **How To: Use Your Wild Yeast Culture to Bake Bread**

Like the other Families of Bread, the Wild Yeast Family has a Representative Bread. This is the *Pain au Levain,* a classic French hearth bread. Literally, the name means *Bread made from a Wild Yeast Culture.*

The *Pain au Levain* is explained with step-by-step techniques and photos. The other formulas in this section all rely on the same procedures. Once you have made the *Pain au Levain* a few times, your confidence will pay off with the other breads in this section.

Section 3 is on pages 51 to 56.

The *Basic Levain* Master Formula and Procedure
starts on page 59.

The *Pain au Levain* Master Formula and Procedure
starts on page 73.

The *Formulas* for more *Wild Yeast Breads*
start on page 137.

Here's the most frequently asked question I hear when baking with wild yeast—whether I'm working with new bakers or accomplished hotline chefs. Take a minute to read this and you'll get a sense of how simple the process is, even though you're working with a wild organism like Yeast.

Don't I Need a Scale to Weigh Ingredients?

A common mantra for baking and pastry work is that *Bakers always use a scale*. For creating the most consistent products, there is no denying that a scale is required.

But when you want to capture wild yeast and then feed it a routine diet of flour and water, your main concern is the vitality of the yeast colony. Not the exact amounts of flour and water.

During this first stage of starting a Wild Yeast Starter, it's fine to use a measuring cup for both the flour and the water. If you don't have a scale at hand, don't let that stand in your way of starting your own Starter.

Just take advantage of a natural phenomenon. Capture some yeast, put it in a jar. Give it food and water, it grows. That's part of the magic and mystery of a Sour Starter.

There is nothing especially critical in how you go about this. Yeast has been doing this on its own for thousands of years. There's no need to be overly precise.

All the yeast needs is its house to be cleaned routinely, and then to be fed more food and water. It doesn't really care about the measurements. In **Section 1—Starting Out**, the amounts of flour and water are listed in cups, because it's simpler.

If your Starter gets more flour one day, then it will be thicker. If it gets more Water the next day, then it will be thinner. The success of the first stage of your Starter depends on routine feeding, not exact measurements. Just like you, some days you'll eat a lot for dinner, some days you'll eat less. It's no more complicated than that.

Once you reach Day 6, you'll have a bubbling colony of yeast cells. Then, Yes! You do want to scale exact weights of water and flour. That's how you establish consistency in your Starter. Consistent texture in your Starter equals consistent flavor in your Breads.

You can weigh your ingredients from the beginning, if you choose. Some bakers get a better feel for the ultimate texture of the Starter by using a scale from Day 1. Other bakers watch the magic before their eyes and are content with scooping flour and water with a measuring cup until the mixture has the correct texture. Either way, the wild yeast will take hold and reward you with a bubbling, flavorful mixture to bake breads.

A Wild Yeast Culture

A Wild Yeast Culture

1. Starting Out

2. Keeping the Culture Alive

3. Baking with a Wild Yeast Culture

1 *Starting Out*

A *Sour Starter* is one of the oldest culinary ingredients. At the earliest of recorded time and most likely by accident, people discovered that when it was left on its own, a mixture of grain and water would start bubbling. They as likely didn't know that this bubbling was caused by the spontaneous action of microbes—*Yeast* and *Bacteria*, to be specific. They discovered that the bubbling mixture had better flavor and texture when it was then cooked. A process which they likely also discovered by accident when some of the wet grain mixture spilled onto hot stones or embers from a fire.

Trial and error probably taught them the mixture remained bubbly as long as they replenished it with some fresh grain and water. To keep the volume of the mixture from overtaking the size of their pottery, they learned to remove some of the mixture before adding more grain and water. This made it possible to share the mixture among the community.

Almost every region of the world has a culinary heritage that includes a *Sour Starter*. This magical bubbling mixture of grain and water was given many names. *Starter* or *Barm*. *Desem, Mother, or Madre.* No matter what it's called, it's still a Wild Yeast Starter and the oldest known way to make leavened bread. There are likely as many different styles for a Sour Yeast Starter as there are culinary traditions around the world.

Product ID—
A Guide to Yeast

There are two kinds of yeast used to ferment dough in a production environment: **commercial yeast** and **wild yeast.**

- **Saccharomyces cerevisiae**, abbreviated *S. cerevisiae,* is the more common type of *commercial yeast.*

- There are several kinds of **wild yeast** associated with Starters. They can be found in the whitish bloom on fruits like grapes and plums. Wild yeast is also found on the outside of whole grains.

Once flour and water are mixed with either kind of yeast, the Dough Fermentation process begins. Fermentation gives the bread baker two benefits:

- Leavening (Raising) the Bread Dough, and

- Producing Flavor Compounds in the Dough

Shelf Life & Storage

S. cerevisiae is a species of yeast that is commercially cultivated. It's the type used in much large-scale industrial bread production. It's similar to the type of yeast used in brewing wheat beers, ales, and porters. It is fast-acting and reliable.

It's available in Fresh, Active Dry, and Instant forms. Shelf life ranges from 21 days for fresh forms to 3 months or longer for dried forms. This type of yeast is used for all the formulas in *How To Bake Bread: The Five Families of Bread®.*

Compared to commercial yeast, the shelf life of a **wild yeast** colony is indefinite. It requires simple but routine care to maintain its health and vitality.

Fermentation Activity Rate

When breads use commercial yeast (*S. cerevisiae*), the fermentation rate is quick. This species of yeast was developed to speed the leavening proces. It quickly produces $CO2$, increasing the volume of the dough. Commercial yeast provides a modest flavor contribution to the dough.

When breads use wild yeast (*S. exiguus*), the fermentation rate is slower. $CO2$ bubbles are still created by wild yeast, but the leavening process takes longer. Because the process is longer, wild yeast fermentation allows more flavor compounds to develop in the dough.

Fermentation That's *Just Wild Enough*

When they have access to water, *Wild Yeast* microbes come back to life. They reanimate. They begin eating any available food source, like the simple sugar molecules contained in the flour. As time goes by, the hard-to-digest starches in the flour are broken into sugar molecules that the yeast can eat, too.

This is the process of *Wild Fermentation*. It needs no control or human intervention. It can happen spontaneously when yeast-covered foods get wet. Wheat, Corn, and Grapes are examples of foods that can start fermenting without any help from us.

Spontaneous (spon TA nee us)

Happening without visible influence or cause. Unplanned and without human interference. Self-generated.

This chapter shows how to take advantage of spontaneous fermentation in your classroom bakery or home kitchen, just by mixing flour and water. It's simple and straightforward. Once the yeast is collected, the process takes about 6 days. Nature does almost all the work.

All you need to do is feed the wild yeast some fresh flour and water each day and keep it safe from insects, fellow bakers, and extreme temperatures.

Grains, and the flour milled from them, are covered with three things:

- *Yeast*
- *Bacteria*
  and
- *Enzymes*

The first two are live organisms. They are in a state of suspended animation on the grain and in the flour, waiting. Add Water—the source of all Life—and the Yeast and Bacteria reanimate.

The last one on the list, Enzymes, is not a live organism. It's a sort of protein. Enzymes are important for the baker because they break starch molecules into sugars to fuel the fermentation process of the dough.

There are different kinds of Enzymes in the flour and each makes different sugar molecules when breaking down the complex starch. Some Enzymes create the sugar Glucose. Other Enzymes produce Fructose, Maltose, and Sucrose.

The reanimated Yeast cells are able to eat only a few selections from this buffet of sugar molecules. In a balancing act of Nature, the thriving Bacteria cells eat the other ones.

When Bacteria eat sugars, they produce Lactic Acid. Lactic Acid is a primary source of flavor development when foods are fermented. It should not be surprising that this type of Bacteria is called *Lactic Acid Bacteria.* Or *LAB's*, as they are often called.

Just Add Water . . .

Once the baker combines Flour and Water, a world of microbes comes to life.

Yeast cells start the fermentation process in the dough, LAB's produce flavor acids, and the Enzymes replenish the buffet line with assorted sugars.

and a Bread Baker

The *Craft* of baking bread is balancing these activities—by manipulating Time, Temperature, and the Type of Flour in the fermenting dough. How the bread baker goes about his craft—the choices that are made at each phase of the process, the aroma and flavor notes that are developed— this is the *Art* of baking bread.

I learned the procedure used in this book from Peter Reinhart when we worked together at the California Culinary Academy in San Francisco. I've adapted it for a bakery classroom where hands-on time is invaluable and where baking may not be possible on a daily basis. The feeding schedule described here, along with the formulas in the next section, is designed for a 5-hour class period, one or two days a week.

In the next section, you'll find Day-by-Day procedures to establish your own Wild Yeast Starter. At the end of this section, you'll have a bubbling, active Colony of Yeast Cells, as anxious as you are to bake bread.

Starting Out

How To: Build an Active Colony of Yeast Cells

1	Collect Natural Yeast	2 to 3 Days Before

Ingredients

1 cup Dark Raisins
4 cups H2O (60° to 70°F)
(See following note about using dechlorinated water)

Procedure

1. In a clean plastic container, combine Water and Raisins.
2. Cover loosely and set aside for 48 to 72 hours, keeping it 60° to 70°F.

Q: How Do I Collect Wild Yeast?

A: Soak Raisins in water.

In a clean plastic container, combine cool Water and Raisins. Cover the container to prevent other things from getting in.

Place the water and raisin container in a safe spot in your kitchen or bakeshop, away from foot traffic. The ambient temperature should be 60° to 70°F. After two to three days, the water will be teeming with wild yeast.

During the first 24 hours, monitor the temperature of the water. If it's warmer than 75°F, transfer the container to the refrigerator. To prevent spilling, place the water container inside a larger container with a flat bottom, like a 2- or 3-quart Lexan®, Cambro® or other commercial food storage container.

That's all. You don't need the water to change color or get darker. You don't need to actually see a collection of yeast cells on the surface. The cells are too small to see with the naked eye. But they're there.

Q: How Do I De-chlorinate Water?

A: Add Vitamin C or let it stand overnight.

If the water in your local area is highly chlorinated, the chemical will slow the action of the yeast. If you've not had good luck with a Wild Yeast Starter, you may need to use de-chlorinated water for this first stage. Just until the yeast colony can establish itself in your Starter. Here are two methods:

The passive method is to fill a container with tap water and leave it, uncovered, in sunlight for the day. Or, let it stand at ambient temperature in the bakeshop overnight so the chlorine evaporates.

A quicker method calls for dissolving some Vitamin C in the water. Because Vitamin C is an acid and lowers the pH of the water, too much can inhibit the growth of the yeast cells.

The amount of Vitamin C you'll need is determined by the amount of chlorine in your water. To use the Vitamin C method, you need to know the parts per million of chlorine in your water. Your local utility or water company can provide this information. Use the internet to find this information and the procedure for de-chlorinating water with Vitamin C.

1 Feed the Wild Yeast   Day 1

Ingredients

1 cup (strained) Raisin Water (60° to 70°F)
1 teaspoon Honey
1 cup Whole Wheat Flour (or White Bread Flour)

Procedure

1. Strain the Raisin Water and reserve it. Discard the fruit.
2. Measure 1 cup of Raisin Water and transfer it to a clean container. A disposable 1-quart plastic deli container is a good size to start with.
3. Blend Honey into the Raisin Water.
4. Add Flour.
5. Stir well.
6. Cover loosely and set aside for 24 hours, about 60° to 70°F.

Q: What Do I Do with the Leftover Raisin Water?

A: Discard it. Compost the raisins.

As a back-up measure in our bakery classroom, we keep this raisin water in the refrigerator for about a week after we start the project. If we have to start over, there's still some raisin water on hand. We discard it once the Starter is established.

Q: What Flour Should I Use?

A: A Yeast Starter can be established with almost any flour. Bread Flour and All Purpose are the better choices. The important thing is the starch—starch breaks down into sugars. Yeast eats sugar.

In a bakeshop, Whole Wheat Flour is recommended for the first feeding on **Day 1**. The whole wheat grain is covered with wild yeast cells. When the whole grains are ground, a large number of yeast cells remain in the flour. This additional yeast helps establish the colony.

Don't use flour that has been bleached or treated with chemicals to whiten its appearance. For example, some cake flours can be chlorinated. Some pastry flours, particularly those manufactured for biscuits and quickbreads, may also be chlorinated. Recall that chlorine can slow the action of the yeast or keep it from setting up its colony in the flour and water paste. Flours treated with bleaching agents develop a slight bitterness in the Starter, too.

1   Refresh the Environment for the Yeast   Day 2

STEP ONE:
Cleanse the Starter Mixture

1. Spoon off any dark grey liquid which may (or may not) appear on the surface of the Starter mixture.
2. Reserve half the Starter mixture in a small container. Discard the remaining Starter, which may include some sediment, too.
3. Thoroughly wash the original container, but don't bleach it.
4. Return the reserved mixture to the original container.

STEP TWO:
Re-build the Starter Mixture

Ingredients

1 cup Water (60° to 70°F)
1 cup Bread Flour (White Bread Flour—not Whole Wheat Flour—is all you need from this day forward.)

Procedure

1. Add the Water, then the Flour.
2. Stir well.
3. Cover loosely and set aside for 24 hours, about 60° to 70°F.

1 — Increase the Amount of Starter Mixture — Day 3

Ingredients

1 cup Water (60° to 70°F)
1 cup Bread Flour

Procedure

1. Add the Water, then the Flour.
2. Stir well.
3. Cover loosely and set aside for 24 hours, about 60° to 70°F.

Q: What should I look for on Day 3?

A: The mixture might still separate, leaving a small amount of liquid on top and sediment on the bottom.

If your mixture looks like this, cleanse it using the same procedure from **Day 2, Step One** (page 20).

If you began this project with a one-quart deli container, you'll need to transfer all the Starter mixture to its permanent home on **Day 3**.

Q: What Kind of Container Makes the Best Home for the Starter?

A: Plastic.

For the formulas in this book, a one-gallon (4-liter) plastic with a round base and a removable lid works well. It's a common size and can be found at a restaurant supply store or on the internet.

Plastic is the preferred material. Glass or ceramic may be used in your home kitchen, but these can break—worse, they can get small chips you might not see. Glass and ceramic containers are prohibited in professional foodservice operations.

The lid should be completely removable and easy to snap back in place. A removable lid is easier to keep clean. Your hands and other tools will be scooping into the Starter every day—make sure you have quick and easy access.

A round base, or footprint, is better than a square or rectangular one. When water and fresh flour are added to the container, it's easier to mix when the container is round. You get fewer lumps.

As a last consideration, select a narrow container, one which is *taller than* (or at least *as tall as*) *it is wide*. These proportions take less shelf space in your refrigerator. More importantly, a container which is taller than wide has less surface area. With a small surface area, less water evaporates and the top of the Starter stays moist instead of forming a crust.

To prep the container, wash it and its lid in hot soapy water. Rinse well and sanitize* them. Let the pieces air dry. Just before using them, rinse the container and the lid in cool, clean water. Dry the outside of the container but the inside can stay wet.

*Use a solution of 1 teaspoon household bleach in 1 quart cool water. Rinse very well with more clear water.

| **1** | **Set Up the Standard Volume** | **Day 4** |

Ingredients

3/4 cup Water (60 to 70°F)
1 cup Bread Flour

Procedure

1. Discard HALF the Starter mixture.
2. Add the Water, then the Flour.
3. Stir well.
4. Cover loosely and set aside for 24 hours, about 60° to 70°F.

Q: What Should I Look For on Day 4?

A: On Day 4, the mixture will appear more homogeneous. It won't separate nearly as much as it did earlier, and any dark gray liquid won't be as visible on the surface. If you continue to see liquid on the surface, cleanse the Starter before feeding it, using the procedure on page 20, **Day 2, Step One**.

A few hours after the Starter is fed on **Day 4**, it will rise to its highest level, stay at that level for 2 or maybe 3 hours more, and then recede, or deflate. To use a beach-side analogy, you'll see a *high tide line*, a ring left around the inside of the container.

The aroma will be milder now. It might still seem like beer, but you should be able to notice a slight fruitiness. Maybe citrus, especially lemon. Or maybe apple. These are two possible notes that might be detected at this stage. You may find other aromatic notes, because the starter process varies according to your region. Changing aroma is part of the discovery process when you establish a Wild Yeast Starter in your own bake shop or kitchen.

Q: *How Much Starter Should I Have?*

A: *By now, you'll have about 32 ounces of Starter mixture.* This is enough to make the two-bread yield for any of the formulas in this section or a single bread from two different formulas. For the formulas in this book, keeping more than 32 ounces of Starter on hand is wasteful.

On **Day 4**, begin the practice of discarding some of the Starter before feeding it. That's right. Stir it up first, to distribute the yeast, and then scoop half into the compost bin.

No need to be precise. Just estimate half the volume of the Starter. If you like, place a strip of masking tape on the side of the container so that the top of the tape marks half the volume of your Starter. This way, you will be removing about the same amount each time you do this step.

Add the Water and Fresh Flour for the **Day 4** Feeding. For easier mixing, thin the mixture by blending in the water first. Then, thicken it with the flour. Put the lid loosely on top and place the container in its fermentation area in the bakeshop or kitchen.

In 2 or 3 more days, your Starter will be established and have a predictable behavior and consistent aroma. That's when the half that's removed can be used to make simple breads or preparations like Pizza, Focaccia, and Pancakes. But not just yet.

| 1 | **Start the Routine Feeding** | **Day 5** |

Ingredients

3/4 cup Water (60 to 70°F)
1 cup Bread Flour

Procedure

1. Discard HALF the Starter mixture.
2. Add the Water, then the Flour.
3. Stir well.
4. Cover loosely and set aside for 24 hours, about 60° to 70°F.

Q: What Should I Look For on Day 5?

*A: **The Starter mixture behaves more consistently now**—* rising to pretty much the same level, keeping that level for a few hours, and then gradually receding. A rhythmic rise and fall of the Starter's volume is the best sign that you've established a strong yeast colony.

Today, repeat the same procedure from **Day 4**. Namely, stir the Starter to distribute the yeast cells. Remove enough of the mixture so its level drops to the half-way mark on your container. Add the Water to thin the mixture. Add the Flour to thicken it.

Replace the lid on the container and return it to its fermentation spot.

TroubleShooting

Begin to monitor the temperature of the mixture. Take a reading every eight or twelve hours, just to determine its average temperature.

The target temperature is 60°F. If your mixture's temperature averages more than five degrees warmer or cooler than the target, it's activity level and aroma profile will vary accordingly.

If it's much warmer, a beer-like aroma will be more dominant. The lemon or apple notes may not be detectable. The bubbles inside the mixture will be larger, the level will rise faster and a little higher, and it will deflate quicker than the example described here.

If it's much cooler than the target temperature, the bubbles will be smaller, the mixture will rise slowly, and it won't rise as high. It is less likely to deflate quickly, and the aroma notes of lemon or apple will be harder to identify. Also, there might be a starchy or paste-like aroma note in the mixture.

Correct the Situation

The easiest thing to change is the Water Temperature when you feed the Starter. Depending on your situation, raise or lower the temperature of your water by five degrees. If this doesn't correct the situation, find another location whose ambient temperature will keep your Starter closer to its 60°F target.

A Guiding Principle

Your Starter mixture might not behave precisely as described in this section. Remember, it's a colony of living microbes and responds to its environment.

If the Starter seems sluggish on **Day 5**, just follow the same feeding procedure for a few more days and the activity level should increase. If it still fails to show signs of activity, you may need to repeat the procedure from the beginning.

Before you re-start, read the FAQs in Section 2 (pages 40–50). You'll likely uncover the reason your Starter was having trouble.

1 Repeat the Routine Feeding — Day 6 and forever

Ingredients

3/4 cup Water (60° to 70°F)
1 cup Bread Flour

Procedure

1. Discard HALF the Starter mixture.
2. Add the Water, then the Flour.
3. Stir well.
4. Cover loosely and set aside for 24 hours, about 60° to 70°F.

Q: What Do I Look For on Day 6 and After?

A: The Starter should behave as it did on Day 5.

It should rise to the same height, remain stationary at that level for a few hours, and then gradually recede.

You'll notice more intense citrus or apple aroma notes. Perhaps your mixture offers a different note or two, grapefruit is a common note at this stage in the process.

Congratulations. Each time the environment is replenished and the yeast is fed, its rhythmic rise and fall reveals a strong and active yeast colony.

You've done it. Built a Wild Yeast Culture—just like the first bakers, thousands of years ago.

Baker's Note

Once you have a reliable and active Starter, turn to *Section 2, Wild Yeast—Keeping It Alive,* beginning on page 31. Moving forward, weighing ingredients on a scale is recommended instead of using measuring cups. Weighing ingredients is the baker's way of creating reliability and consistency in the Starter and all the breads made from it.

Q: *When Can I Use the Starter to Bake Bread?*

A: *If you observe the mixture rise and fall in the container, keeping a sort of rhythm, your Starter is strong enough to leaven all sorts of simple breads.*

Instead of using Active Dry, Instant, or even Fresh Cake forms of commercial yeast, you can use some of your Wild Yeast Culture.

The flavor will be mild and you won't get the sour intensity that comes with using an older, more mature yeast culture. But your Wild Yeast Colony is thriving and active enough to use.

Q: *What about Fruit Flies?*

A: *It's not unusual to find one or two fruit flies hovering over your Starter while it sits on a shelf in the bakeshop. All insects are a threat to food safety.*

Best practice: Especially during warmer weather, keep a lid on your Starter container whenever it is *on the floor.** If you still discover an inquisitive fruit fly or two, move the Starter to the refrigerator.

Q: *What Temperature Should the Starter Be?*

A: *Like any microorganism, yeast cells have a preferred temperature range. You can establish a Sour Starter at any temperature between 40° and 90°F. Within that, the preferred temperature range is 60° to 70°F.*

The steps described in Section 1 are designed for a 6-day process, keeping the Starter mixture near a target temperature of 60°F. A bakeshop with an ambient temperature of 60° to 70°F is ideal for this.

---

*On the floor is bakeshop lingo. It means *the item is @ ambient temperature. In a safe area and protected from contaminants.*

Warm temperatures make microbes work faster. Yeast cells pollute their environment with CO2 and alcohol faster than you can feed them. The environment becomes toxic to them. Their activity rate slows, some yeast cells die.

At 85°F, the Yeast is still able to establish a colony, but the Starter mixture develops off-flavors from the alcohol. Sometimes it smells like stale beer.

Correct the Situation

If the ambient temperature of your bakery or kitchen is warmer than 80°F, use a *warm-then-cool* routine with your Starter, like this:

Let the Starter mixture spend the first part of its day (the *warm* part*) on the floor*. Let it spend the rest of the day—and overnight—in the refrigerator or retarder. As long as the Starter spends an average of three or four hours *on the floor* daily, both you and the Yeast will be successful.

If you use this *warm-then-cool* routine, remove the yeast container from the refrigerator at the start of your shift. After an hour, the Starter will have lost its chill. It may not be as warm as 60°F, but what's important is that it's not at refrigerator temperature. Temper the Culture to about 60°F before you feed it.

Feed your Starter according to its daily schedule. Once the fresh flour and water are combined with the Starter, set the mixture aside for two to three hours before returning it to the refrigerator or retarder.

Two to three hours *on the floor* is enough for the yeast to start eating its new food supply, give off CO2 and Alcohol, and start to multiply once again. When the container is transferred to the cooler environment, the yeast activity continues. It just slows down.

Compared to another Starter that sits *on the floor* overnight at a constant temperature, the *warm-then-cool* Starter will appear less active. It's just cold. When it warms to ambient temperature it once again shows bubbling signs of life.

This *warm-then-cool* routine fits a five-hour shift.

Q: What If I Can't Feed the Starter Mixture Six Days in a Row?

*A: **If you've been unable to give daily care to your new Starter for the first 6 days, you should expect to find sediment at the bottom of your container and a layer of dark liquid on top.***

There likely will be a few fruit flies hovering nearby. And the whole mixture will probably smell like alcohol.

The Starter mix is overripe. The food source is depleted, the environment is toxic for the yeast cells. The yeast cells can still be revived from this situation, but it's easier to start over.

Scrape everything directly into the compost bin. Wash, rinse and sanitize the container. Let it dry thoroughly. Then start the process again.

2

Keeping the Culture Alive

At the end of Stage 1, the Starter is strong enough to replace commercial yeast in simple breads, especially flatbreads. The flavor profile of the mixture develops over the next week with routine feedings and a little care.

A Starter No Longer

In Stage 2, the Starter becomes a **Culture**. The difference is that in a Culture, the flour and water becomes home to another colony of microorganisms—*Bacteria.* They set up camp in the mixture, sharing the environment and food source with the wild yeast.

The bacteria contribute their varied flavor notes to the mixture while the wild yeast provide leavening power. Maintain a balance between these two colonies in your Culture and your breads will be well-textured and have complex flavor profiles.

This section shows how to develop a thriving bacteria colony in your Wild Yeast Starter. First, some background about the bacteria in your region.

LAB's—Lactic Acid Bacteria

Recall (from page 14, *Nature's Instant Bread Dough*), that the Wild Yeast and Bacteria found in flour reanimate once they get wet. Spontaneous fermentation of the flour begins.

Flour contains Enzymes that pre-digest the starch molecules, similar to the way Enzymes in saliva help pre-digest the food you're chewing so more nutrients are available to your body. In any flour/water mixture, Enzymes break down flour into smaller molecules of sugar. These sugars are quick food for the Yeast and Bacteria microbes.

There are a number of different bacteria strains found naturally in the flour. For breadbakers, the important ones are the Lactic Acid Bacteria. These are usually abbreviated as *LAB's*.

Fortunately for the baker, the LAB's work together with the Wild Yeast in what's called a symbiotic relationship.

During fermentation, LAB's create acid flavor compounds which give the dough complex aroma and flavor. These acids are the source of the sourness in the Starter and in your breads. The two categories of acid compounds important to bread bakers are **lactic acid** and **acetic acid**.

Symbiosis (sim bee O sis)

A relationship between two different kinds of living things that cooperate with each other and share a common environment.

A Symbiotic Pair:
Banana Slugs and California Redwood Trees

This bright yellow mollusk has no shell. It's found in the deep redwood forests of Central and Northern California.

The ancient redwood trees send up seedlings along the forest floor. Instead of eating them, the banana slugs clear the surrounding environment for the seedlings, eating the plants that compete with the redwoods for light, water, and nutrients. In return, the redwoods provide the slugs with the cool, moist habitat they need to survive.

The relationship between the humble banana slug and the coast redwood is a valuable and long-standing one. In an unusual and endearingly quirky choice, the University of California, Santa Cruz, nestled among these ancient giants along the California coast, adopted the slimy, bright yellow banana slug as its mascot.

The Changing Aroma from Stage 1 to Stage 2

In **Stage 1**, the first six days of your Starter, the Yeast is hard at work setting up a colony in the flour paste. Yeast digests the available sugars and gives off alcohol in the process. A dominant aroma of the flour/water paste during this stage is beer.

By the end of the first six days, the action of the Yeast becomes more predictable. A routine is established within the colony. The alcohol aroma is still present but its character, or style, has changed. It seems more like wine now. And its intensity is lower.

Meanwhile, recall that Bacteria are also found naturally on flour.

In **Stage 1**, the Bacteria establish their own colony in the Starter. In fact, they are more effective than the Yeast at setting up their community and can do it in about half the time that it takes the Yeast.

When you first detect slight notes of citrus or tree fruits like apple, that's the signal that the Bacteria colony has taken hold in your Starter. But the Yeast colony is still establishing itself—the alcohol aroma from the Yeast still dominates the aroma profile.

In **Stage 2**, local Bacteria in your environment set up colonies of their own in your Starter. The bacteria vary from one starter to another. The particular combination yours will have depends on *how often* you feed it, *how much* you feed it, *in what temperature range* you maintain it, and *how long* you ripen it.

Stage 2 takes about six days more, maybe ten in colder months. During **Stage 2**, you can smell the changing aroma in your Starter as notes like apple and grapefruit become even more prominent.

Local Bacteria Provide Complex Aroma and Flavor

Some parts of the world have given rise to specific fermentation procedures that foster unique combinations of local Bacteria and other micro-organisms. These combinations ferment certain foods into products that have become world famous and have a distinctive flavor of the region where they are produced.

GOVERNMENT-CONTROLLED LABELS

French food heritage includes appreciating a food or beverage for the qualities it derives from its region of growth. This is what is meant by *terroir*.

This concept is the foundation of the French classification and labeling system known as *appellation contrôlée* (*controlled name*).

The statement that the beverage called *Champagne* can originate only in the region of France with the same name is an example of *appellation contrôlée*. In contrast, a bubbly wine from another region is correctly classified as a sparkling wine, according to the philosophy of *terroir*.

Terroir (tare WAHR)

The word *Terroir* usually describes a vineyard and the character of the wine it produces. The term refers to the flavors and mouthfeel of a wine that are distinct to grapes grown in that region of the world.

Terroir comes from the French word for earth, *la terre*, which is the base for other words like *terra cotta* or *terrine*.

Appellation Contrôlée foods are produced according to terms defined by the French government.

The low-moisture, dense butter with its slight saltiness produced in the northwest region of France is the only product that can be labeled *la Beurre Normande* (Normandy Butter) in France. In American grocery stores, the European product *Plus Gras*® is an example of this style of butter.

The label *Roquefort* can only be applied to cheese aged in the prehistoric caves in the south of France near the town of the same name. Local bacteria and yeast molds give this sheep's milk cheese the chalky, mineral character that marks an authentic Roquefort.

These foods reveal the intricacy, variety, and pride that is the French concept of local flavor. *Terroir*.

DENOMINAZIONE DI ORIGINE CONTROLLATA, D.O.C.

Italy has a comparable system for its food products, called **DOC** (*Controlled Label of Origin*). At the highest quality level within this system is the label **DOCG** (see pull-out).

The emblem with the rooster found on some bottles of Italian red wine can only be applied to *Italian Chianti Classico* wines whose grapes are from, and whose production is carried out entirely within, the legal boundaries of the province of Tuscany.

Bread holds such a revered position in Italian cuisine that the government has created a unique guarantee to protect the heritage of its regionally produced breads. This is the designation **igp.**

When **igp** is used to identify an Italian bread, it designates not only its region of origin but also a formula and procedure that have been sustained through centuries of baking. **Igp** represents the Italian pride of place for locally produced foods.

Pane Casereccio di Genzano is an example of an **igp** product. Known familiarly as the *Pope's bread*, it can be officially baked only in Genzano, the small town located about 19 miles south of Rome. The baker's percent for water and for salt are a matter of public record, along with the minimum fermentation time of the *Biga*, a type of yeast starter used in Italy.

An **igp** bread is part of the cultural and economic backbone of its community. *Pane di Genzano* evokes a heritage and a history, a tradition that is as unique as the town where the bread is baked.

DOCG

DOCG stands for *Denominazione di Origine Controllata e Garantita* and means *identification of origin checked and guaranteed.* It's the consumer's guarantee that the food product is what it says on the label and that it comes from the area specified.

On a wine bottle, for example, this label indicates the producers followed the strictest regulations possible to make that wine. The wine was tested by a committee that guaranteed the geographic authenticity of the wine and its quality. Only a handful of Italian wines qualify for **DOCG** status.

Getting Ready for This Section—
Controlled Fermentation

Better flavor in your breads is achieved with consistent care of your Wild Yeast Culture. The next section shows easy ways for you to do this. You'll find answers to a lot of frequently asked questions. And lots of information about what's going on at the microbe-level in your Starter.

At the end of this section, you'll have confidence in the leavening power of your Wild Yeast Culture and you'll be proud of its unique aroma and flavor profile. You'll be ready and anxious to bake the variety of wild yeast breads included in the formula section.

Sorting through and organizing the vast amount of information on yeast and bacteria cultures was a challenge. The author is indebted to Megan Fisklements, Ph. D., from U.C. Davis, and to Sandor Ellix Katz for their cheerful assistance and sharp eye in preparing this chapter. For a more scientifically precise description of the whole process, pick up a copy of Mr. Katz's New York Times Bestseller, *The Art of Fermentation*, Chelsea Green Publishing, 2012.

Keeping the Culture Alive

When the Starter reaches a consistent activity level, it's called a *Culture*. With proper care are routine feedings, a Wild Yeast Culture can be sustained indefinitely.

To sustain the Wild Yeast Culture, a baker uses a 3-step system.

A	Divide It . . .

A1	Reserve 1/3 of the Culture . . .

Before any dough mixing is begun on a given production day, a small portion of the fermented Culture is removed from its original container. It's put aside in a safe place. This can be a separate area of the bakeshop or sometimes back in the refrigerator, if the ambient temperature of the bakeshop is higher than 75°F.

A2   and use 2/3 of the Culture to make breads

At the end of the production workday, whatever has not been used from the larger portion of Starter can be discarded or composted. Recall that throughout the day, the Culture continues to ferment. Its flavor profile becomes more pronounced while its leavening power slowly decreases. If left long enough, the Culture can over-ferment.

In a production environment, over-fermented Culture causes product inconsistency and disrupts the schedule. Leftover Culture is discarded or composted if unused by day's end.

In your home kitchen, any unused Culture can certainly be saved, especially if this would otherwise seem wasteful. In a shop, the baker might keep some unused Culture on hand for a small project or to do formula testing. But it won't go back into the Culture used for production.

B   Feed It . . .

Recall that some of the Culture is being kept safe, away from the production area. Before the shift ends, this reserved portion is rebuilt to its original amount. The Culture is given water and fresh flour. In baker's language, this is called *Replenishing the Culture.*

Replenish

In casual language, the routine re-building of a Sour Starter with fresh flour and water is called *Feeding the Starter.*

In technical articles and in commercial production, this process is called *Replenishing the Culture.*

Ripe = Proper Fermentation

Each time the Culture is given Fresh Flour and Water, it needs to ferment before you can use it. Once the Fermentation Stage is completed, the Culture is aromatic and bubbling with activity. A baker says that the Culture is *ripe*.

Always use a *ripe* Culture to produce consistent flavor and texture in your breads. (Specific steps for ripening your Culture are described later in this section.)

C		& Ferment It

The mixture ferments for 2 to 3 hours *on the floor*. After that, it is transferred to the refrigerator or retarder to complete the *Cool Fermentation* for 8 hours or more. (Much more detail about fermenting the Culture follows.)

**The next day, the Culture is ripe,
and can be used for bread production.**

The entire process—Steps A, B, and C—is repeated.

Be Consistent

Consistency is the key to sustaining your Culture. Like many living organisms, the Yeast performs better when it has a routine. Feed the Culture regularly and your breads will reward you with consistent flavor and texture.

Guidelines for Sustaining your Wild Yeast Culture

I	Schedule	Get your Culture on a routine schedule.
II	Flour	Weigh your Culture* before you feed it. Match its weight with Fresh Flour. When you replenish, the Fresh Flour weighs the same as the reserved Culture. (*This assumes you've already separated 2/3's of the ripe Culture needed to bake your breads for the day.)
III	H2O	Give your Culture **5 parts H2O** to **4 parts Fresh Flour**.
IV	Fermentation	Use the 2-stage fermentation schedule for your Culture: **Stage 1:** 2 hours on the floor and then . . . **Stage 2:** 8 to 22 hours or longer, in the refrigerator or retarder.
V	Tempering	Bring your ripe Culture to 60°F before using it.

FAQs

Baker's Tip

Prevent scaling mishaps, write the *Feeding Ratio* on the side of your container.

Q: How Often Do I Need to Divide and Feed My Culture?

A: Select a routine that fits your schedule.

Feed your Culture based on how often you use it. Most bakeries feed their cultures daily. If the production load is large, they may feed the culture twice a day. Small bakeries can feed their yeast culture every other day. In your home, the Culture can be replenished twice or even once a week. The frequency of feedings can vary to fit any situation.

Q: When I Feed It, How Much Fresh Flour Does My Culture Need?

A: Use a ratio of 1 part Fresh Flour to 1 part Culture.

Always use weight, like ounces and pounds. Don't use volume, like cups or quarts. If you have four ounces of Culture to feed, you need four ounces of Fresh Flour. With this system, you are always replenishing the Culture with a consistent amount of food—a percent based on the actual weight of the Culture.

Feeding Ratio

When replenishing a Wild Yeast Culture, the amount of water compared to the amount of fresh flour is called the **feeding ratio**. For example, **five** ounces of water and **four** ounces of fresh flour is a **feeding ratio** of **5 to 4**.

Q: How Much H2O Does My Culture Need?

A1: Use a ratio of 5 parts H2O to 4 parts Fresh Flour when you feed your Culture.

For example, for 5 pounds of water, use 4 pounds of fresh flour. Or 500 grams of water to 400 grams of flour. Weighed in ounces, pounds or grams—the **Feeding Ratio** is constant.

This 5 to 4 ratio works well in a classroom bakeshop or a home kitchen—it's quick to measure and easy to mix. *The Culture in this book uses the Feeding Ratio of 5 to 4.*

It works no matter how much Culture you have on hand:

	Example A	Example B
IF:		
Reserved Culture weighs	400 grams	100 grams
THEN:		
H2O weighs	500 grams	125 grams
Fresh Flour weighs	400 grams	100 grams

A2: Hydrate your Culture @ 125% whenever you feed it.

Within the industry, bakers talk about their Cultures in terms of hydration—the baker's percent of water to flour. *The Culture in this book has a hydration of 125%.*

With Baker's Percent, you can easily calculate how much water and flour you need to replenish *any* amount of Culture. In this example, suppose you have reserved 300 grams of Culture. To replenish it, follow these steps:

	Procedure	Example	
1	Weigh the Culture.	*300 g*	*Culture (Reserved)*
2	Weigh an equal amount of Fresh Flour and set it aside.	*300 g*	*Fresh Flour (New)*
3	Weigh the H2O: A. Multiply the weight of the Flour by 1.25 B. In this example, that's 375 g C. Scale 375 g H2O and set that aside.	300 g $\times 1.25$ $= 375 \text{ g}$ $= 375 \text{ g}$	*H2O (New)*
4	Replenish the Culture: A. Thin the Culture with the H2O, B. Thicken the Culture by adding the Flour, C. Stir well.	*= 975 g*	*TOTAL* *Replenished Culture*

(For more about Baker's Percent, see Appendix 1)

Photo Gallery #1   Quick Steps for Routine Feeding

A: No. The replenished Culture must Ferment before you can use it.

Once it's fed, the Culture is diluted with fresh flour and water and it does not contain enough yeast cells to effectively leaven a main dough. About half of the aroma and flavor compounds have been removed from the Culture, too. To re-energize the yeast activity and to develop its full flavor, Ferment the Culture each time you feed it.

Ferment the Culture at 2 Different Temperatures

- Stage 1--*Floor Time* @ 70° to 80°F
- Stage 2--*RFG (Refrigerator) Time* @ 35° to 50° F

The Baker's Strategy

The Yeast and the Bacteria colonies prefer different temperature ranges. By changing the temperature of the Culture from ambient temperature to refrigerator temperature, the baker supports the symbiotic relationship between these micro-organisms.

Warm temperatures favor the Yeast Colony

In your bakeshop or kitchen, an ambient temperature of 70° to 80°F is desirable. This relatively warmer environment boosts the activity of the Yeast as it eats the new sugars.

Cool temperatures favor the LAB Colony

Refrigerator temperatures should range from 34° to 38°F. If you have a Dough Retarder, set it at 50°F.

The LAB's prefer cooler temperatures. The cool temperature slows the activity of the Yeast, giving the LAB's time to develop more flavor acids in the dough.

Q: I Fed My Culture Yesterday, then I Fermented It. Now Can I Use It?

A: Not just yet. Let the Culture lose its chill after you remove it from the refrigerator.

Temper the Yeast Culture

When it's cold, a Culture is thick, hard to mix, and does not blend uniformly in a main dough. Let it come to ambient temperature for an hour before using it.

If you need it sooner than that, place the container in a bain marie filled with water that is 90°, but no hotter. To keep the container from tipping over and collecting water from the bain marie, put a light weight on top of it. A small plate that sits flat is usually enough.

When there's too much water in the bain marie, the container can bobble and float. This is a dangerous situation for your Culture. Remove some of the water from the bain marie and place a heavier weight on top of the container.

After 15 minutes, stir the Culture with a spoon. Let it stand 15 minutes more, re-warming the water in the bain marie if needed.

The Culture should be 60° or a few degrees warmer when you use it. Stir it once more before measuring what you need. Re-distributing the yeast and LAB colonies before measuring the Culture brings consistent flavor and leavening to your doughs.

Q: Can't I use the Culture directly from the refrigerator? What if I'm in a hurry?

A: You certainly can use the Culture directly from the refrigerator if your schedule is tight. One way is to use warmer water when mixing ingredients for the main dough. The temperature of the Culture rises as you combine it with the other ingredients.

Using hot water to mix dough is a quick fix. But it doesn't develop your skill as a baker. A baker's goal is to create a rhythm within the breadbaking practice, not to rush through steps trying to adjust things along the way. Schedule time to temper your Culture.

Is My Wild Yeast Culture Ripe?

Because they survive shipping better that way, the bananas that arrive at your local grocery store are often under-ripe. The fruit is firm and the flavor notes have low intensity. There's a raw, unripe character to the aroma profile.

Ripening the banana is left to you. Ripening is the job of the naturally occurring enzymes on the fruit. Whatever method you choose, you're giving them the time and favorable conditions to soften the banana's texture and develop its flavor.

A ripe banana has a creamy mouthfeel and a sweet, round, and complex flavor. Similar to the mouth drying sensation of red wine, there's a touch of astringency in the finish. The aroma is sweet, earthy, and there's a note of honey. You've got to seize that moment when the fruit is ripe.

If not, the enzymes continue to ripen the fruit. The texture becomes mushy, the surface of the banana turns brown, and there's an alcohol off-note in the aroma.

At this stage, the fruit is over-ripe. It's still edible and makes very flavorful Banana Pancakes or Muffins. But its chance to appear in a showcase venue like a tropical fruit tart or pattern the meringue topping of a cream pie has passed.

Your Wild Yeast Culture goes through a similar ripening process. When it's just been fed, you can still detect the culture's aroma notes, but their intensity is diminished. The fresh flour adds a raw character to the aroma and flavor profile. At this stage the culture is analogous to the hard, non-aromatic banana you've just brought home from the grocery store.

As the Wild Yeast Culture ferments, the acid intensity develops. You can discern aroma notes unique to your environment. Notes like apple, white wine, yogurt, or grapefruit. Use the culture when it's ripe and it reveals its full aroma and flavor character in your breads.

The culture can over-ripen if it sits too long. The flavor notes intensify, an alcohol off-note develops, and the acidity dominates. Altogether, these notes overpower the delicate aroma and flavor profile of the fermented wheat flour in the culture. When you use an over-ripe culture to make a dough, the sour taste overpowers the fermented wheat flavors of the bread's interior and the caramelized sweetness of the crust.

Give your culture time to ripen. Use it at its peak of flavor so it makes the best contribution to your breads.

**The same principle applies to ripening a Basic
Levain before using it to make a main dough.**

At a temperature of 60° to 70°F the Culture is pliable, even pourable. When combining ingredients, a quick gesture disperses the Culture in the water. It blends evenly when the flour is added.

When you carry out the Phases of Bread in a gentle, rhythmic way—especially Ingredient Mixing, Development, and Shaping—the improvements in texture and flavor bring a quality to the final loaves that is more than the sum of its parts.

Use ingredients at correct temperatures.
A Hotline Analogy

Forget about the yeast cells and LAB's for a minute. Picture how you combine ingredients when you're cooking. A Hollandaise sauce, for example.

Warmed, melted butter @ 145°F* is whisked into an equally warmed base of egg yolk and lemon juice. Done. Ready to serve!

Cool melted butter, at 70°F, can also be emulsified. But in the end, the Hollandaise sauce will be cold. It will need time and more of your attention to be brought to a correct temperature before you can serve it.

*The Professional Chef,
Culinary Institute of America,
9th Edition by Wiley

Q: *It Seems Like I'm Throwing Out a Lot of Unused Culture!*

A: **To control food costs in a production environment, the amount of discarded Culture should be kept as small as possible.**

It's easy to put controls in place so you have enough for your baking needs without being wasteful. Here are two techniques for a classroom bakeshop or home kitchen:

Mark the *Fill Line* on the Container

To keep a consistent amount of Culture on hand, put a mark on your container to indicate the halfway level. This is the *Fill Line*.

A piece of masking tape wrapped around the container is a quick way to standardize how much Culture you need before replenishing.

With a *Fill Line* in place, the baker scoops portions of the Culture as needed throughout the day. By the end of the shift, the volume of Culture in the bucket will be to the **Fill Line**. If there's still too much, he scoops until the level of the Culture matches the **Fill Line**. Excess Culture is composted or shared.

Subtract the *Tare Weight* of the Container

Say your **container weighs 4 ounces**. When you place it on a scale, the scale reading will always include those four ounces of the container's own weight. Whether the container is empty or full.

When it's time to replenish your Culture, follow these steps:

1 Zero your scale.

2 Place the container—and however much Culture is in it—on the zeroed scale. In this example, let's say the **Culture and container together weigh 10 ounces**.

3 **Subtract 4 ounces from the 10 ounces.**
(Recall that the *tare weight* of the container is 4 ounces.)

4 **That leaves 6 ounces of Culture in the container.**

Q: What if I Already Have a Starter from another Baker or Chef. Can I use It for the Formulas in this Book?

A: Yes. But . . .

Any Starter that is viable can be used for the bread formulas in this section. This *new* Starter, let's call it **Starter X**, must be modified so its hydration is 125%. That means **Starter X** is replenished, or fed, with 5 parts of Water for every four parts of Flour.

Here's a quick way to change the hydration of *Starter X* **so it is the same as the Culture used in this book.**

1. Place a container on a sale. Zero the scale.

2. Add the **Starter X** to the container. Note its weight.

3. Separately scale the same amount of Fresh Flour. Set it aside.

4. Multiply the weight of the **Starter X** by 1.25. Scale the same amount of Water.

5. Add the Water to **Starter X**. Blend. Add the Flour. Blend.

6. Ferment as usual. **Starter X** can be used the following day.

Baker's Note

The procedure on this page is an approximation and is useful for a small amount of Starter Culture. It's quick to use and gets any other Starter ready for the formulas in this book within 24 hours.

With only one feeding, this method doesn't give your new Starter an exact hydration of 125%. But it's quite close and works for the formulas in this book. With each feeding after that, the hydration of the new Starter gets closer to 125%.

More precise (and complicated) methods for changing the hydration of a Culture can be found online and in technical resources. The more precise you need to be, the more intricate will be the math.

*A: **Probably not. But it will take some attention to revitalize it.***

When storing your Culture for a long time, you may encounter Surface Mold and a build-up of Alcohol. You can save a dormant Culture from these situations and revitalize it with a 2-step process.

There are two steps to revitalizing a dormant Yeast Culture:

1. Cleanse the Culture

and

2. Re-Build the Culture

Through another miracle of nature, an active Yeast Colony can defeat many other invading micro-organisms. But when it becomes dormant, especially during long-term storage, other microbes can invade the sleeping Colony's home.

Mold can establish its own colony on the surface of a dormant Yeast Culture. It's easy for these invaders to set up camp in the airspace between the top of the Culture and the lid of its container. All these surfaces—the underside of the lid, the walls of the container and the perimeter of the culture itself—are potential territories for invading microbes.

Dormant

Definition: Not currently active, but capable of becoming active. Like a *dormant* volcano that could erupt at any time.

When Yeast and Bacteria are *dormant*, they are in a state of suspended animation. They aren't active but they're still alive.

Cleanse the Culture

If you discover Surface Mold on your culture, use a damp paper towel to wipe away as much as possible from the inside wall of the container. Discard the towel and wash your hands.

Run a teaspoon under cool water and spoon off and discard an inch or more from the top of the Culture to reveal the clean, light tan mixture below. Scoop out a half cup or so of this clean Culture and transfer it to another container.

Compost the rest of the Culture. Clean and sanitize the original container. Flush it well with clear water and return the reserved Culture to it.

FOOD SAFETY WARNING: If you see any bits of yellow, orange, or reddish growth on your culture or on its container, discard the culture entirely.

If the container is re-usable, wash it in hot soapy water. Rinse it. And then sanitize it. Allow the container to dry throughly overnight. Rinse it with clear water once again before using it for your Culture.

If you are in doubt or in any way hesitant about the food safety of your Culture, better to throw the entire thing away.

Alcohol Build-Up

A gray liquid collects on the top of the Culture during long-term storage under refrigeration. Known as *hootch,* this dark liquid is alcohol. If you feed your Culture daily, you likely won't see this murky liquid.

Depending on your feeding schedule, you may sometimes find more or less hootch. If small amounts accumulate, just spoon them off and discard them.

An eighth-inch layer or more of hootch is a sign that your Culture has over-ripened. The Yeast are sluggish or even dormant, but they're alive. The Culture must be revitalized before it can be used.

Here's what to do:

Cleanse the Culture

When hootch appears, carefully remove it. Either ladle or spoon it. Sometimes, the top of the Culture itself has a grayish or even black appearance, depending on the last time it was fed. Carefully spoon away as much of this dark layer as needed until you can see the creamy, light tan Culture beneath the surface layer.

Baker's Tip

When a Yeast Culture is stirred, it's harder for Surface Mold to form. Develop a habit of stirring your Culture every day, even if you don't divide and replenish it daily.

How To Revitalize a Dormant Culture

1. CLEANSE THE CULTURE

To cleanse your Culture after a prolonged rest period, simply siphon or spoon off the surface mold and/or alcohol and discard it. Then scoop off and discard all but about a half-cup of the creamy, tan Culture.

Wash and sanitize the container. Flush it once again with clear water and return the reserved Culture to the container.

2. RE-BUILD THE CULTURE

Allow 3 days of routine Feeding (Replenishing) for your culture to regain its leavening power and flavor profile.

The longer the Culture has been dormant, the more days of routine feeding it will need before it's a reliable leavener for your breads. A Culture that has been dormant for three months or longer needs 6 or 7 days of routine feedings before its characteristic flavor profile returns.

Baker's Note

Store some back-up Culture in your freezer. To use it, thaw the Culture and then feed it for 3 or 4 days. It is soon teeming with yeast bubbles, LAB's, and familiar aroma notes.

3

Baking with a Wild Yeast Culture

The World of Levains

Levain is a French term referring to a naturally fermented leavener that's used to make a main dough. The classic French *Pain au Levain* literally translates to *bread made with a natural leavener*.

When making a Levain, the ratio of water to flour to wild yeast culture can vary. As strict as classic French culinary guidelines can sometimes be, there are few rules when it comes to making a Levain.

The hydration of the Levain can vary. There are *Stiff Levains* with hydrations as low as 55%. To visualize just how firm this is, recall that dense, firm Bagel dough has a hydration of 56%. There are *Liquid Levains* with hydrations as high as 120%. The Wild Yeast Culture in this book has the same thickness.

The flavor of the Levain varies. Some bakers routinely make their Levains from whole grain flours—wheat, rye, or oats. Some use strictly white flour.

The acid profile of the Levain can be manipulated simply by adjusting its fermentation schedule. Levain fermented for 18 hours at 50° has a different acid character than one that ferments 6 hours at 70°. To distinguish acid characters in bread, see the section on *Palate Development*, pages 210–211.

This gives artistic choice to the baker. Simply by using a different Levain, a baker can bring a variety of flavor and texture profiles to his breads.

Culinary Analogy—The Roux

The roux, pronounced ***Roo***, is a thickener for a sauce, soup, or other flavorful liquid, like pan drippings that are made into a gravy. It's made from equal measures of fat and flour that are cooked together in a saucepan before the liquid is added. In classic French cuisine the fat is Butter.

There are three types of roux: *White*, *Blonde*, and *Brown*. In addition to the color, each brings unique aroma and flavor notes to the liquid it ultimately thickens. How to cook and use the roux, plus other foundation practices of the Saucier*, are strictly proscribed in ***Le Guide Culinarie*** by Escoffier** and are still practiced by generations of classically trained chefs.

A *White Roux* is cooked for 2 to 3 minutes. It thickens Milk into a White Sauce called a *Sauce Béchamel* (**Bay** sha mel).

A *Blonde Roux* is cooked for 5 to 6 minutes, time enough to encourage aroma notes of lightly toasted hazelnuts from the flour. Chicken stock thickened with a blonde roux is called *Sauce Velouté* (**Veh** loo tay).

A *Brown Roux* is cooked for 8 to 10 minutes. The toasted flour develops notes of caramel, toasted bread, or the flavor of the grill marks on a steak. Use a brown roux to thicken beef or game stock or even chicken stock made from roasted

---

* In the hierarchy of the the classic French kitchen, referred to as *la Brigade de Cuisine*, the *Saucier*'s role is to prepare master sauce bases called *Mother Sauces*. During hours of service, the *Saucier* makes *à la minute* modifications to individual portions of these *Mother Sauces* to accompany menu items. For example, a whole cauliflower may be topped with *Sauce Mornay*, a Béchamel flavored with Gruyère or similar cheese, and then baked.

** Georges Auguste Escoffier compiled ***Le Guide Culinaire*** (*The Culinary Guide*) to codify preparations and procedures for the French restaurant kitchen. It first appeared in 1903 and is a benchmark for classic French culinary arts. Many of Escoffier's principles continue to influence the basic curriculums of professional culinary schools.

poultry bones, like the rich stock found in Cajun/Creole cooking. Thickening a Browned Veal Stock with this roux creates a *Sauce Espangnole* (Es pan **yole**).

Functionally, the roux thickens a liquid. From a sensory perspective, the initial cooking of the roux contributes specific aroma, flavor, and textural attributes to the sauce or soup it's used to thicken.

To follow the roux analogy, the function of the Levain is to leaven the main dough, opening its interior structure to large, irregular air cells. On a sensory level, it brings a unique flavor profile and acid character to the bread depending on the type of Levain the baker selects.

Each combination of a Levain's hydration, the type of flour it uses, and its additional fermentation time develops specific aroma and flavor notes. Building flavors by using different Levains is an integral aspect of the baker's craft.

The following Levains are used in this book. They give a broad representation of flavor possibilities and can inspire your further development as a bread baker.

Collection of Levains

Basic Levain (White Flour)

Barley Levain

Whole Wheat Levain

Rye Levain

Spelt Levain

1-Build Levain (White Flour)

2-Build Levain (White Flour)

Baking with a Wild Yeast Culture

Once it is established, the Wild Yeast Culture can be used to make a main dough. The yeast provides leavening power so commercial yeast is not required. The LAB colony delivers a distinctive flavor profile. Many naturally fermented breads are made directly from a Wild Yeast Culture.

Often, a baker builds additional flavor notes and types of acidity into the culture instead of using it as is. He does this through a system of *Builds* or *Elaborations*.

A *Build* is a *derivative*, or *secondary*, culture that has a unique feeding formula and fermentation schedule. Instead of all white flour, for example, a portion of the Wild Yeast Culture can be fed 95% White Flour and 5% Rye. It is fermented for 5 hours more at 70°F and then spends additional time in the refrigerator or cooler.

The result is called a **Levain**. Once the Levain is ripe (that is, has completed its full fermentation) it is used to make a main bread dough, like a *Pain au Levain, Honey Rye Bread,* or *Oatmeal & Raisin Porridge Bread* and the other breads in this book.

This extra step of *building* develops a more complex flavor profile in the final dough. The process also tempers the acidity of the Wild Yeast Culture.

The *build* energizes the colony of wild yeast cells, too. This makes a Levain more reliable in leavening a main dough than using the Wild Yeast Culture itself.

The breads in this book follow this sequence:

Step 1   Build a *Levain* from the Culture

This section shows you how to build a **Basic Levain**. The procedure is similar for the other flavor Levains you'll find in this book.

Step 2   Make a *Main Dough* from the Levain

Following this section, the **Master Formula for Wild Yeast Bread** shows you how to prepare the classic French *Pain au Levain*. The procedure is similar for all the breads in this book.

Master Formula for Wild Yeast Levain

Wild Yeast Levain

BASIC LEVAIN

Family: Wild Yeast Dough

		8-hour shift ddt°= 70°F	5-hour shift ddt°= 76°F
	Mise en Place	H2O @ **70°**; Starter Culture @ 70°	H2O @ **84°**; Starter Culture @ 70°

Wild Yeast Culture

The Culture must be ripe to make a Basic Levain. To test for ripeness, refer to the notes on pages 38, 42, and 44.

Temper the Wild Yeast Culture

Remove the Wild Yeast Culture from the refrigerator or retarder at least 1 hour before using it so it comes to ambient temperature.

If you need to temper (i.e., *warm*) the Culture quickly, use the procedure on page 43.

Water Temperature

For a 5-hour shift, the **ddt° (desired dough temperature)** for the Basic Levain is 76°F. With that in mind, the Mise en Place shows that Water should be at 84°F and the Culture at 70°F when you mix the Levain.

This is based on the observation that the Ambient Temperature in a bakery classroom averages 76°F. The Flour temperature is usually close to that, but it can be two or three degrees cooler.

Based on these assumptions, the Mise en Place specifies Water at 84°F.

Before mixing a Levain or Main Dough, Bakers adjust the temperature of the water (warmer or cooler), in response to the temperature of the bakeshop and of the flour itself. We want the dough to be at a specific temperature when it comes off the mixer so we can proceed directly with Fermentation. Troubleshooting a mixture that's too warm or too cool is inefficient and creates inconsistent results in our breads.

We call this the *desired dough temperature,* or ddt°. It's sometimes called *Target* or *Arrival Temperature.*

About *Mise en Place* Temperatures

Water temperatures listed for Mise en Place are based on
these assumptions:

- The *ambient temperature* of your bakeshop *is
  76° F*
- Let's say your *Flour is 74°F*
  (Flour temperature is generally a few degrees
  cooler than the bakeshop.)

So if you . . .
   scale water at **84°F**
   and temper your Starter Culture to **70°F**

then your . . .
   Basic Levain will have a temperature close to 76°F.

In winter, the bakeshop temperature is lower. At the start of a
morning shift when the kitchen is colder, the Flour may be as
cool as 60°. You'll need warmer water to bring the temperature
of the Basic Levain to its *ddt°* of 76° for the 5-hour shift.

During warmer months, Flour can arrive at your receiving
dock at temperatures of 80°F or sometimes higher. That, plus a
warmer kitchen, means you'll have to use colder water to manage the temperature of your Levain and main dough.

Wild Yeast Breads have better flavor and more consistent leavening when the *ddt°'s* of the Basic Levain and the main dough
are both on target.

When first starting to make breads with wild yeast, use the
Quick H2O Temp° Formula on page 61 (for the Basic Levain)
and on page 74 (for the Main Dough). With a little experience,
you will learn the average temperatures in your shop and intuitively adjust your H2O temperatures for consistent breads.

In extreme conditions—summer months or the middle of winter, when the Flour and Bakeshop are noticeably warm or cold—you need to adjust the temperature of the Water before mixing the Levain. For accuracy, a baker always calculates the Water Temperature based on his environment. A Quick H2O Temp° Formula for Basic Levain follows.

In this example, the Bakeshop is 76°F and the Flour is 74°F. The Culture is cold, at 60°F. Using the Quick Formula, you can see the Water needs to be 94°F so the Levain has a temperature of 76°F.

Quick H2O Temp° Formula for Basic Levain

Mise en place:

- Take the temperature of the Wild Yeast Culture
- Take the temperature of the Flour
- Take the ambient temperature of the Bakeshop

	Actual temp°	Target temperature ddt°	Difference	
Flour	76°	76°	0°	
Ambient°	74°	76°	+ 2°	
Wild Yeast Culture	60°	76°	+ 16°	
H_2O	???	76°	+ 18°	94°F

In this example, the Bakeshop (ambient°) is 76° and the Flour temperature is 74°F. The Wild Yeast Culture (out of the refrigerator for one hour) has a temperature of 60°F.

Using this formula, the water temperature must be 94°F so the Basic Levain temperature will be 76°F.

		8-hour shift ddt°= 70°F	5-hour shift ddt°= 76°F
2	**Ingredient Mixing**	Combine Water & Starter Culture; add Flour	same

A. Scale Culture into mixing bowl

This formula is designed to be made by hand. Select a stainless steel work bowl and run it under some hot water to warm it. Shake out excess water but don't dry the bowl.

The easiest way to handle the Culture is to measure it directly into the stainless steel workbowl. Put your mixing bowl on the scale. Zero, or tare, the scale.

Pour in the Culture.

B. Add Water to the mixing bowl

Again, zero the scale. Measure the Water directly onto the Culture. Use a spatula or dip your fingers in water and by hand, thoroughly dilute the Culture in the water.

If you're apprehensive in using this one-bowl method, scale the water in its own container first. Once the Culture has been measured into the bowl, just pour the Water on top of it.

C. Add the Flour

Add about **half** the Flour to the Culture/Water mixture. Blend briefly. Add the remaining Flour and blend thoroughly.

D. Mix until *Take Up*

Make sure the ingredients are well combined. If you're using a plastic hand scraper, smear the mixture across the bottom of the workbowl. Scrape up the entire mixture, flip it over in the bowl and smear it one or two more times, using the scraper's rounded edge.

Photo Gallery #2   Basic Levain

		8-hour shift ddt°= 70°F	5-hour shift ddt°= 76°F
3	**Development**	Stir until blended	same

Combine the ingredients well.

The *Basic Levain* does not need to be Developed. Proceed directly to the Fermentation Phase.

		8-hour shift ddt°= 70°F	5-hour shift ddt°= 76°F
4A	**Fermentation** *On the Floor*	5h 00 @ 70° (70% hum);	2h 00 at 76° (70% hum)

Select a plastic container to ferment the Levain

Plastic is recommended. Other non-reactive materials such as ceramic or glass are suitable for your home kitchen. In a bakeshop these materials can break, creating a physical contamination hazard. Even one small chip from a ceramic bowl is a painful discovery later when your hands are developing the dough.

The amount of Levain should fill the plastic container at least one-fourth of its total volume, never more than half. For this formula, a one-quart plastic deli container is a good choice for the Levain while it ferments. Coat the inside of the plastic container with pan spray—the Levain will be easier to remove.

Transfer the Levain mixture to the fermentation container

Use a plastic scraper. Dip it first in water and use one sweep to catch as much of the Levain as you can manage.

Use your fingers dipped in water to get the Levain into the plastic container.

Make a final sweep through the workbowl for the remaining Levain and wipe the scraper over the rim of the plastic container.

Baker's Tip

Instead of using pan spray, rinse the container first with plain water.
Once your hands get a feel for the Levain's behavior, you'll find that rinsing the container first with a little fresh water is all you need.

Baker's Tip

Keep a small Lexan® or similar container of water on your workbench to store the plastic scraper and to rinse your fingers while working.

Clean the inside walls of the container

To prevent dried bits forming on the surface, compact the Levain in the bottom of the container. Scrape any mixture from the walls of the container, too. The easiest tool to use is your fingers dipped in fresh water.

As a final touch, dip your fingers in water and pat down the surface of the Levain, smoothing it. The water prevents a surface skin from forming while the Levain ferments.

Take the Levain's Temperature

Use a calibrated thermometer in the center of the Levain. Meanwhile, put a piece of masking tape on the side of the plastic container so you can record all the Fermentation details in one place.

Cover the plastic container

Select a flexible plastic cover that fits your container. Plastic wrap won't be secure enough.

Leave the lid slightly ajar to let carbon dioxide (CO_2) gas escape. Under a tight-fitting lid, CO_2 may build up pressure and force the lid open. Physical contaminants can then fall into the container.

Tag the Levain

The Basic Levain has a 2-Stage Fermentation. For the 5-hour shift, it looks like this:

Stage 1	***On the Floor***	2 hours at 76°F
Stage 2	**RFG time**	20 to 28 hours more in the Refrigerator

When making a Fermentation Tag for the Levain, divide it into sections. One for **On the Floor Fermentation** and one for **Cool Fermentation**.

The Basic Levain ferments in 2 Stages, like the Wild Yeast Starter. The Floor Fermentation supports the yeast colony. The Cool Fermentation, in a dough retarder or refrigerator, supports the bacteria colony. See page 42.

Stage 1 *On the Floor* Fermentation

	Floor Fermentation		Cool Fermentation	
Name & Product	Start FLOOR time (t°)	End FLOOR time (t°)	Start RFG time (t°)	End RFG time (t°)

Start FLOOR time

Write the starting time for the Floor Fermentation stage on the tag.

Calculate the ending time and write that on the masking tape tag. Leave a "**(°)**" symbol to remind you to check the Levain's temperature at the end of the Floor Fermentation Stage.

In this example, let's say the Fermentation Tag has these times recorded on it:

Keep the Levain at its target temperature— for a 5-hour class, the target is 76°F.

	Floor Fermentation		Cool Fermentation	
Basic Levain (for *Pain au Levain*)	12:00 Monday (70°)	2:00 pm Monday (°)	2:00 pm Monday (°)	9:00 am Tuesday (°)

Select a safe spot in your bakeshop to ferment the Levain. The goal is to maintain the Levain's temperature as close to 76°F as is reasonable.

Consider the *actual* temperature of the Levain. If the Levain's a chilly 65°F, select a spot in the bakery that is approximately 85°F. Likewise, a warm Levain ferments better in a cooler spot.

End FLOOR time

After 2 hours, take the Levain's temperature again. Write this on your fermentation tag. Don't worry if the Levain is a little warmer or cooler than 76°F. At least, not the first or second time. If it continues to be a problem, look for another spot in your bakeshop.

Monitor the Levain's temperature to learn if that particular fermentation spot was a good choice or not. Once you find that *sweet spot* in your bakeshop where the Levain can ferment at its target temperature, you're well on your way to producing consistent flavor in your wild yeast breads.

Stir the Levain

Dip a spoon in water and stir the Levain. Just enough to eliminate CO_2 and to distribute the yeast and LAB colonies once more.

As a final touch, dip your fingers in fresh water and pat down the surface of the Levain, smoothing it. Replace the lid on the container, still slightly ajar. If you're more comfortable with a snug-fitting lid, poke 2 or 3 holes in it first. CO_2 still collects in the container for the first couple of hours once the Levain is in the refrigerator.

Write the ACTUAL time that you transfer the Levain to the refrigerator on the fermentation tag. This may be a little earlier or later than you had planned.

This is valuable information once the main dough is baked. There may be a new flavor in the final bread—for better or worse. This can be traced back to a fermentation stage that was shorter or longer than intended. Don't let the opportunity to improve your breads slip by. Monitor your Levain at each step.

Reading a Fermentation Tag for Basic Levain

The sample Fermentation Tag now looks like this:

	Floor Fermentation		Cool Fermentation	
Basic Levain (for *Pain au Levain*)	12:00 Monday (76°)	2:00 pm Monday (78°)	*1:30* ~~2:00 pm~~ Monday (78°)	9:00 am Tuesday (°)

- The Levain temperature has risen during the floor fermentation. The spot where the Levain was sitting was warmer than expected. Two degrees plus or minus either way is not something to worry about. If it's too hot, look for a different spot to ferment your Levain next time.

- The Levain was transferred to the refrigerator a half hour earlier than its scheduled time. Perhaps it was a mistake or kitchen clean-up had begun. Either way, it is important to make this notation on the Fermentation Tag.

  Tomorrow, when you evaluate the baked bread, this information will help you understand how the particular flavor of this bread was affected. For now, there's nothing that can be done about it.

- Keep everything else on schedule. At 9:00 am Tuesday, the Levain should be removed from the refrigerator and tempered on the floor, as scheduled.

Most of the Levains in this book follow this fermentation schedule. When the pattern is standardized, you learn it more quickly. Once it becomes second nature, you are free to modify the fermentation schedule to fit your situation.

	8-hour shift ddt°= 70°F	5-hour shift ddt°= 76°F
4B Fermentation	+ stir for 10 seconds	+ stir for 10 seconds
	+ 16 to 24h 00 in RFG	**+ 20 to 28h 00 in RFG**

Stage 2 *Cool* Fermentation

Leave the Levain undisturbed while it ferments an additional 16 to 24 hours. Remember to bring it to ambient temperature at least one hour before using it tomorrow.

Baker's Tip

When you transfer the Levain to the re-frigerator, make sure to place it on a flat surface. You don't want to find your plastic container knocked on its side with fermented Levain flowing through the wire shelving in the refrigerator.

Baker's Insight
8-hour Shift or 5-hour Shift

The Basic Levain formula is on the next page. In the *Procedure* section, you'll see two sets of times and temperatures.

For a 4- or 5-hour class session, use the *5-hour shift* schedule on the right-hand side. Use the *8-hour shift* schedule on the left-hand side in a production bakery. The steps are the same for both schedules.

For the 8-hour shift, the desired temperature for the Levain is 70°F

Once it is mixed, give the Basic Levain a 5-hour Floor Fermentation. Then transfer it to the refrigerator or retarder for 16 to 24 hours. (It can stay chilled for up to 48 hours, if needed.)

For the 5-hour shift, the desired temperature for the Levain is 76°F

In a 5-hour class, give the Basic Levain a 2-hour Floor Fermentation. Then transfer it to the refrigerator or retarder for 20 to 28 hours. (Like the 8-hour version, it can also stay chilled longer.)

One schedule isn't better than the other. Based on the situation, the baker can vary the combination of time and temperature for the Floor Fermentation.

Basic Levain

Formula

Ingredient	BP%	4-1/2 or 6 Qt		8 Qt	20 Qt
		Ounces	Grams		
Water	50%	1 oz	25 g	50 g	90 g
Starter Culture, ripe	150%	3 oz	75 g	150 g	270 g
Bread Flour	100%	2 oz	50 g	100 g	180 g
Yields		6 oz	150 g	300 g	540 g
enough to make main dough @		2# 2 oz or 950 g main dough		1,800 g main dough	4,100 g main dough

Procedure, Basic Levain

		8-hour shift ddt°= 70°F	5-hour shift ddt°= 76°F
1	Mise en Place	H2O @ **70°**; Starter Culture @ 70°	H2O @ **84°**; Starter Culture @ 70°
2	Ingredient Mixing	Combine Water & Starter Culture; add Flour	same
3	Development	Stir until blended	same
4A	Fermentation *On the Floor*	**5h 00 @ 70°** (70% hum)	**2h 00 @ 76°** (70% hum)
4B	Fermentation *RFG*	+ stir for 10 seconds + 16 to 24h 00 in RFG	+ stir for 10 seconds + 20 to 28h 00 in RFG

Master Formula
for
Wild Yeast
Bread

Recommended tools for working with wild yeast doughs.

(counterclockwise from left to right) one-gallon plastic storage bags, 2-inch soft bristle pastry brush, felt marking pen (medium tip), insta-read thermometer (spring-operated) or insta-read thermometer (digital), wire cooling rack, oven peel (wood or metal), round banneton, straight edge plastic bench scraper, oval banneton, curved edge plastic bowl scraper.

The bench is covered with a 3-foot piece of linen couche.

PAIN au LEVAIN: Representative Dough

Family: Wild Yeast Dough
Ingredient Mixing Sequence: Autolyse

This section continues the step-by-step process for the main dough. It assumes you are making one loaf of *Pain au Levain*, using the hand method for the Mixing and Development phases. If you prefer to use a tabletop or stand mixer, refer to Appendix 1.

Phase One: Mise En Place

1	Mise en Place	H_2O @ 92°F; Levain @ 70°F	ddt° = 78°F

Temper the Levain

Remove the Levain from the refrigerator or retarder at the time indicated on the fermentation tag. Let it come to ambient temperature for at least one hour. The Levain should be 70° or a few degrees warmer when you use it.

Stir it once more before measuring what you need for mise en place. Distributing the Yeast and LAB colonies just before measuring the Levain gives more reliable leavening and consistent flavor to your main dough.

Water Temperature

The ***ddt°***, or target temperature, for the *Pain au Levain* Main Dough is 78°F. The Mise en Place recommends that the water be 92°F. This is based on the assumption that your Bakeshop temp° is 76° and your Flour is 74°. To determine the precise water temperature, use the **Quick H2O Temp° Formula** *for* **MAIN DOUGH**. (For more details about controlling the temperature of your dough, see Appendix 1.)

> ### Baker's Tip
>
> Follow the Fermentation Schedules and always use a ripe Levain to main a main dough. To review how to check for ripeness, refer to pages 44 and 64–68.

Quick H2O Temp° Formula
for Main Dough

Mise en Place:

- Take the temperature of the Levain
- Take the temperature of the Flour
- Take the ambient temperature of the Bakeshop

	Actual temp°	Target temperature ddt°	Difference	
Flour	74°	78°	+ 4°	
Ambient°	74°	78°	+ 4°	
Levain	60°	78°	+ 18°	
H_2O	???	78°	+ 26°	104°

In this example, both the Bakeshop (ambient°) and the Flour temperatures are 74°F.

The Levain for this example (out of the refrigerator for one hour) has a temperature of 60°F instead of 70°F.

Using this formula, the water temperature must be 104°F so the main dough temperature will be 78°F.

Note: The **Quick H_2O Temp° Formula** does **not** take into account the *Friction Factor*. *Why not?* See the discussion on page 75.

Baker's Tip
100°F is Hot!

If the *Water Temperature* for the main dough must be 100°F or higher, don't add the Levain directly to it. Instead, gradually lower the water's temperature by adding some of the flour to it. Specifically,

1 Add enough of the flour from the main dough formula so that the mixture is similar in texture to the Levain.

2 Then, add the Levain to the water/flour mixture and blend it by hand or with a plastic scraper.

3 Proceed with the *Ingredient Mixing Sequence* as indicated. In most cases, this would mean adding the remainder of the flour and then the salt.

Why there's **no *Friction Factor***
in the **Quick H2O Temp Formula—Main Dough**

Most textbooks include another value when determining water temperature for a dough. It's called **_Friction Factor_** and it has to do with the heat that's generated as the dough is beaten against the mixing bowl by a mechanical dough hook.

With production runs (and here, we're talking about 100 kilograms of dough and larger), *Friction Factor* is a big deal in raising the temperature of the dough during its Development Phase. In small batches, like one or two loaves at a time, it's not that significant.

Friction Factor is different for every combination of dough weight, machine type, and speed at which the kneading takes place. In a book about algebra, *Friction Factor* would be very popular. It's a variable, after all, and algebra is all about solving for **x** when things around it keep changing. Lucky for us, this is a book about baking bread.

I've found it better to present readers with no more information than they really need to start making their own breads. I just use the basic temperatures— the Flour, the Bakery itself, the Starter Culture. Things your thermometer can measure for you. In the whirlwind that is a bakery, this method gives an approximation that works.

I appreciate the value of being *close enough*, especially when there are bigger things on the table, like learning how to develop a dough by hand without using too much pressure. Or learning how to tell when the bread is proofed and ready for scoring. As a bread baker, I focus on using my hands and teach my students to do the same.

So am I wrong for letting you think that a baker doesn't really need to account for *Friction Factor*? Well, that depends. If you were the Production Manager for a commercial bakery, responsible for hundreds of thousands of loaves daily, then yes. I'd be wrong for not teaching you *Friction Factor*.

In a bakery classroom, I'm unconvinced that more time spent calculating a precise answer to the water temperature question actually benefits the young baker. The more measuring used to generate the answer, the more possibility for being wrong. Besides, and if you want to get technical about it, why stop at the *Friction Factor*?

What about the air resistance as you knead the dough? On hot, humid days there's more than on dry, cold days. Or the temperature of the wooden or stainless steel bench? That makes a difference, too. What about the span of your extended hand—from the tip of the thumb to the end of the pinkie? A wider span heats dough up more. These effects may be small, but each is big enough to keep you from calculating to a decimal point what the temperature of the dough will be when you or a machine are done handling it.

My point—there's a time at which we can become too precise in our methods. This is one example, and there will be more to follow. This is a good time to put your faith in the ART part of baking, and leave the ARITHMETIC part of it alone for the moment.

Later, when the yeast bug bites you hard, you'll want to learn more about *Friction Factor* and how each machine manufacturer calculates it given the amount of dough, the type of machine, and the hydration of the dough itself. This is great stuff to look up while your dough is fermenting. For now, we'll rely on a calibrated thermometer and things we can actually measure—Flour, the Ambient temp in the Bakery, the Starter Culture, and the Water. That's a pretty good start.

2	**Ingredient Mixing**	Autolyse

Autolyse—Step by Step

A. Add Levain to the mixing bowl

Select a stainless steel work bowl and run it under some hot water to warm it. Shake out the excess water but don't dry the bowl.

Put your mixing bowl on the scale.

Zero, or tare, the scale.

Add the Levain.

The easiest way to handle the Levain is to measure it directly into the stainless steel workbowl.

Artisan Skill

Dip your hand in fresh water and then quickly scoop some Levain from the container into the stainless bowl.

B. Add Water

Again, zero the scale. Measure the Water directly onto the Levain. Use a spatula or dip your fingers in water and by hand, thoroughly dilute the Levain in the water.

If you're apprehensive in using this direct scaling method, measure the water in a separate container first. Once the Levain is measured into the bowl, just pour the water on top of it.

C. Add the Flour(s)

First, add the Whole Wheat Flour to the Levain/Water mixture. Blend thoroughly.

Then, add the Bread Flour.

When a main dough calls for white flour plus another type(s) of flour, blend the varietal (non-white) flour with the Levain/Water mixture first. White flours like bread flour and all purpose flour absorb water quickly. Whole grain flours require slightly more time to hydrate.

Varietal flours can have a higher protein content, like Semolina, or they may be Whole Grain Flours containing parts of the Germ or Bran. Either way, the varietal flour needs more time to absorb water before the white wheat flour is added.

A Whole Wheat formula, for example, often calls for both Whole Wheat Flour and Bread Flour. The baker blends the Whole Wheat Flour with the Levain/Water first and lets the mixture stand for five or ten minutes so the whole grain flour hydrates.

When there is only one type of flour in the main dough, no matter if it's bread flour or something else, simply add all the flour to the Levain/Water mixture at once.

D. Add the Salt

Salt is the last ingredient added. Sprinkle it evenly over the top of the flour.

E. Mix until *Take Up*

Use your hand or a plastic bowl scraper to combine the ingredients until *Take Up*. Recall that this means all the flour(s) is moistened and no dry flour is visible in the bowl—on the walls of the bowl or especially at the bottom, underneath the mass of dough.

Most of the doughs in this family are hydrated at 70%. It won't take much work to reach *Take Up*.

The Meatloaf Method

As you combine the ingredients, you'll find that the moisture concentrates inside the dough and the dry flour stays on the outside. You might think you can incorporate the dry flour into the wet dough by kneading. Don't do it.

Photo Gallery #3   The Ingredient Mixing Sequence

Don't start Developing the dough until all the flour has been moistened. Dry flour has trouble incorporating, the more the dough is developed.

It's much quicker and more thorough to cut into the dough with a scraper, tossing pieces of dough together. Do this in the stainless workbowl or scrape everything onto the bench, whichever is easier. Use a plastic scraper in the stainless bowl, a metal scraper on the bench.

My students have nicknamed this cutting technique the *Meatloaf Method*. It's easy, quick, and clean.

THE *MEATLOAF METHOD*

The *Meatloaf Method* is not like the folding technique, that gentle lifting and stirring gesture used to incorporate whipped egg whites into a soufflé base, for example. There is no delicate volume to maintain when mixing dough ingredients. The goal is just to get all the flour wet.

1 Use a plastic scraper to bring flour from the outside edge of the bowl toward the center. Deliberately cut into the thick, damp part of the dough so that the dry flour can get moist.

2 Take one broad sweep with the scraper around the inside wall of the workbowl to get all the dry flour and bring it into the center.

3 Finally, you will reach a point where the bowl no longer serves its purpose. In fact, you may find the bowl actually makes it harder for you to continue cutting into the dough.

At that point, *Scrape the entire contents of the bowl* onto the work bench. Don't add any flour to the bench. You've already got enough dry flour that needs to get wet.

4 Use the straight side of the plastic scraper when working on the bench. Starting at the edge of dough farthest away from you, make a series of parallel cuts into the dough at about one-inch intervals. With each gesture, cut downward until the plastic scraper hits the bench. Keeping the flat edge of the scrape in contact with the bench, gently push the one-inch strip of dough about two inches away from you.

The gentle pushing makes the strips of dough curl under themselves as they move. You'll see how efficiently this helps the dry flour absorb moisture.

5 Use both hands to gather all the dough strips into a single mass on the bench. Then rotate the entire batch a quarter-turn.

Make another series of parallel cuts through the dough, this time cutting the strips into blocks or cubes of dough. When the scraper hits the bench, push the dough cubes away from you.

Check inside the dough, you'll find no dry flour lumps. If you do, keep chopping to break them down and moisten them.

6 Use your metal bench scraper to form the dough into one large mass. It doesn't need to be smooth, just collected in one mass.

Photo Gallery #4   The *Meatloaf Method*

Culinary Analogy

The ***Meatloaf Method*** is similar to the basic knife skill of cutting a vegetable into large dice. A potato, for example, is first cut into long rectangles, about one-half inch on each side. The rectangles are gathered three or four at a time and turned on a right angle, 90 degrees

They're cut once again at one-half inch lengths, giving them the squared-off look of dice.

F. *Autolyse* dough for 15 minutes

Dip your fingers in fresh water and pat the surface of the dough. This smooths the dough and prevents it from drying.

The **autolyse** step requires the dough to rest, undisturbed, for 15 minutes. Unless your workspace is limited, lay your scraper on the dough. Invert your (scraped out) stainless workbowl over the dough and scraper. Place a piece of masking tape on the bowl to identify which main dough you are working on. Take note of the time and write that down on the tape, too.

If you need to move the dough from the bench for the *autolyse* period, simple scrape it into your stainless workbowl. Use your fingers, dip them in water, and brush the inside of the bowl with them instead of using pan spray. There's no need for plastic wrap directly on the surface of the dough, but cover the bowl itself to keep out physical contaminants.

All of these steps:
1. Adding Levain to the Water,
2. adding the Flour and the Salt,
3. mixing to *Take Up* and
4. letting the covered mixture rest for 15 minutes

are summarized in baker's shorthand by **Autolyse Sequence**. These are the same steps for all breads in the Wild Yeast Dough family. Take a look at the formula for *Pain au Levain* at the end of this section. You will see that a baker merely writes **Autolyse** to summarize all these steps of the *Ingredient Mixing Sequence*.

Baker's Tip
Cover your Scraper.

Left uncovered on the bench, bits of dough on the scraper will dry by the time the autolyse is finished. Unless you need your bench scraper for another task, lay it on top of the dough mass and then cover the whole assembly. When you remove the workbowl, your scraper will be where you need it, and any dough left on it will still be moist.

We stand upon the achievements of those who have come before us.

In this case, the late Professor Raymond Calvel. With a respected career as a scientist and researcher under his belt, Professor Calvel turned his attention to French bread and its heritage. A heritage that by the 1980's in France had become all but forgotten, judging by the commercially produced baguettes that filled retail and wholesale shelves throughout France at the time. Spurred by his activist personality, he wrote a book which became much more than that. It was to be a declaration, a call-to-arms for craft bakers, pleading for the revival of the taste and tradition of French bread baking.

Le Goût du Pain appeared in 1990. Written in a uniquely poetic language with imagery and passion, his book could not be ignored.

The book uncovers wheat milling procedures and flour types, dough mixing variations, and proper shaping techniques. There's an investigation into the organic acids created during fermentation—the ones principally responsible for bread's aroma and flavor. The chapter on *Crust* is almost 15% of the technical section of the book.

With its English translation, Calvel's ***Taste of Bread*** became the official flag of the Artisan Bread Revolution in America in the last quarter of the 20th century.

The Autolyse

Perhaps his greatest invention is the ***Autolyse***, pronounced ***auto lees***. Exactly what did Professor Calvel mean by the word *autolyse?* He specified a rest period of 15 to 20 minutes once the water and flour are thoroughly mixed.

Why the rest period? The flour fully hydrates so it is easier to manipulate, stretch, fold or knead into shape. And the proteins link up, starting the gluten network which ultimately holds everything together.

(A little science here . . .)
There are two charactistics of gluten that form the dough's structure.
Elasticity and ***Extensibility***.

Elasticity makes the dough contract, so a bread can keep its shape while proofing. *Extensibility* helps the dough stretch while it stays relaxed. This characteristic lets the baker gently lengthen logs of Ciabatta dough without deflating the large air cells he's built inside the dough.

In addition, there are flour enzymes called **protease**. These are activated during the *autolyse*. **Protease** enzymes break down some of the **elastic** gluten to increase the dough's *extensibility*. (Appendix 1 has more details on balancing these two characteristics of gluten in your breads.)

In the end, the dough literally develops itself during for 15 to 20 minute rest. This leaves plenty of time for other tasks in the shop.

> ### Professor Calvel's original guideline was clear— the autolyse contains only flour and water.

Yeast? No, that begins fermentation of the flour before the gluten has formed.

Salt? No, that tightens the gluten, making the protease enzymes work harder.

How about a Pre-Ferment, like a Biga, a Sponge, or a Levain?
None of the above. A pre-ferment brings acid to the flour/water mixture and this also tightens the gluten while the enzymes are trying to relax it.

Since Professor Calvel first introduced the autolyse, several advancements in baking production and technology have forced small compromises here or there.

Instant Yeast? It's OK, now. The fact that Instant Yeast takes longer to hydrate than other types of yeast was the first challenge to Professor Calvel's guideline.

The decision? If the main dough calls for Instant Yeast, it's now accepted practice to include it in the autolyse.

Pre-Ferments? Sometimes. Put simply, a preferment is a mix of water, yeast and flour that is independently fermented before it is added to the main dough ingredients.

The water, yeast and flour for a preferment are subtracted, or *borrowed*, from the total ingredient weights in the bread formula. Some preferments use so much of the total water and so little of the flour, there's not enough water left to hydrate the flour that's left behind.

The decision? If he needs all the water in the formula, the baker can now combine the preferment into the **autolyse.**

As the slope gets more slippery with each paragraph, the honored Professor's theory has graciously bowed to the practical solution along the way.

This reduces the chance of forgetting an ingredient during the Mixing Sequence. It's best practice for learning how to prepare these breads.

Once you've developed confidence with this type of bread, do a controlled experiment or two. *Autolyse with salt* versus *Autolyse without salt.* Experience for yourself what happens. Taste the results, note any differences. If it's worth it, by all means make a modification to your procedures. That's the **Art** of baking.

But first, make sure you know the mechanics of the procedure—the **Craft** of baking bread.

Phase Three: Development

3	Development	Speed #2, 2 m; + Rest 5 m; + Speed #1, 2 m	*Improved*

Development—Step by Step

The purpose of the Development Phase is to better organize the protein structure that started during the Autolyse. With gentle, rhythmic handling, the gluten structure becomes uniform and a smoother surface appears.

A. On Medium Speed, develop dough for 2 minutes

Initial Development

Use your metal bench scraper to develop the dough by hand, directly on the bench. Don't add additional flour. You need the dough to stick both to the bench and to the scraper while the gestures of your hand stretch the dough. Stretching makes the gluten network firmer and organizes the structure.

Sensory/Tactile Skill

Take a minute to get acquainted with the dough, now that it has completed the autolyse stage. Poke it, push it, grab a small piece and stretch it. Dip your fingers in **bench flour** (a small bowl of bread or all-purpose flour kept on your workbench) so the dough won't stick to you.

As you gently stretch some of the dough, can you see how the gluten window has already begun to develop? Except for the shaggy, rough or uneven appearance of the dough mass, it often looks at this stage like a dough that has already been developed, or kneaded.

Specifically, start at the 12 o'clock position on your bench. With the flat side of the scraper held about 45° to the bench, draw the scraper through the dough toward the 6 o'clock position. As you do this, move the scraper side to side in a zigzag motion. This is the ***Fishtail Technique*** used to develop the Focaccia and other slack doughs (Appendix 1).

Use a medium or low amount of pressure. Too much pressure rips the gluten chains and is uncomfortable for your hand.

Once you've made one complete pass through the dough from 12 o'clock to 6 o'clock, scrape the entire mass of dough into a mound and flip it over onto itself.

Repeat the whole process, 12 o'clock to 6 o'clock. Draw the scraper through the dough, moving right to left, until the scraper has travelled across the entire surface of the dough. In one broad gesture, scrape up the dough and invert it.

Continue to develop the dough with this technique. Work uniformly, repeating the sequence of movements. The more routine your gestures, the better organization your hand brings to the main dough.

Stop developing after 2 minutes. Recall that the autolyse built the foundation of the protein network. Only a brief time is needed to organize the structure now.

Using the bench scraper in a repeating pattern and with consistent pressure brings an open crumb structure to the final bread. The cells are random in size, from 1/8th-inch to 1-inch or larger. The cell walls glisten when the bread is sliced and the crumb is tender, moist and creamy to chew.

When the bench work is rough, tough or uneven, the bread's interior has cells walls look dry and have a non-reflective finish. When chewed, the interior is crumbly and rough on the palate.

Photo Gallery #5A   Initial Development

B. Rest dough 5 minutes

As before, use your bench scraper to gather the dough into a ball. Place the bench scraper on top of the dough and cover everything with the stainless work bowl.

This is a short rest period, just 5 minutes. Set a timer if possible. It's easy to get distracted with another bakeshop task. Plus, you don't want to stand and wait—there always some dishes that need washing or a bench that could be scraped clean.

C. On Low Speed, develop dough for 2 minutes more

Final Development (*Clean Up* Stage)

Uncover the dough and use the zigzag motion to develop it for two minutes more. Work with the same speed as before but, this time, use even less pressure. Keep the dough moving and change directions smoothly as your scraper goes through the routine—from zigzagging, to scraping, to inverting the dough.

Photo Gallery #5B   Clean-Up (Final Development)

D. *Windowpane* and Check for Salt

Use your scraper to cut off a piece of dough no more than one inch in diameter. Roll it between the palms of your hands.

The dough will be sticky. Don't add extra flour. The stickier the dough, the quicker your hands should be moving in opposite directions to roll it into a ball.

VISUALIZATION

Picture how dough develops on a mixer. It rolls and tumbles between the dog-legged hook and the side of the workbowl. Its surface is smooth and shiny, it doesn't rip or tear. Translate this sense of rhythm to your bench-work.

Artisan Bench Skill— Windowpane a Slack Dough

The stickier the dough, the less pressure you need from your hands. Use quick and light gestures, rounding the dough for no more than 3 or 4 seconds. Longer than that and your hands get warm from friction, making the dough stick to your palms.

When that happens, start again. Peel, scrape and rub the dough from your hands. Rub them together with some bench flour. Use a new, cooler piece of dough.

It is unlikely that after an autolyse, two periods of active development and a five minute rest that the dough ball does not have enough gluten. If you're having trouble window-paning this particular dough and there is another baker or two at hand, just have them try it with you. Even though the dough ball is tacky, you will be able to stretch it gently and see the translucent gluten window.

Drop the dough ball in some bench flour and roll it around, like a Mexican Wedding Cookie or Russian Teacake. Place the flour-coated ball directly on a dry part of the bench. With an up-and-down motion, use your fingers to flatten the dough into a small disk.

Dip your fingertips in bench flour once more and pick up the disk. Gently stretch it until you can see the windowpane. You will not be able to stretch the dough as much as you can with Intensive Development doughs like Baguettes. But you will be able to see the thin, trampoline-like layer of dough as you stretch it.

Photo Gallery #6   Windowpane the Dough

Taste the dough (a quick lick of the windowpane) to check the salt level. The dough should taste slightly salty. In fact, the salt intensity is often higher than the sourness at this step in the dough's progress.

Discard the small piece of dough and wash your hands before resuming work.

All of these steps:
1. Initial Development on Medium Speed,
2. a 5-minute rest, then
3. a Final Development on Low Speed,
4. Checking the Windowpane and
5. Tasting for proper salt intensity

are summarized in baker's shorthand by the term ***Improved Development***. These are the same steps for all doughs in the Wild Yeast Dough Family. Turn to the complete formula for *Pain au Levain* at the end of this section. You will see that all these steps are abbreviated by what bakers call ***Improved Development***.

By learning the *Improved Development Technique* for *Pain au Levain*, you've also learned how to make a variety of other Wild Yeast Doughs like *Rosemary Raisin* and *Apple Walnut Farmhouse Bread*. After making three or four breads from the Wild Yeast Family, the procedure will become second nature.

Questions about assembling any of the formulas in this section? Refer back to the details of this chapter and your questions will be answered.

Phase Four: Fermentation

Ferment the Pain au Levain Main Dough in 2 Stages		
Stage 1	FLOOR Fermentation	2 hours @ 78°F with 1 Degas & Fold after an hour
Stage 2	COOL Fermentation	16 to 24 hours more @ 35°F to 50°F in the Refrigerator or Retarder

Fermentation—Step by Step

Fermentation—Step by Step

Recall (from page 42) that the Yeast and Bacteria colonies prefer different temperatures for optimal growth. The warm temperature of a bakeshop fosters the Yeast activity, encouraging the cells to digest the sugars in the main dough. Then, the cool temperature of the refrigerator slows the Yeast activity. This allows the LAB's opportunity to develop more flavor acids in the dough.

Stage 1
Floor Fermentation

4A	**Floor Fermentation**	1h 00 m @ 78° (70% hum); + Degas and Fold; 1h 00 @ 78° (70% hum)

1. Ferment the Main Dough for 1 hour

A. Prep the Fermentation Container

Select a 4-quart plastic container with lid for a single loaf of *Pain au Levain*.

For a larger batch, choose a container whose ***volume*** is approximately three times the ***weight*** of the formula yield. This will make sure the lid stays on if the dough more than doubles in size while fermenting. Coat the inside of the container with pan spray or a neutral-flavored oil first.

Baker's Tip

Can I Use Olive Oil?

Consider the flavor profile of the bread when choosing an oil to coat the inside of a fermentation container.

Olive oil would be appropriate for an *Olive Rosemary* bread or *Roasted Garlic and Parmigiano* rolls. A light-flavored oil like Canola or Safflower would be appropriate for the French *Pain au Levain* or *Apple Walnut Hearth Bread*.

B. Round the Dough

One final time before leaving the main dough to ferment, form it into a round. It may seem unnecessary that the dough have a specific shape when it's just going to stay in a plastic fermentation container for the next several hours. But this is an opportunity to practice your dough rounding skills on the bench, and a baker can never have too much of that.

Handling the dough and learning how it feels helps your hands monitor its changes through the Fermentation, Shaping and Proofing phases. Take any opportunity to improve your sense of touch. It all translates to better quality bread.

Baker's Tip

In a bakeshop, it's wise practice to write your name on the tag, too. If anything unusual happens during the Fermentation Phase, a fellow baker can notify you.

C. Take the Temperature of the Dough

Use a calibrated thermometer in the center of the main dough to register its temperature. Meanwhile, put a piece of masking tape on the side of the plastic container.

D. *Tag* the Dough

Write the time of day on the tag, along with the dough temperature. Ideally, the dough will be 78°. A few degrees plus or minus is okay the first few times.

<table>
<tr>
<td> **4A**</td>
<td>**Floor Fermentation**</td>
<td>1h 00 m @ 78° (70% hum);
+ Degas and Fold;
1h 00 @ 78° (70% hum)</td>
</tr>
</table>

2. Degas and Fold the Dough

After one hour of floor fermentation, degas and fold the dough using these steps:

1 Take its temperature, using the same thermometer you used initially. Record this on the fermentation tag. (In this example, the dough is 78°F.)

2 Lightly flour your bench, lightly flour the top of the dough.

3 Invert the container onto the floured bench, allowing the dough to fall onto the bench. Lift the container and lightly flour the top of the dough.

4 Gently and with floured hands, press down evenly on the dough to release the carbon dioxide and alcohol.

5 Round the dough.

6 Return the dough to the plastic container, lightly spray or oil the top of the dough, and replace the lid.

Photo Gallery #7   De-gas & Fold

ddt° is 78°F

Keep the dough at its target temperature throughout the Fermentation Phase. It takes some trial and error to find just the right spot in your bakeshop, but keep looking until you find it.

<table>
<tr>
<td>**4A**</td>
<td>**Floor Fermentation**</td>
<td>1h 00 m @ 78° (70% hum);
+ Degas and Fold;
1h 00 @ 78° (70% hum)</td>
</tr>
</table>

3. Ferment the dough on the floor for 1 hour more.

This is the end of Stage 1—Floor Fermentation.

4B	Cool Fermentation	18 to 24 h 00 @ 50° (70% hum)

Ferment the Main Dough for 18 to 24 hours @ 35° to 50°F

Use this procedure:

1 Take the dough's temperature once again.

2 Degas and fold the dough, using the same procedure.

3 Return the dough to the container.

4 Lightly spray or oil the top of the dough and replace the lid.

5 Transfer the dough to the refrigerator or retarder.

Place the dough and its container on a sheet tray. Find a secure spot in the refrigerator. If you store the container on a rolling rack in the walk-in, be sure to use a full sheet tray under it. Share the extra space with other doughs. A half sheet on a rolling rack can be hard to see. It gets pushed onto the floor when a full sheet tray is slid onto its rung.

Baker's Tip

Keep the Dough on Its Schedule

Any change to the schedule once the dough starts its Fermentation Phase will ripple through the rest of the day in the bakeshop. Other bread projects, with their own timetables, will fight for the baker's attention while he's busy *fixing* something else.

By shift's end, there will be competition for oven space. Rarely a good result comes from that situation. Loaves get crammed into small oven spaces, decks are overfilled, the oven gets less temperature recovery time between bakes. In general, lots of breads get baked at lower temperatures than they want to. All bread suffers when a doughs falls behind on its schedule.

Reading a Fermentation Tag
for Pain au Levain Main Dough

The Fermentation Tag for a Wild Yeast Dough has two separate components. The first is for *Floor Fermentation* and the second for *Cool Fermentation*.

Here's a sample of a completed schedule:

	Floor Fermentation			Cool Fermentation	
Pain au Levain Main Dough	1:00 pm Tuesday (78°)	2:00 pm Tuesday (79°)	3:00 pm Tuesday (79°)	3:00 pm Tuesday (79°)	10:00 am Wednesday (°)

The Main Dough completed its Development Phase at 1:00 pm. The **arrival temp°** (the actual temp° of the dough when it goes into its fermentation container) is spot-on @ 78°F.

- Before the De-gas & Fold, the dough temp° is taken again. The temperature has risen slightly, but is still in range. Better to have a dough get slightly warmer during Floor Fermentation instead of getting cooler.

- Looks like we've found a sweet spot in the bakeshop for fermenting doughs. Only one degree higher than when we started, and holding steady.

- Another De-gas & Fold before the dough is moved to the cooler. The *End time* for the Floor Fermentation is the same as the *Start time* for the Cool Fermentation.

- In this example, class begins the following day at noon and we'll need the dough ready for Shaping at the start. Is there a fellow student or colleague available at 10:00 am to lend a baker's hand?

Most of the Bread Formulas in this section follow the 2-Stage Fermentation Schedule shown here. Some breads, like the *Apple Walnut Farmhouse Bread* and the *Honey Rye Hearth Bread* don't need the second stage, the Cool Fermentation. In those cases, just use the Floor Fermentation portion of the Tag.

5	**Shaping**	Temper dough 1h 00 *on the floor*
		Scale @ 2# 2 oz piece
		Form as gentle round
		Bench rest 20 m
		Final Form as Round or Boulot

Shaping—Step by Step

A. Temper dough 1h 00 *on the floor*

Move the main dough from the refrigerator to a warm spot in the bakeshop. Recall that the desired temperature for a Wild Yeast Dough is 78°F.

Leave the plastic cover on the dough while it's tempering. When possible, select a spot where the ambient temperature is 80° to 86°F. Too much hotter and your main dough warms unevenly.

The outside of the dough ferments quicker as its temperature rises. Meanwhile, the interior stays cool and ferments slowly. The result is uneven proofing for the final shapes.

Take the dough's temperature after an hour. So long as the dough is at least 68° to 70°F, you can begin to work with it. It will continue to warm and reach 78° to 80°F once the Shaping Sequence is finished.

Baker's Note

Plan enough time to temper your dough

Depending on the ambient temperature of your bakeshop, cold dough can sometimes take up to 2 hours to temper. Sometimes a baker may need to temper a dough quickly. He may move the dough to an overly warm spot, like a proof box set at 90°F or even higher. The outside of the dough warms quickly but the interior stays cold.

To correct for this, the baker gives a punch and fold to the dough every 15 to 20 minutes, maybe. This moves warm dough to the interior while exposing colder dough to the outside. Sounds good, so far.

But every punch and fold of the dough reawakens the elasticity in the dough. More elasticity means more proofing time is needed. Otherwise, the bread is dense and has a tight crumb when it bakes.

B. Prepare your oven, plan your baking schedule

If this bread will be the first bake of the day, preheat your oven while the dough is tempering. If your bakeshop uses a community baking schedule for a number of different bakers and bread projects, sign up for a designated oven deck and baking time.

(For Oven Settings, see below in *Phase 7—Décor & Baking*)

Scale @ 2# 2 oz piece
Form as gentle round
Bench rest 20 m

Final Form as Round or Boulot

A. Scale @ 2# 2 ounces

The basic formula yields between two pounds and two pounds four ounces. This is enough for one boule or two smaller ones at about one pound each. When working with a larger yield of dough than this, portion it on a scale and not by eye.

B. Form dough as gentle round(s)

Before the dough is placed in the proofing basket, degas it and form it into a gentle round. This step prepares the gluten structure for the final shape. The brief handling eliminates CO_2 and alcohol from the dough while distributing the Yeast and LAB colonies. Use only enough flour to make the dough manageable.

Bench rest the dough rounds on an inverted sheet tray lined with a silicone baking sheet. This frees workspace and you can move them to a warm spot if needed.

There are no precise measurements or size for this first shape, no particular diameter. For boules weighing two pounds, a 7- or 8-inch diameter is average. A one-pound boule can be 5 to 6 inches in diameter—about the length of a benchscraper.

Don't make the rounds too tight. A light touch and gentle motions keep larger air cells inside the bread.

Photo Gallery #8   The Shaping Sequence

C. Bench rest 20 m

Lightly coat a section of your work bench with oil or pan spray. Place the dough round—seam facing down—on the oiled bench. Lightly coat the top of the dough with oil or pan spray.

Cover with a piece of plastic wrap. Rest it for 20 minutes. Write the start and stop times on a piece of masking tape and stick it on the plastic.

D. Prep your proofing basket(s) now

For one loaf weighing about 2 pounds, select a banneton that is:

Round—10" (diameter) x 3" (depth)

or

Oval—11" (length) x 5" (width) x 3" (depth).

Invert the basket and, with one or two quick gestures, rap it on the bench. This releases flour or dried bits of dough that may be caked inside from a prior use.

Line the banneton with rice flour, brown or white. There should be a visible layer of flour in the basket, so use more than you would if you were lining a cake pan. Set the prepared basket aside.

Baker's Tip

Use a scrubbing tool, like a 99-cent drinking glass scrubber from the hardware store. With no more than moderate pressure, brush the interior of the basket. Harder pressure damages the basket, causing it to splinter. Pieces of the reed basket end up inside the dough as it proofs.

5	**Shaping**	Temper dough 1h 00 *on the floor*
		Scale @ 2# 2 oz piece
		Form as gentle round
		Bench rest 20 m

Final Form as Round or Boulot

A. Final Form as Round(s)

When the 20-minute bench rest is finished, remove the plastic cover from the dough round. Lightly dust a clean section of the bench. Lightly dust the top of the dough round.

Using the metal bench scraper, scoop up the dough and invert it onto the lightly dusted bench. Lightly dust the (new) top of the dough.

1 With flat hands, gently flatten the dough round into a disc, eliminating CO_2. Tap gently downward on the dough with a flat hand—don't press or stretch the dough outward. It doesn't need to be perfectly round. Let the dough take any shape as it gives under the gentle pressure of your hands.

2 Fold the top edge of the dough to the bottom edge; gently tap the top of the dough to eliminate air pockets. Give the dough a quarter turn.

3 Bring the (new) top edge of the dough to the bottom edge as before; tap the top of the dough to remove air pockets. Give the dough one more quarter turn.

4 Fold the top edge of the dough to the bottom edge; tap to remove air pockets.

5 Use a scraper to invert the dough round.

There may be two or three edges of the dough that stick out and give the dough a less than round appearance. One at a time, gently tuck each piece under the dough. The weight of the dough keeps these pieces in place.

6 Round the dough, using the ***Two-Handed Rounding*** gesture described here. Or use the ***Poker Chip*** gesture (Appendix 1), whichever is more comfortable.

Proofing baskets can be lined with linen. These are well-suited for high hydration doughs, rye breads, and porridge breads.

Baker's Tip
Travelling on the Bench

The dough doesn't need to travel far across the bench with each push or pull gesture. About two inches or maybe three each time. This keeps surface tension in the dough.

When the dough covers too much distance, like 4 or 5 inches, seams are exposed and surface tension disappears. The bottom of the dough becomes the top.

When seams are exposed, the bread flattens as it proofs. It bakes even flatter.

Two-Handed Rounding Gesture

Let's say the dough ball is at the 6 o'clock (6:00) position on the bench.

Using your **left hand**, push the dough ball away from you, toward the 12:00 position on the bench. Remove your left hand from the dough.

Cup your **right hand** and use it to draw the dough back toward the 6:00 starting position. As you do this, the dough will slowly curl against the bench and start to rotate counterclockwise. Don't deliberately turn the dough, let it grip the bench and rotate on its own.

Lightly flour your hands once again. Repeat the sequence of gestures—push away with the left hand, pull the dough back with the right hand. Let the dough rotate itself as it grips the bench.

Only one hand is on the dough at a time. Use your **left hand** to push away, **right hand** to draw the dough back.

Continue until the dough is round. Three or four times for the whole process is enough. Don't make the dough too round or too tight. When you see the first signs of a blister on the surface of the dough, *Stop*. That's round enough.

Even a *flour-free zone* isn't enough sometimes. In a dry and breezy shop, you need to keep the bench moist, too. A hand-held water mister or a damp towel to wipe across the bench are effective solutions.

Photo Gallery #9   Two-Handed Rounding Gesture

Baker's Tips

If you've practiced the Poker Chip gesture (Appendix 1), your hands know what the dough itself feels while it's being rounded. Focus on the leading edge of the dough to see that it grips the bench and curls under as it moves.

- Keep the heel of your hand in contact with the bench.

- Use your metal scraper to clean your bench. Rounding dough is easier when there's no flour on the bench.

If you have time, let the dough ball sit on the bench for a minute or two before it goes into its banneton. This brief rest lets the weight of the dough settle on itself, closing the seam that faces down. The momentum from the rounding process fades and the dough ball relaxes.

If your proofing basket has yet to be prepped, now's the time for that (refer to page 96).

B. Transfer the dough to the prepared banneton

Scoop up the dough with a metal bench scraper. Transfer it to the banneton.

Artisan Baker Skill

Seam Up or Seam Down in the Banneton?

I know as many bakers who put the dough seam facing up in the banneton as those who put it seam facing down. I've heard convincing arguments for each way. This is my strategy:

Same Day Bake? Seam Facing Up.

When the dough proofs and bakes on the same day, keep the seam facing up in the banneton. When the proofed bread is ready for the oven, the baker inverts the bread from the banneton onto the loading peel. This puts the seam facing down in the oven. The seams are more likely to stay closed and sealed when they are placed directly on the hot surface of the deck.

The part of the dough that was facing down in the banneton is now facing up. It's a smooth canvas ready for decorative scoring—the artist's signature.

Next Day Bake? Seam Facing Down.

Sometimes the dough is scheduled to proof slowly in the refrigerator and bake the next day. In this case, don't invert the dough, put the seam facing down in the basket. Throughout the Cool Fermentation, the weight of the dough forces the seam to close.

Try it both ways. Pick your preference. Once you do, be consistent so your breads are uniform.

Baker's Tip

Lightly coat the dough round with flour so it doesn't stick to the banneton

1 Dust a section of the bench with your choice of flour.

2 Pick up a boule of dough with a scraper.

3 Place it onto the floured bench and gently roll it around so the bottom half is coated with flour.

4 Use your scraper and transfer the dough to the banneton, floured side facing down.

Photo Gallery #10   Into the Banneton

Baker's Tip

Mix Up the Grains

Use a variety of Flours and Ground Grains to give a distinctive look to different breads. If you have two or three types of breads that all bake in the same round shape, use a different flour or ground grain mixture to identify each variety.

Semolina, Whole Wheat Flour, Cracked Wheat, and Pumpernickel Meal make attractive toppings for your breads. Use any of these alone or in a blend.

Phase Six: Proofing

6	**Proofing**	1h 30 @ 78° (70% hum), covered; + 30 m more, uncovered

Proofing—Step by Step

1h 30m @ 78°F (covered)

Gently tap on the dough so it settles in the banneton. With pan spray or a neutral-flavored oil, lightly coat the top of the dough. Cover with plastic, so the dough doesn't form a skin as it proofs.

Give the dough room to rise

Don't wedge the plastic between the dough and the proofing basket. Just lay it on the dough and let the excess plastic rest against the inside of the banneton. As if you were lining a pie pan with flaky dough.

When the plastic is wedged between the dough and the wall of the banneton, unmolding the dough is difficult.

Don't wrap the entire banneton, either. This creates an air gap between the dough and the plastic, making the dough surface dry.

Baker's Tip

Need some humidity quickly? Try a small stockpot of water simmering on a nearby burner.

Or use a spray bottle to mist water on the plastic-covered banneton to keep the bread moist while it proofs.

Place the covered banneton on a sheet tray and set it where the ambient temperature is 75° to 80°F. A humidity level of 70% to 80% is ideal. Make sure the breads are not in a draft—this extends the proofing time.

Is your oven pre-heated?

Verify your oven settings—a fellow baker may have been using your intended oven space in the meantime.

6	**Proofing**	1h 30 @ 78° (70% hum), covered; + 30 m more, uncovered

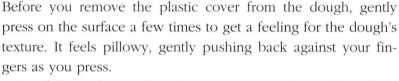

plus
30 m more @ 78° (uncovered)

Before you remove the plastic cover from the dough, gently press on the surface a few times to get a feeling for the dough's texture. It feels pillowy, gently pushing back against your fingers as you press.

Carefully peel away the plastic cover. Now, the surface of the dough can relax even more.

Once uncovered, give the dough an additional 30 minutes proofing time. Look for two characteristics at the end of this stage:

Baker's Tip

Recycle these plastic covers on other doughs whenever possible. They can be stored in the refrigerator for a few days.

1 **The surface of the dough is dry to the touch**
A dry surface makes oven loading a smoother process. The dough doesn't stick to the peel.

2 **The dough fully proofs**

How To: Test for Full Proof

I use several different techniques to judge the proper proof level on a *Pain au Levain*.

The **first** is what my students call the *Jell-O® test*. I call it *Tilt and Wobble*.

Hold a banneton with a fully proofed dough inside. Gently tilt, roll and wobble the basket back and forth. No sudden or excessive gestures.

The surface of the dough will ripple and flow as it responds to your gestures.

The **second** is the *Rare-Medium-Well test*.

With this hotline technique, a chef presses on the pad of his non-dominant hand, directly under his thumb. On what palm readers call the *Mound of Venus*, shown by the arrow in the first photo below.

By changing which finger of the left hand touches the thumb, the firmness of the pad changes. Forefinger and thumb for **Rare**, Middle Finger and Thumb for **Medium** and Ring Finger and Thumb for **Well Done**.

   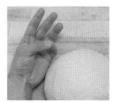

RARE	MEDIUM	WELL DONE	TOUGH
Press on the thumb pad for *Rare*.	Press on the thumb pad for *Medium*, . . .	*Well Done,* and . . .	*Tough, Dry Steak.*

For a hotline chef, these textures correspond to the firmness in a piece of protein as it cooks, like a grilled steak or a sautéed chicken breast (Appendix 1).

To modify this technique for the bakeshop, just press on the soft, un-flexed pad of your palm, just below the thumb. Don't touch any finger to the tip of the thumb.

You'll feel very little elasticity or push-back from the pad. A fully proofed *Pain au Levain* feels like this.

Photo Gallery #12   Proofing Tests

Getting More from Your Home Oven

Introduction

To simulate a professional oven in the home, there are several techniques a resourceful baker can use. The ingenious method of preheating a cast-iron pot in your oven, with something like a *Le Creuset* or *Lodge*, comes to mind.

When your bread is proofed and ready to bake, you carefully remove the preheated pot (and its lid) and place it on top of the stove. Transfer the dough inside the pot, replace the cover, and then return the assembly to the oven. When baked this way, the bread delivers a crackling, aromatic crust and a moist, tender interior.

Jim Lahey popularized this technique with his *No-Knead Bread* innovation. In *Josey Baker Breads*, the eponymous baker offers his riff on the process. In *From the Wood-Fired Oven*, Richard Miscovich works with a cast-iron combo cooker.

The *oven stone—*aka *pizza* or *baking stone—*is another way to modify a home oven to get bakeshop results. In his books, Peter Reinhart bakes on an oven stone to deliver crustier bread with toasty aroma notes.

I've used all of these methods for different types of doughs and in different ovens. I've had success with all of them and can recommend any one as a valuable contribution to the home baker's skill set.

**The technique I describe here
requires two oven stones, not just one.**

**To simulate the heat distribution of a hearth
or commercial bread oven in your home,
bake your bread not just ON an oven stone,
but UNDER one, too.**

Backstory

In the part of my life when I'm not writing, I enjoy time as an itinerant baking instructor travelling for hands-on classes, demos, and workshops. I routinely discover all sorts of ovens, brand new ones to literally seasoned veterans.

At the time of this story, I was baking in a *leaky* oven (meaning it was poorly insulated with more heat escaping into the kitchen than staying inside the oven). It was what line chefs often call a *roasting oven*, its chamber large enough to turn out two 30-pound turkeys on Thanksgiving. Inside the oven, the top rack was about 6 inches from the oven ceiling, the middle rack about 15 inches.

As we know, heat rises. The ceiling of the oven chamber is hotter than the oven's floor. In order to get a dark crust color, the bread has to be close to this super-heated part of the oven while still being low enough for heat to penetrate its thickest part without burning the exterior.

Baking on the top rack was not an option. With an average height of 4 inches, a one and one-half pound boule of dough would have only 2 inches of headroom. Its top would burn before the bread was baked through.

On the other hand, baking on the middle rack would leave about 10 inches of empty space between the oven ceiling and the top of the bread. That's too far away for the crust from the deflected heat the ceiling provides. It would be like grilling a hamburger a foot from the coals. The burger will cook through, but it won't have dark brown grill marks and the caramelized meaty flavor that comes with them.

Turns out the sweet spot for a one and one-half to two-pound boule of Pain au Levain is around 4 inches from the oven ceiling. And that's when it hit me. By stacking five inverted sheet trays on the middle rack, I could elevate the bread to where it wanted to be. But I couldn't expect the bottom crust to get enough heat through the multiple layers of insulation the sheet trays provided.

That takes us back to the main reason for baking directly on an oven stone. So in the Jenga™-like construction I was creating in the oven chamber, now I had an oven stone sitting on top of the five sheet trays. By stacking sheet trays and an oven stone into the oven chamber, I was literally reducing its capacity. I was concentrating the heat into a smaller and smaller space.

So then I asked,
Instead of raising the height of the bread, couldn't I lower the height of the oven ceiling? In other words, instead of just baking ON an oven stone, I wanted to bake UNDER one, too.

The idea of using two oven stones was a flash of lightning and reminded me that much of our culinary history is steeped in random discovery. I tried to imagine what it was like when Man first discovered how to bake yeasted bread thousands of years ago and I was humbled to feel a brief connection with one of our oldest civilized rituals.

Technical Information—Thermal Mass

The oven stone is a sponge, soaking up more heat the longer it preheats in the oven. After an hour, the stone becomes a dense core of retained heat.

Interestingly, this doesn't increase the temperature of the air in the oven chamber. What it does is keep the air temperature constant, closer to the oven's set point and for a longer time. The heated core slowly releases retained heat as the air temperature cools, like when the door is opened or because the temperature of the dough is much lower.

This property is what baker's know as *thermal mass*. It's the basic principle of preparing a wood-fired masonry oven, letting the flames die, and sweeping out the ashes. The breads are baked with the heat stored in the masonry.

It's not just a question of how the masonry in the oven absorbs the heat. It's equally as important how that heat is released and where this core of thermal mass is placed with respect to the food being cooked.

Baking directly on a pre-heated oven stone concentrates more heat along the bottom of the bread. A single oven stone does a good job of simulating the masonry floor of a hearth or pizza oven.

It's easy to see how the concentrated bottom heat delivers a thicker, crisper bottom crust to your bread. How this affects the interior of bread, what bakers call the *crumb*, deserves an explanation.

The *crumb* represents the size of the air cells in the bread and also how they are distributed. A well-made *Ciabatta*, the Italian *Slipper Bread*, has air cells one-half inch in diameter or larger. These cells are randomly distributed throughout the bread and words like *large, open,* or *irregular* better describe this crumb structure. A *sponge cake* (not a bread, but an effective image in this discussion) has small air cells, evenly distributed. Its crumb would be called *fine, tight, or uniform.*

The *coup de feu* (a French cooking term meaning a *kick of heat*) that comes from baking on the oven stone quickly changes water in the dough to steam. In turn, this steam raises the height of the bread and opens the interior cell structure. The open, irregular crumb that is characteristic of breads baked directly on the oven hearth highlights the tender, chewy texture of wild yeast breads.

A single stone in your home oven benefits the bread's crumb and its bottom crust. However, it doesn't address how heat is delivered to the top crust of your bread.

When a Neapolitan style pizza is baked at temperatures of 700° to 800°, it's not the surface of the hearth—the *deck*—that's being referred to. It's the temperature in the upper part of the oven—the *dome*. The dome is the super-heated oven zone responsible for what the top of your pizza looks like. The caramelized cheese, the toasted edges on the onions, and the char on the edge of the crust.

To simulate the two heat zones of a hearth oven or commercial bread oven in your home oven, use two oven stones. One to bake the bread *ON* and the other to bake the bread *UNDER*.

Placing the stone on the top rung in the oven literally reduces the size of the oven chamber. It concentrates the heat into a smaller space and creates a micro-climate of even heat beneath the stone. To recall an earlier analogy, the hamburger is closer to the coals now.

This is what baking in a cast-iron pot does. It creates a small oven inside a larger one. When the core of heat is placed closer to the baking bread, the crust browns and caramelizes. It's the caramelization that brings more flavor and texture contrast between the crust and the crumb.

Oven Set-Up and Baking Procedure

This sketch shows two oven stones and one empty baking tray.

Preheating (and Mise en Place)

1. While the oven is cold, adjust the baking racks.
2. Place one oven stone on the top rung and the other on the middle rung. Place the empty baking tray on the floor of the oven or on the lowest rung.*
3. Set the oven to 500°F. Preheat the oven for at least 30 minutes, one hour is preferred.
4. Five minutes before baking, pour warm water onto the empty baking tray at the bottom.
5. Shut the oven door.

* Certain oven manufacturers say DO NOT place anything directly on the floor of the oven since it can interfere with the heating element. For safety, refer to your oven's instruction manual or inquire through the manufacturer's website. If in doubt, just place the empty tray on the lowest rung in the oven.

This example uses the Baking Chart for the Pain au Levain (pages nnnn)

Stage I—Oven Spring (the first 8 minutes)

1. Load the scored bread onto the oven stone on the middle rung. Quickly shut the door. Be careful! Escaping steam can burn you.
2. Set the oven timer for 8 minutes. This is the *Oven Spring* stage of baking. Don't disturb the bread during this stage.
3. When the timer sounds, crack the oven door to release the initial rush of steam. Then open the door completely to eliminate the remaining steam.
4. Working quickly and carefully, remove the tray of water. Shut the oven door once again.

Stage II—Dry Baking (the second 8 minutes)

1. Reduce the oven thermostat to 435°F.
2. Set the oven timer for 8 minutes.
3. When the timer sounds, vent the oven again.
4. Check the bottom crust, assessing whether it can withstand the final 8 minutes required by the baking schedule. Make any necessary adjustments. (See the discussion on page nnnnn)
5. Shut the oven door.

Stage II—Dry Baking, continued
(the third and final 8 minutes)

1. Reset the oven timer for the final 8 minutes.
2. When the timer sounds, check the bread's internal temperature and assess its crust.
3. Remove the bread or continue baking as necessary.

1 Oven Stone + 1 Baking Tray

If you have only one stone, set up your oven this way:

Place the oven stone on the top rung and leave the middle rung empty. At the bottom, place the empty baking tray as before.

When ready to bake, invert your proofed bread onto the back of another baking tray. Score it, and then transfer the whole assembly onto the empty middle shelf.

At the two-thirds mark through baking, assess the bottom of the bread to make sure it's not taking too much color. If it is, carefully remove it with a pair of gloved hands, leaving the tray in the oven.

Invert another cool tray on top of the hot one in the oven. This creates an air gap between the two trays, mediating the direct heat that reaches the bottom crust.

Return the bread to the oven to finish its bake.

Oven Safety

Use a pair of metal tongs to move the baking tray two inches forward so it's easier to fill it with water. Use a gloved hand to push the tray back.

When removing the water tray, use the tongs again to bring it forward so it's easy to grab.

Baking gloves are recommended over kitchen towels. It's easy for the corner of a towel to find its way into the hot water, causing a spill or a burn.

Baker's Tip:
Poor Crust from a Crowded Oven

Bake only as many loaves as your oven can accommodate at one time. To determine the ideal amount of bread your oven can handle, consider its inside dimensions:

How high is the oven chamber?
Most home ovens do not have enough vertical space for two shelves of bread to bake at once.

The higher one tends to burn its top crust while the lower one burns its underside. When the loaves are rotated, the breads get too dark on the remaining sides.

How wide is the oven chamber?
Generally, it's a question of whether the oven is wide enough to accommodate both loaves.

When you place two loaves on the same oven shelf there needs to be at least four inches of space between them. Also, there needs to be at least three inches of space between the side of the loaves and the oven wall. If your oven meeets these requirements, you can bake two loaves simultaneously on one shelf.

Baker's Tip:
Juggling Two Loaves

Baking two loaves at once
Ideally you can load both at the same time. This is often not possible in a home kitchen because you need a large loading peel or another pair of hands. Keep the oven door open as briefly as possible. Have the second loaf ready to load—scored and on its own peel—before loading the first one.

Baking one loaf at a time
When baking only one loaf at a time, let the oven recover (i.e., return to its original heat settings) before baking the second loaf. To slow the proofing of the second loaf, transfer it to the refrigerator about 15 minutes before you bake the first one. No need to cover it with plastic while it waits.

When the first loaf is almost done baking, pull the second one from the refrigerator. Let it sit at ambient temperature while the first loaf finishes its bake. While the first loaf is cooling, re-set the oven according to the Baking Chart. Remember to replace the empty tray on the bottom of the oven or lowest rung. Preheat it for five minutes, and then another five minutes once you pour the water onto the tray. This gives your oven a full ten minutes between bakes.

Meanwhile, prepare the second loaf for baking. If it has developed a dry skin on its surface, score it as usual. Then, spray it with a hand-held water mister before loading into the oven.

7	Décor & Baking	Score; See **Baking Chart**

Décor & Baking—Step by Step

A. Prepare a loading peel

Select a wood or metal peel for loading your bread and wipe it with a clean dry rag. Lightly dust the peel with semolina, bread flour or a blend of the two.

B. Make sure the dough doesn't stick to the banneton before inverting it

1 Holding the banneton in both hands, use the two-handled *Tilt and Wobble Technique* described above to loosen the dough from the sides of the basket.

If the dough sticks in the crevices, sprinkle some Semolina around the outer rim of the dough where it contacts the banneton. During the *Tilt and Wobble*, the Semolina slowly makes its way between the dough and the wall, letting the dough pull free. A second sprinkling of Semolina is sometimes necessary.

Cornmeal v. Semolina

Dusting a loading peel with Cornmeal is a stylistic preference of some craft bakers. It's used for some loaves that are sold whole, as in a retail bakery.

In a food service operation, where loaves are sliced for sandwiches or served as table breads, Cornmeal is coarse and makes slicing difficult. Semolina is finer so is preferred here.

If you don't have Semolina, you can just use a dusting of bread or whole wheat flour on the peel. Flour won't burn as quickly as Cornmeal, either.

2 Dust the surface of your proofed dough with bread flour to make sure its surface is dry. Quickly and surely, invert the dough onto the peel. Don't slam the banneton onto the peel. This can flatten or deflate the dough.

3 Rest the inverted banneton on the peel for a few seconds, letting the dough fall from its own weight. Don't shake or bang the banneton.

4 Use both hands to gently remove the banneton from the peel. Lift the basket on an angle to loosen the dough.

5 Move the dough to the front edge of the peel. If there is too much rice flour on the dough, use the back of your fingers to brush some away.

6 Use a plastic scraper to remove excess semolina or flour from the peel, it can quickly burn on the deck. Plus, it can be blown onto the bread when steam is injected into the oven.

Photo Gallery #13   From the Banneton to the Loading Peel

C. Score with a serrated knife or baker's lame (*lahm*)

Fixed or Replaceable Blade?

The blades on professional scoring tools may be fixed or replaceable. The advantage of the replaceable style is that the baker can change his blade when it gets dull. Fixed blade lames have a limited number of loaves they can score.

When one corner of the blade becomes dull, a blade that is replaceable can be rotated. With its four corners, one replaceable blade scores four times as many loaves as a fixed-blade lame.

SAFETY FIRST

Swapping out double-edged razor blades by hand can be a fearful task. Some bakers prefer the fixed blade style for that reason.

Discard a dull razor blade carefully. For safety, wrap it in a piece of masking tape before putting it in the landfill bucket.

Blade Shapes

There are two shapes for the razor blade—straight or curved. One shape is not more **correct** than the other. As with every art, each baker has a preference for the shape of the blade. It depends on how he signs his loaves.

Straight blades create patterns of straight lines, like the ones in the pattern guide on page 120.

Curved blades allow the baker to draw arcs, curves, and flowing lines.

Lames on display at *Europain* Bakery Trade Show

Lames are like paintbrushes for the artist

At *Europain*, the bakery exposition held just north of Paris each Spring, vendors have walls of displays for new versions of the *lame* each year. Some are of the switchblade-type so the tool closes and protects the blade and the baker from injury. Still others have removable plastic or stainless covers that fit snugly over the blades.

Baker's Tip

When learning to score proofed loaves, a 5- or 6-inch serrated blade, similar to the one on a steak knife, is a valuable tool. Its lightweight design and scalloped teeth are ideally suited for slicing through protein networks, the kind you find in a properly developed dough and in a grilled steak.

The individual teeth let the knife grip the surface of the dough at several points simultaneously. The blade gets a quick hold on the surface and makes an incision. You get a feel for how little pressure is actually required to score breads. This increases your confidence in scoring and you quickly advance to using the lame.

TIPS FOR SCORING

Straight Lines

It's easier to create a scoring pattern with a combination of straight lines. For this style, a straight edge is recommended. Refer to the Pattern Guide for examples.

It's all about the surface tension

Visualize the surface tension on the dough before scoring it. Look at the dough from the side and see how gravity pulls the profile outward and down. Note how the top of the dough flattens while the sides bulge slightly outward.

If you start at the center of the dough on the top, the first cut releases this tension and the sides of the dough flatten. Further cuts continue to flatten the overall appearance of the bread.

Use small cuts to release the surface tension of the dough

Small cuts release small amounts of surface tensions gradually. Your scoring pattern will remain more intact as the dough rises during the Oven Spring stage of baking.

Rotate the dough as you score

Visualize your scoring hand as a fixed machine and rotate the dough for each cut.

Instead of drawing the blade across the dough from different directions, repeat the scoring gesture from the same position each time. Rotate the dough to expose a new part of the dough's surface for each cut.

Score from the bottom up

To make a sand-dollar pattern (page 120), draw the knife from the bottom of the bread toward the top as you score—this keeps more surface tension in the dough. When you draw your knife downward across the dough surface, the downward pressure flattens the bread.

Photo Gallery #15   Scoring the Sand Dollar Pattern

Score quickly!

When using a serrated knife, position the blade on the bread *where you want the score mark to begin*. Then, quickly draw the knife across the surface to make the incision. Rest the blade on the surface of the dough and rapidly draw the knife across the surface. The teeth of the blade grip the dough easily.

If using a razor blade, you need a sort of running start before the blade contacts the dough. A razor blade can't make an incision from a stopped position. It needs to be in motion, building momentum, before it can make that first cut. That's why the serrated steak knife is a good tool when learning to score.

Change the angle of the blade as it moves across the bread

Look at the bread's profile from the side. From left to right, the profile curves upward, reaches a high point, and then recedes downward. Keep this shifting profile in mind as you score the bread.

In slow motion, visualize how your hand will first draw the blade in an upward motion and gradually level off as it travels over the top of the boule. To finish, your hand will gradually draw the blade at a downward angle as the blade travels down the slope of the bread.

With just the slightest change of angle as the blade is drawn across the dough, the depth of the score is more even. During the Oven Spring stage of baking, the design blossoms as the bread expands.

Photo Gallery #14   Follow the Curve of the Dough

Don't press down on the dough

Let the weight of the blade do the work. Knives have enough weight to anchor the teeth on the surface of the dough and make the first cuts. No downward pressure from the baker's hand is needed.

Baker's Tip

A craft baker makes scoring breads look easy. The easier he makes it look, the more practice you know went into his skill. Don't worry if your first score marks aren't exactly what you had in mind. Use each result to critique your own skills. Make your next scores better.

Even the best bakers have stories of frustration recalling their first tries at scoring. The better the baker, the funnier the story usually is.

Visualization

Before scoring a production run of breads, I take a moment to visualize how a concert violinist draws his bow with light and sustained pressure—at the beginning, middle, and end of its travels—across the strings. The sound it creates is uniform, consistent and unmodulated. That's the hand gesture I visualize and try to bring to my breads when scoring them.

Curved Lines

Creating the *ear*

When a bread is properly cut with a lame, the score mark seems to *peel back* during the Oven Spring. The lame slips beneath the surface of the dough, creating a small *flap* of dough that overlaps the incision. The surface tension of the dough tugs on this flap, widening the cut. The result is a sliver of crust standing higher than the rest of the surface. It's thin and bakes faster. It gets caramelized and crispy. Bakers call this the *ear*.

Make score marks uniformly deep

This allows the bread to expand evenly as it rises during the *Oven Spring*.

Hold the tool so only *one corner* of the blade comes in contact with the dough

20 degrees to the surface of the dough is recommended. Don't hold the entire edge of the razor blade level with the dough surface.

Tilt the blade away from you

If there's writing or the manufacturer's name on the blade, you should be able to see it when the blade is held at the proper angle. Some bakers visualize that the lame is a spoon and use it to score through the dough surface as if they are going to scoop up a small bit of sauce or warm ganache from a bowl.

SCORING PATTERNS

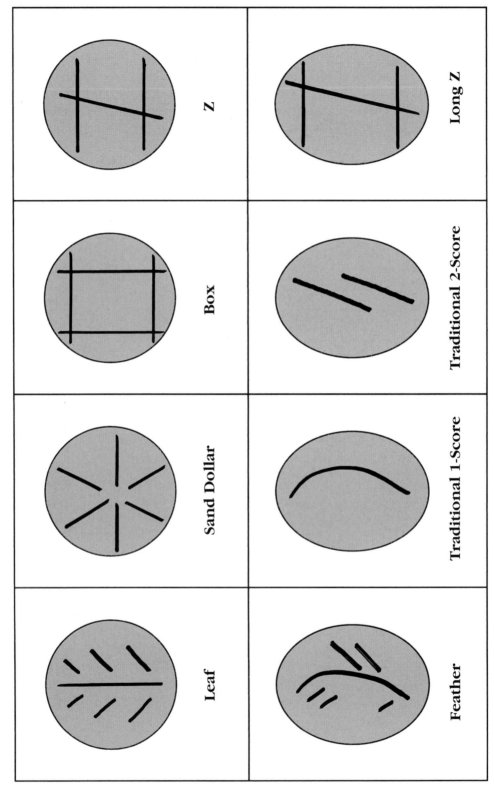

Z

Long Z

Box

Traditional 2-Score

Sand Dollar

Traditional 1-Score

Leaf

Feather

Visualization

In one of the more poetic descriptions of a cooking process I've ever read, Chinese scholar, chef, and cookbook author Barbara Tropp* captures on the written page the concert of sensations, thoughts and cooking chemistry when a simple vegetable stir-fry is properly prepared by a chef who is as well-seasoned as his wok. Her image sizzles from the page as if watching the synchronized movements of a ballet dancer or a full-court press from an NBA team.

The steps are seamless and in rapid motion. No gesture is wasted and no time unutilized. That is the essence of beauty in a technique-intense activity. Getting your proofed breads into the oven and properly steamed falls into the same category of skill.

Her advice is to visualize the entire sequence of movements. And to repeat them consistently each time. Same oven, same loading spot, same amount of steam. Until the gestures are automatic, with a rhythm you can repeat without thinking about it.

Here are the steps in the loading and baking sequence I have found to be most successful for students. Each baker, each oven and every boule of dough is a unique combination. Some modifications will present themselves the more you practice. But shortly, the discipline rewards you with beautifully consistent breads.

The Modern Art of Chinese Cooking: Techniques and Recipes, Barbara Tropp, William Morrow Cookbooks, 1996.

ARTISAN WORK HABITS

Use a soft-bristle oven brush with a long handle to sweep semolina and flour from the bottom of the deck before each bake. A stiff-bristle brush can be used but requires more effort.

A. Prepare the surface of the deck

Make broad, sweeping motions across the deck. Two passes with the brush and your deck is clean. For an oven that holds two full-size sheet trays, a 20-inch bristle with a 36-inch handle works well.

With gloved hands and rolled-down sleeves, position the brush in the oven against the right-hand wall. Sweep the entire deck surface from the right to the left. Angle the bristles into the left-hand corner and draw the collected debris toward the front of the oven.

DO

- Wear gloves.
- Use a smaller brush to sweep the crumbs and bits from the front edge of the oven.
- Hold a flat metal container, like a reusable aluminum pie tin, in one hand and sweep the crumbs out with the other hand.
- Set the small brush and metal container aside for the next use. Make sure the crumbs are not hot when they are emptied into the compost bin.

DON'T

- Don't sweep crumbs onto the bakeshop floor. They make the floor slippery and create a safety hazard.
- Don't use a plastic container for the crumbs. In direct contact with the hot deck or oven door, it melts.

B. Take the *sting* out of the hot deck

When it's the first bake of the day and the ovens have been pre-heating for more than an hour, the surface of the deck gets very hot. Even if the bottom oven element is set to a low heat position, the deck stone still absorbs a lot of heat. The first breads loaded onto the deck receive a shock from the built-up heat, like the first pancake poured on a hot griddle.

Take the *sting* out of the deck with a wet oven mop or similar tool. Here's how:

1 Take an empty plastic bucket (2- or 3-gallon) and fill it halfway with warm water. If you are right-handed, set this on the floor next to the right-hand side of your oven. Reverse, for lefties.

2 Use a clean kitchen rag. Immerse it in the water and thoroughly soak it.

3 Lift the rag from the water and wring it gently. Lay the wet rag over the scrubbing head of a stiff-bristle oven brush— not the soft-bristle brush used for dry sweeping the deck.

4 Starting on the right hand side, mop the deck from the back wall to the front in one gesture. Moving to the left, reposition the brush against the back wall and mop toward the front of the oven. Halfway across the deck, remove the brush and wet rag from the oven.

5 Careful! Peel off the rag and drop it in the water. Dip it once or twice to rinse it. Then draw the rag out of the water again. Hold it over the bucket until it is just dripping slowly and lay it across the brush as before. Pick up where you left off and mop the left half of the deck.

6 Return the rag to the water and set the oven brush aside. Move the water bucket away from the oven top a safe area.

Photo Gallery #11   Prep the Oven Deck

WARNING!

The danger of steam burns aside, this technique is not without its risks.

In the bakeshop, the water bucket itself and the possibility of a wet floor are safety hazards. In the oven, if there is too much water or the rag sits on one part of the deck too long, the thermal shock can cause the deck to crack.

SAFETY FIRST

Use caution when mopping the deck with this technique. The wet rag gets very hot. Peel it carefully off the brush and use a dry hand or pair of tongs.

If you use a glove, don't let it get wet. A wet oven mitt is a safety hazard for the entire shop.

Nothing gives you a burn faster than grabbing a hot sheet tray with a wet mitt. Nothing.

Stage I—Oven Spring
The first 8 minutes

Oven	Stage I	¿Steam?	Vent @	Stage II	Duration	Int. temp°
Deck	500° (9.9.1) [3.3.1]	10 secs	8 m	435° (6.6.0) [2.2.0]	+ 8 m • • • • • • • • • • check*/rotate + 8 to 10 m more	200°
Rack (w/ convection + oven stone)	440°	10 secs	8 m	390°	+ 8 m • • • • • • • • • • check*/rotate + 8 to 10 m more	200°

Note: These are heating element settings. *About a Commercial Deck Oven,* Appendix 3, explains how these operate.

ERGONOMICS

For better control, keep the front edge of the peel touching the deck once it is placed in the oven chamber. If the peel's not making contact with the deck, the breads can slide off to the left or right.

QUICK & SURE

Before loading, make sure the manual vent control is in the *closed* or shut position.

From the moment the oven door is opened, load breads quickly. With multiple loaves, have as many of them scored and on peels (or other loading tools), ready to go.

The longer the oven door is open, the more heat is lost. The breads bake more slowly and have less volume.

1 **Load the bread onto the deck**

Grab the peel with both hands and have a baking partner open the oven door for you. Insert the peel into the oven, resting its front edge flat on the deck.

Push the peel into the oven to position the bread where you want it to land on the hearth. Then, tilt the handle of the peel upward, keeping the front edge of the peel in contact with the deck. A small angle of 20 degrees is enough of a sliding board for the bread.

Again, keeping the front edge of the peel on the surface of the deck, move the peel forward and back, deeper into the oven and then back toward the front, creating momentum so that the bread slides by itself toward the front edge of the peel.

With less pressure now, continue moving the peel forward and back. Smoothly draw the peel toward you, still keeping its front edge touching the deck. As the peel is drawn out, the bread slides onto the deck.

Photo Gallery #16　**Loading Bread onto the Deck**

2 Inject steam into the oven chamber

Inject steam into the oven chamber for a total of 10 seconds. Oven models have different mechanisms for introducing steam. Most often there is a button that can be pushed and held down for a *count of ten* or there is a knob that can be rotated right or left.

During this entire stage, keep the oven door closed and the manual oven vent in the **closed** position.

Don't Over-Steam Your Breads!

Once the breads are loaded, inject steam into the oven chamber for a count of 10 seconds. If your oven injects steam slowly, depress the steam button, hold it for a count of ten seconds, and then release it. Keep the oven vent closed.

If your oven set-up injects steam rapidly, so strongly that it sometimes blows the breads across the surface of the deck, then use a pulsing on-off motion. Depress the steam button and then release it. Repeat this 10 times.

Either way, be careful not to get too much steam in the oven chamber. When there's too much steam in the oven chamber, it condenses on the surface of the bread and drips down the side. The bottom gets gummy and the wet starch glues the bread onto the deck.

Assuming the oven door is well-sealed, never inject so much steam that it visibly seeps out around the edges of the oven door. This is a safety hazard and can cause steam burns to you or your fellow bakers.

3 Set the oven timer

This is the Oven Spring stage of baking.
Set the timer for 8 minutes.

The bread needs a high heat and a moist environment to expand to its full size. Don't open the door during this stage.

Oven	Stage I	¿Steam?	Vent @	Stage II	Duration	Int. temp°
Deck	500° (9.9.1) [3.3.1]	10 secs	8 m	435° (6.6.0) [2.2.0]	+ 8 m · · · · · · · · · · check*/rotate + 8 to 10 m more	200°
Rack (w/ convection + oven stone)	440°	10 secs	8 m	390°	+ 8 m · · · · · · · · · · check*/rotate + 8 to 10 m more	200°

4. Vent Steam from the Oven

When the timer sounds, turn it off. Then, pull the manual handle or lever on the oven to release steam from the oven chamber. Every oven model is different, but most have a knob that is pulled out.

The vent itself is usually located along the top rear of the oven chamber. There may be a single vent in the center or one in each of the top corners. Either way, about 90% of the accumulated steam escapes via this route.

To remove the remaining 10% steam, open the oven door. Roll down your sleeves and place a mitt on your hand. Stand back from the oven to avoid a steam burn.

Slowly open the door so steam escapes gradually, then open it completely. Leave the oven door open for a *count of ten* to thoroughly vent it. Then shut the door.

Keep the vent in the ***open*** position for the remainder of the bake.

Oven	Stage I	¿Steam?	Vent @	Stage II	Duration	Int. temp°
Deck	500° (9.9.1) [3.3.1]	10 secs	8 m	435° (6.6.0) [2.2.0]	+ 8 m ··········· check*/rotate + 8 to 10 m more	200°
Rack (w/ convection + oven stone)	440°	10 secs	8 m	390°	+ 8 m ··········· check*/rotate + 8 to 10 m more	200°

Stage II—Dry Baking

The second 8 minutes

1. Reduce the Oven Temperature and Element Settings

Reduce the oven thermostat to 435°F.
Adjust the element settings to 6.6.0 or 2.2.0, depending on your oven model.

2. Re-set the Oven Timer

Set the timer for 8 minutes.

They are inflated with steam and expanded CO_2 bubbles. The crust is fragile.

3 Vent the Oven again

When the timer sounds, turn it off. With a gloved hand, carefully vent the oven a second time. Even though the physical vent is already *open*, wild yeast breads continue to give off steam as they bake.

4 Check the Bottom Crust

Use a pair of gloved hands or a metal oven peel to remove a test bread. Shut the oven door. Tilt the test bread to inspect how brown the bottom crust has become.

The bread is still scheduled for 8 more minutes in the oven. Ask yourself if the loaves can withstand this or if they will burn.

CASE I The Bottom Crust is Light Brown

In this case, you've got a good balance of heat across the bottom elements in your deck and the breads are baking evenly. Return the test bread to the oven, shut the door.

CASE II The Bottom Crust is Already Dark

Insert an inverted sheet tray or oven rack between the deck and the breads so they don't bake directly on the hearth for the next 8 minutes. Here's how:

A Shut the oven door and gather your mise en place. Grab a baking partner to lend a hand.

B Don't remove the breads from the oven. Their baking slows down and their crusts get thick and leathery.

C When you're ready, use gloved hands and a metal peel to move the breads from the right side of the oven to the left. Have your partner insert the oven rack or inverted sheet tray on the right side of the deck.

D Move all the breads on top of the rack or sheet tray. Then have your partner insert an oven rack or inverted sheet tray on the left side of the deck.

E Re-distribute the loaves evenly across the whole deck. Work quickly yet safely.

5 Re-set the Oven Timer

Set the timer for 8 minutes more. Keep the door closed and the vent *open*.

Oven	Stage I	¿Steam?	Vent @	Stage II	Duration	Int. temp°
Deck	500° (9.9.1) [3.3.1]	10 secs	8 m	435° (6.6.0) [2.2.0]	+ 8 m •••••••••• check*/rotate + 8 to 10 m more	200°
Rack (w/ convection + oven stone)	440°	10 secs	8 m	390°	+ 8 m •••••••••• check*/rotate + 8 to 10 m more	200°

Baker's Tip

If the bread still needs more time, you've got an oven problem and you need to troubleshoot the entire baking schedule. Perhaps the top elements don't get as hot as they should and need to be set one position higher in order to properly brown the crust. Maybe the element settings are appropriate but the oven temperature needs to be increased by 25 degrees.

Any of these changes can solve your issue. But continuing to bake the bread at this point develops a thick crust and dries out the interior.

Stage II—Dry Baking (continued)
The third and final 8 minutes

When the timer sounds, turn it off.

Use a pair of gloved hands or a metal oven peel to remove the bread. Shut the oven door.

1 Check the Bread

Invert the bread the bench. Insert an insta-read thermometer into the center of the bread. ***The interior of the Pain au Levain is done when its temperature reaches 200°F.***

But that's only the inside. The crust must also pass its own test.

If the crust is dark brown, smells toasty and is hard when flicked with your finger or tapped with the back of a spoon, the bread is done.

2 Remove the Bread

Remove it and set on a rack to cool for at least 1 hour.

—OR—

(see next page)

1 Check the Bread

If the internal temperature has not yet reached 200°F or if the crust does not suit you, return the bread to the oven and continue baking. Keep your eye on the bottom crust that it does not burn.

2 Re-set the Oven Timer

Re-set the oven timer. This can take an additional 4 or 5 minutes. Depending on your oven, it can take slightly longer.

3 Remove the Bread

Once this additional time has elapsed, remove the bread. Any additional oven time dries the bread (see *Baker's Tip*).

Baker's Tip

Am I Supposed to Rotate the Breads?

Breads are not cakes. Cakes bake more evenly when rotated, usually halfway through their total oven time. Not breads. Breads like to stay in one spot.

There may be one side of your oven that bakes slower. In that case, those loaves will need to stay in the oven longer.

Keep your eye on the rest of breads, the majority of them. Remove them when they're done. Then, move the *slower* loaves into the hotter spot and let them finish up.

When you move all the loaves around on the deck, the oven temperature drops. All the breads on the entire deck bake slower and they all become drier.

The Most Important Steps

A. Clean out the oven

Use a soft bristle brush or oven brush to sweep out any semolina, flour or crumbs on the floor of the deck. Use the technique described on pages 121–123.

B. Re-set the Oven Thermostat and Element Settings

Think ahead to the next baker. Return the oven to its original settings. For Wild Yeast Doughs the settings are:

❖ Oven @ 500°F

❖ Element settings @ 9.9.1 or 3.3.1, depending on the oven model

❖ Manual Oven Vent **closed**

C. Allow Time for Oven Recovery

The oven needs at least 5 to 10 minutes to regain thermal mass. Always build a minimum of ten minutes oven recovery time into your schedule.

Re-set the oven timer as a reminder.

Phase Eight: Cooling & Ripening

Wear oven mitts. Hold the bread in one hand and gently turn it over, use the other gloved hand to brush browned semolina or flour from the bottom. Place the bread upright on a screen or wooden board. Allow it to cool at least one hour.

Ripening involves little more than letting a bread rest on a rack after it has completely cooled. The protein structure sets and the starches become firm, losing their gummy texture. Residual CO_2 and alcohol leave the bread. After a 4 to 8 hour ripening phase, wild yeast breads have improved flavor and texture (Appendix 1).

Warm foods have more aroma and flavor intensity than cold foods. You can return the bread to a 375°F oven before serving to re-crisp the crust and restore its just-baked character.

Pain au Levain

Formula, Main Dough

Ingredient	BP%	4-1/2 or 6 Qt Ounces	4-1/2 or 6 Qt Grams	8 Qt	20 Qt
Basic Levain (from above)	20%	4 oz	120 g	240 g	500 g
Water	70%	14 oz	400 g	800 g	1,725 g
Whole Wheat Flour	20%	4 oz	120 g	240 g	500 g
Bread Flour	80%	1 #	450 g	900 g	2,000 g
Salt	2.5%	1/2 oz	14 g	30 g	64 g
Yields		2# 2 oz	950 g	1,800 g	4,100 g

Procedure, Main Dough

1	Mise en Place	H₂O @ 92° ; Levain @ 70°	ddt°= 78°
2	Ingredient Mixing	Autolyse	
3	Development	Speed #2, 2 m; + Rest 5 m; + Speed #1, 2 m	*Improved*
4A	Floor Fermentation	1h 00 m @ 78° (70% hum); + Degas and Fold; 1h 00 @ 78° (70% hum)	
4B	Cool Fermentation	18 to 24 h 00 @ 50° (70% hum)	
5	Shaping	Temper dough 1h 00 *on the floor* Scale @ 2# 2 oz piece Form as gentle round Bench rest 20 m Final Form as Round or Boulot	
6	Proofing	1h 30 @ 78° (70% hum), covered; + 30 m more, uncovered	
7	Décor & Baking	Score; See **Baking Chart**	

Pain au Levain

Baking Chart

Pain au Levain
@ 2# to 2# 2 oz

Oven	Stage I	¿Steam?	Vent @	Stage II	Duration	Int. temp°
Deck	500° (9.9.1) [3.3.1]	10 secs	8 m	435° (6.6.0) [2.2.0]	+ 8 m • • • • • • • • • • check*/rotate + 8 to 10 m more	200°
Rack (w/ convection + oven stone)	440°	10 secs	8 m	390°	+ 8 m • • • • • • • • • • check*/rotate + 8 to 10 m more	200°

* **Check** means inspect bottom crust. If it is browning more than the top crust and appears it would burn with additional baking, elevate the loaves onto the back of an inverted sheet pan placed directly on the hearth.
Rotate loaves only if necessary.

When it's time to feed your Wild Yeast Culture...
Zero your scale. Weigh the Culture and its container together. Subtract the *tare weight* of the container to determine the *Initial Weight* of the Culture.

Multiply the Initial Weight of the Culture by **1.25** to determine how much Water you need. Add the Water and stir.

Scale Fresh Flour to equal the Initial Weight of the Culture. Add the Flour.

Blend well.

Dip your fingers in water to wipe down the wall of the container.

To make a Basic Levain...
Place a bowl on the scale and zero the scale. Spoon Ripe Culture into the bowl.

Zero the scale again. Add Water. Blend the Culture with the Water.

Zero the scale a third time. Add Flour. Blend so all the Flour is wet.

Smear the mixture against the side of the bowl with a plastic scraper.

Transfer the mixture into a plastic container. Dip your fingers in water to remove all the Levain from the scraper.

Press the mixture into the bottom of the container. Clean the wall of the container with wet fingers.

Take the temperature of the Levain mixture. Cover the container. Place a Fermentation Tag on the container.

Ferment the Levain on the floor for two hours (or as directed). Then transfer to the refrigerator for cool fermentation overnight. Temper the ripe Levain to ambient temperature before using it.

#3 INGREDIENT MIXING SEQUENCE

Mise en Place for Main Dough (left to right):
Water, Ripe Levain, Whole Wheat Flour, Bread Flour, Salt

Zero the scale, place a bowl on top, and zero the scale again. Dip your fingers in water to transfer ripe Levain to the mixing bowl.

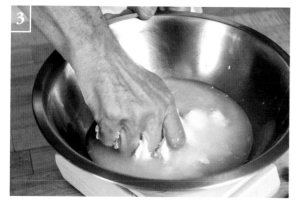

Zero the scale a third time. Calculate Water Temperature using the *Quick H2O Temp° Formula* (see Index). Add Water to Levain. Blend together, keeping the Levain below the surface of the water for easier mixing.

Add the Whole Wheat Flour. Blend until all flour is wet.

Add the Bread Flour. Don't sift it. Finally, sprinkle the Salt evenly over the top.

Cut into the ingredients with a plastic bowl scraper. Don't fold the flour as you would for a cake batter.

Scrape the walls clean. Scrape the bottom of the bowl and turn the mixture over.

Continue cutting into the dough until all the flour is wet. Depending on the size of the bowl, it might be easier to turn the mixture onto the bench.

Baker's Tip:
Clean a scraper by keeping it flat on the bench and using another scraper to do the work.

Cut into the mixture.
Starting at the part farther from you, *Cut* the dough mass into 1-inch strips. Each time the scraper hits the bench, *Push* the strip of dough *Away* from you.

Cut & Push Away. This technique opens the moist interior of the dough and draws in the dry flour. *On a wooden bench, a metal scraper works better. Use a plastic scraper on a stainless or ceramic surface.*

Gather the dough strips together. *Rotate* the pile of strips on a 90-degree angle.

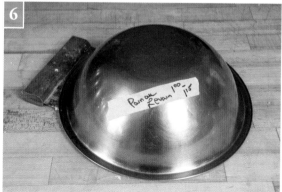

Repeat the whole sequence: **Cut, Push Away, Gather, & Rotate.**

Once all the flour is wet, push the dough side to side with your scraper, gathering it into a round. *Dipping your scraper in water keeps it from sticking to the dough.*

Autolyse
Cover the dough mass. Mark the time. Rest the dough for 15 minutes.

After the Autolyse...
Stretch the dough to see how much gluten has developed.

Zig-zag a metal bench scraper through the dough, left to right and back again, as you draw the scraper toward you.

Use just enough pressure so you can see strands of protein *Stretch* in the dough. Too much pressure rips the dough, making the bread crumbly when chewed.

After one zig-zag pass through the dough, *Scrape* it, pushing it toward its top edge. Use the scraper to *Fold* the top third of the dough toward you. Repeat the process (Steps 2, 3, and 4) for two minutes. **Zig-zag, Stretch, Scrape, & Fold.**

A mini Autolyse
The dough looks jagged and rough. Gather it together with your scraper dipped in water. Let the dough rest on the bench for 5 minutes. *If the dough is sticky, let it air dry without a cover. After the 5-minute rest, a tacky dough is easily formed into a smooth shape.*

If your bakery is cool or has low humidity, cover the dough instead. Meanwhile, clean your hands with bench flour.

Using less pressure now...
gently *Stretch* the dough across the bench.

Gather the dough toward you with the scraper in your right hand. Invert the dough onto itself.

Repeat the **Stretch & Gather** technique for one minute.

Clean your hands with bench flour. For one minute more, use just your hands and a light pressure to develop the dough, making it as smooth as possible.

Ready for Fermentation...
Round the dough gently. It doesn't need to be perfectly smooth at this time.

Lightly oil a container and use a scraper to transfer the dough. Loosely cover the dough with oiled plastic, don't tuck it underneath.

Test the Gluten Structure. Use a piece of dough the size of a Tablespoon. This dough is sticky but don't add flour to it. Roll it between your palms, not your fingers. Keep your fingers open. Air flow keeps the dough from sticking.

Drop the dough ball into bench flour. Roll it around to coat the outside.

Flatten it with the heel of your hand. Use quick and light gestures, up and down.

The dough windowpanes quickly because of the Autolyse. Flour your fingers. Use the pads of your fingers (not your fingernails) to stretch the dough. The dough is slack and sticky so don't overstretch it. A bit of elasticity is all you need to see.

Baker's Tip: Don't add flour during the Development Phase. If the dough sticks to the bench or sticks to you, use less pressure as you push the dough away from you.

Baker's Tip: Scrape the bench clean and rub your hands with bench flour to clean them. Move the dough to a dry area on the bench to reduce sticking.

Monitor the Fermentation Activity of the Dough.
Take the dough's temperature before handling it. Adjust the remainder of the Fermentation Schedule if the dough is too warm or too cool.

Dust the top of the dough with flour. Dust the bench with flour.

Dip your plastic scraper in flour and free the dough from its container.

Invert the dough onto your bench. Let the dough fall from the container by its own weight. Dust the top of the dough with flour.

Gently De-gas the dough. Work from the center of the dough outward.

Grab one edge of the dough. Stretch it outward. Keep the dough flat and parallel to the bench so it doesn't tear.

Lift the edge up and over the center of the dough, folding it in half.

Flatten the dough with your hand. Don't poke with your fingers.

Grab one corner of the dough along the fold. Stretch the dough outward.

Fold the dough in half again and flatten it with your hand.

Grab the remaining corner of the dough along the first fold and stretch it. Lift, fold, and flatten the dough once more.

Use both hands to invert the dough. Gently tuck the edges underneath. With a scraper, return the dough to its Fermentation container. Cover with plastic, as before.

Divide

If you divide your dough by eye, use a scale to check its weight. This develops your skill and accuracy.

First Form

Place dough on a lightly floured bench. Grab the top and stretch it lightly.

Fold the top so it meets the bottom edge of the dough. Keep the dough loose, the first form is a gentle round.

Rotate the dough 90 degrees. *Grab* the top and stretch gently. *Fold* it to meet the bottom edge of the dough once again. Repeat the process: **Rotate, Grab, & Fold.** Invert the dough. Tuck loose ends underneath.

Bench Rest

Coat the dough with oil or pan spray. Cover the dough with plastic, leaving some space where the dough meets the table so it can expand. Rest the dough for 20 minutes.

Final Form

Lightly flour the bench. Invert the dough with a scraper. More gently this time, repeat Steps 2, 3, and 4. Round the dough on the bench using the the *Two-Handed Rounding Gesture* or *the Poker Chip Gesture* (see Appendix 1).

Be sure there's no flour on the bench. Your dough needs surface tension to round smoothly.
In a dry or drafty kitchen, a damp cloth helps your dough grip the table as you round it.

With your left hand, push the dough directly away from you, travelling no more than 2 or 3 inches across the bench. Watch how the leading edge of the dough grips the bench and tucks itself under the moving dough.

With your right hand, pull directly toward you, returning the dough to its starting point. Don't try to rotate the dough. The dough rotates by itself as its leading edge grips the bench.

Use the heel of your hand and your little finger to push or pull the dough. Don't grab the dough with your thumb or first three fingers.

When the first blisters appear on the surface, the dough is round enough.

To check your skill, invert the dough with a bench scraper. Proper rounding leaves a swirled center on the bottom of the dough that bakers call the *navel*.

Don't leave the bench. The moment the Heel of your Hand is lifted from the bench, the dough loses surface tension and all rounding stops.

Gluten stretches in two directions. ① The top stretches toward your hands as the heel cups the dough and pushes forward. ② At the same time, the gluten on the leading edge stretches and tucks underneath.

#10 INTO THE BANNETON

Line the Banneton (Reed Proofing Basket) with Rice Flour, brown or white. Use more flour than if you were lining a cake pan.

Dust your bench with Rice Flour. Roll the dough so the rice flour comes about an inch up the side of the dough round.

Floured side facing down, place the dough in the prepared Banneton. Using a bench scraper to transfer the dough keeps it round.

Settle the dough into the Banneton with light pressure.

Drape lightly oiled plastic over the dough but don't tuck it between the dough and the side wall of the banneton. Leave space for the dough to expand.

Proof loaves for 1 hour 30 minutes at ambient temperature (or as directed), don't use a proof box. Remove the plastic cover and proof for 30 minutes more. When the top surface of the dough is dry, the inverted bread slides easily onto the deck.

#11 PREP THE OVEN DECK

Oven Tools (left to right): Soft-bristle oven brush, Wire-bristle oven brush, Rag for mopping deck, Metal tray for oven debris, Soft-bristle hand brush, Oven mitts.

Wear gloves. A soft-bristle oven brush sweeps debris from the deck. Use long gestures and work from one side of the oven to the other.

Use a hand brush with soft bristles to remove debris from the oven. Sweep hot crumbs into a metal container.

Dunk a rag in warm water. Wring it gently and drape it over an oven brush with wire bristles.

Starting at the back of the oven, move quickly but surely. Use long gestures to draw the wet rag to the front of the oven. Be careful of steam burns.

Draw the wet rag along the front edge of the deck to collect debris from the crevices.

#12 PROOFING TESTS

Tilt & Wobble
Use both hands to tilt the banneton left to right, forward and backward. The dough will wobble like properly-cooked Cheesecake, Flan, or Crème Brûlée.

Rare-Medium-Well
Press the dough with a floured finger. It feels like a rare-cooked steak or burger.

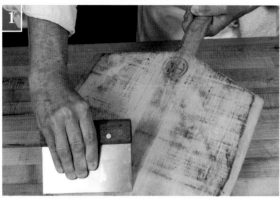

Clean your oven loading peel. Use a metal bench scraper on a wooden peel (as in the photo) or use a clean rag on a metal peel.

Dust the loading peel. Semolina is used here.

Before inverting a proofed bread, lightly dust the top with Flour.

Gently ***tilt and wobble*** the banneton with both hands so the bread pulls free from the wall.

Move quickly now…
Place your left hand on the top of the bread as you invert the banneton.

Quickly pull your left hand away as you place the banneton flat on the loading peel. Let the bread fall onto the peel by its own weight, don't bang the banneton on the peel.

Remove the banneton with two hands. Lifting on an angle helps release the bread.

Hold the blade at a 45-degree angle to the bench as you draw the knife **upward**.

Position the bread at the leading edge of the loading peel.

Hold the blade parallel to the bench as you draw the knife **across** the top.

Use a scraper to clean excess flour or semolina from the peel. The bread is ready for Scoring.

Hold the blade at a 45-degree angle as you draw **downward** to finish the score mark.

#15 SCORING THE SAND DOLLAR PATTERN

Start scoring with the Heel of the Knife, the point where the blade meets the handle. Draw the blade up the side of the dough from the bottom toward the top. Score only the sloping side of the dough, not the top.

Rotate the dough. Repeat the scoring gesture. Rotate and repeat until you have four, five, or six score marks.

#16 LOADING BREAD ONTO THE DECK

Position the peel in the oven and rest its leading edge on the deck surface. Tilt the handle upward 20 degrees. Move the peel forward and backward so the bread slides onto the deck. Keep the leading edge of the peel touching the deck, don't bounce the peel up and down.

Draw the peel out of the oven. Keep the leading edge of the peel touching the deck. Hold the peel parallel to the floor so the semolina doesn't spill.

After the Bench Rest, lightly dust the dough round with flour and invert it. Gently stretch it into an elliptical shape. Bring the top edge of the dough to the centerline. Press with enough pressure so the dough sticks.

Press with the pads of your fingers, not your fingernails. Draw your fingers away from the dough on an angle instead of lifting straight up. You won't stick to the dough.

Bring the bottom edge of the dough to the centerline. Press to close the seam. Draw your fingers away on the angle, as before.

Bring the top edge of the dough to meet the bottom edge, folding the dough in half. Use the pads of yours fingers to close the seam.

Pinch the seam to seal it. Taper the ends by holding your hands on a sharp angle. Keep the heels of your hands on the bench and roll the *Bâtard* forward and backward. Don't stretch the dough outward to the right or left.

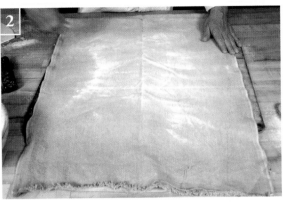

Dust your bench with Rice Flour. Place breads seam facing down on the floured bench while you prepare the *Couche*.

Lay the Couche over the back of an inverted sheet tray or bread proofing board. Dust the Couche with rice flour. Use a flat hand to gently rub flour into the cloth.

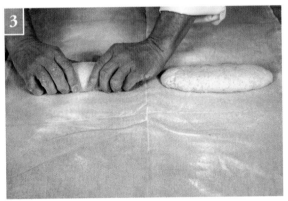

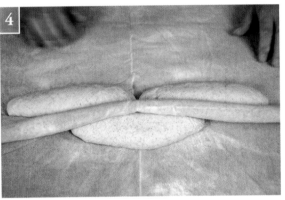

Seam facing up now, place breads a few inches apart on the Couche. Keep them far enough from the side edges of the Couche so there's enough material to cover them while proofing.

Form a pleat an inch higher than the breads to allow for expansion and snugly fit breads on each side. Align the thick part of one bread with the tapered ends of the others.

Fold extra material so it lays flat on top of the breads. Wedge a bench scraper under the side of the Couche to keep things snug. Proof loaves on the floor when using Couche.

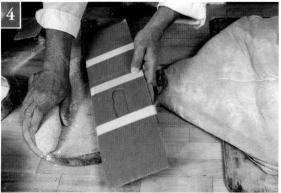

Unload the Couche starting with the bread on your far right-hand side. Grab a *Transfer Peel* with your **left hand**. Place its leading edge about an inch or two from the **left edge of the bread**. Press down to anchor the Transfer Peel onto the Couche.

Your right hand does the work... Gather material in your **right hand** so it moves closer to the bread. Draw the Couche up and toward your other hand. Be swift and sure, you need momentum to invert the bread onto the Transfer Peel.

Peel back the Couche with your right hand. Make sure the bread sits firmly on the Transfer Peel.

Transfer the bread onto a Loading Peel dusted with flour or semolina.

Arrange breads about 3 or 4 inches apart on the Loading Peel. Move them to the leading edge so they slide easily onto the deck.

Score your loaves. Long, overlapping slashes are typical for Bâtards. Load your breads directly onto the hearth.

Following the 2nd *Stretch & Fold*, the dough rounds rest on a Silpat® on an inverted baking tray. If needed, the dough pieces are easily moved to a warmer area.

Adding the Porridge

With floured fingers, quickly stretch the dough on its North-South axis.

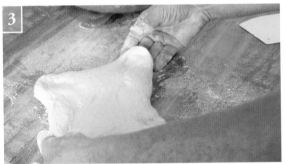

Stretch the dough on its East-West axis, then stretch the dough into a round shape.

Spread *half* the porridge mixture over the dough round. (In the photo, it's grits and goat cheese.) A spoon dipped in water makes this easier.

Using a plastic scraper to help...

fold the dough in half, encasing the porridge.

Spread *half the remaining* porridge mixture over the dough.

Using a plastic scraper, fold the dough in half again.

Spread the *remaining* porridge mixture over the dough. Fold it in half one last time, enclosing as much of the porridge and filling as possible.

Turn the whole assembly over so the seam faces down. Cover with a piece of lightly oiled plastic. Let rest on the bench for the remainder of the Fermentation time, 30 minutes or as directed.

For the final form,
Invert the dough onto a lightly floured bench. Stretch & Fold the right side of the dough...

and let it fall over the center of the dough. Repeat with the other 3 sides.

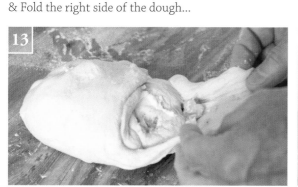

While folding, enclose any loose porridge.

When you finish, invert the folded dough onto a floured bench. Let it rest 5 minutes seam-side down before transferring it into a lined proofing basket.

A Porridge Bread is slack and moist. For easier removal, line your proofing basket with a linen or cotton cloth, then dust it with rice flour.

Protect the dough with a lightly oiled piece of plastic. Don't tuck it tightly between the dough and the cloth, allow space for the dough to expand.

AROMA AND FLAVOR NOTES
FOR BREAD

© MICHAEL KALANTY, 2015

CRUMB

1. **SWEET**/DAIRY
2. **SOUR**/FRUITY
3. **SOUR**/DAIRY

CRUST

4. **ROASTED**
5. **FRUITY**
6. **RESINOUS**
7. **TOASTY**
8. **SWEET**

GRAIN CHARACTER

SIMPLE   **MODERATE**   **COMPLEX**   **OVER-FERMENTED**

KEY

1. MILK, BUTTER, DIACETYL (POPCORN BUTTER)

2. GREEN APPLE, GRAPEFRUIT, LEMON, VINEGAR

3. FRESH CHEESE, BUTTERMILK, PLAIN YOGURT, AGED CHEESE

4. BAKED ONIONS, DARK BEER, BAKED CHESTNUT, CHEESE GRATIN

5. FIG, RAISIN, STEWED FRUIT

6. FRENCH ROAST COFFEE BEANS, VANILLA BEAN, AGED BALSAMIC VINEGAR

7. MALTY, POPPED GRAINS, NUTTY

8. BUTTERSCOTCH, TOFFEE, CHOCOLATE, MOLASSES

RAW STARCH, RAW GREEN BEANS, PEASHOOOTS, STRAW, DRY YEAST

COOKED SPAGHETTI, STEAMED POTATOES, COOKED OATMEAL, YEASTY CHAMPAGNE

COOKED WHOLE GRAINS, COOKED DRIED BEANS, GREEN OLIVE, FLINT, SLATE, MINERAL

BEER, GRAPEFRUIT PITH, "TURNED" RED WINE, SHERRY

Collection of
Bread Formulas

Modern Breads

Ancient Grain Hearth Bread with Barley Levain and Spelt

DESCRIPTION

Barley, one of a group of cereals called *ancient grains*, was grown as early as 8,000 BCE. When *Ulysses* sailed on his adventures in **The Odyssey**, the epic poem reports he stocked Barley for the ship's galley.

Barley Flour is ground from the whole grain grain. It is mild in flavor and brings a nut-like character to a bread's flavor profile.

Barley is used in the production of beer. Barley Malt, in syrup or dry form, is manufactured from grains of barley that have sprouted. When they're boiled in a solution of Malt Syrup and water prior to baking, Bagels take a rich mahogany color, a semi-gloss finish, and a sweet crust.

Barley is a member of the Grass Family but is a different class than Wheat. Barley Flour has more vitamins and minerals but a lower percent of gluten than a comparable amount of Wheat Flour.

The Levain for this bread is made with Barley Flour. Pre-Fermenting develops richer grain flavor and adds flexibility to the Barley Flour's gluten structure.

For a discussion of Spelt Berries and flour made from them, see page 190.

PRODUCTION

Barley Flour produces Malt Sugars in the main dough as it ferments. Malt encourages rapid crust browning. Recall that Bagels are poached in a mixture of Malt Syrup and water before baking to encourage rapid browning, too.

SPECIFICATION

To prevent an overly dark crust, the oven temperature for this bread is reduced by 25°F throughout the whole bake. Compared to the *Baking Schedule* for *Pain au Levain*, the times remain the same, as do the *Steaming* and *Venting* steps. But the oven needs to be cooler.

Quick crust browning makes this dough a wise selection for burger buns. Especially with the slight nuttiness of the bread, this is a distinctive bun for sliders or full-size burgers. Pairing your signature burger with a house-made Barley Bun substantiates a higher price point. Especially for a bar menu, Barley Buns, Burgers, and Beer are a natural pairing.

Scale slider rolls at 3 ounces. Full-size burger buns are 4-1/2 ounces. For proofing the buns, line a sheet tray with parchment, spray it with Pan Spray, and then dust it with Semolina.

Whole Spelt Berries may be added to the main dough. Soak them and then cook them as described on pages 191–192. Cool them (and season them with salt, if they taste flat) before adding them to the main dough.

Ancient Grain Hearth Bread with Barley Levain and Spelt

Formula, Barley Levain

| Ingredient | BP% | 4-1/2 or 6 Qt | | 8 Qt | 20 Qt |
		Ounces	Grams		
Water	67%	2-1/3 oz	65 g	110 g	300 g
Starter Culture, ripe	100%	3-1/2 oz	100 g	170 g	450 g
Barley Flour	100%	3-1/2 oz	100 g	170 g	450 g
Yields		9 oz	265 g	450 g	1,200 g
enough to make main dough @ (Spelt Berries not included)		2# 2 oz or 950 g main dough		1,800 g main dough	5,100 g main dough

Procedure, Barley Levain

		8-hour shift ddt°= 70°F	5-hour shift ddt°= 76°F
1	Mise en Place	H2O @ **70°**; Starter Culture @ 70°	H2O @ **84°**; Starter Culture @ 70°
2	Ingredient Mixing	Combine Water & Starter Culture; add Barley Flour	same
3	Development	Stir until blended	none
4A	Fermentation *On the Floor*	**5h 00 @ 70°** (70% hum)	**2h 00 @ 76°** (70% hum)
4B	Fermentation *RFG*	+ stir for 10 seconds + 16 to 24h 00 in RFG	+ stir for 10 seconds + 20 to 28h 00 in RFG

Ancient Grain Hearth Bread with Barley Levain and Spelt

Formula, Main Dough

Hybrid Levain

Ingredient	BP%	4-1/2 or 6 Qt		8 Qt	20 Qt
		Ounces	Grams		
Barley Levain (from above)	50%	8 oz	225 g	400 g	1,170 g
Water	63%	10 oz	285 g	515 g	1,470 g
Honey	7%	1 oz	30 g	55 g	160 g
Dry Yeast*	0.4%	2 g	2 g	4 g	10 g
Spelt Flour	12%	2 oz	50 g	90 g	300 g
Bread Flour	88%	14 oz	400 g	720 g	2,040 g
Salt	2.8%	1/2 oz	13 g	23 g	65 g
Soaked or Cooked Spelt Berries** (optional)	22%	3-1/2 oz	100 g	180 g	500 g
Yields (Spelt Berries not included)		2# 2 oz	950 g	**1,800 g**	**5,100 g**
Number of pieces		See *About Formula Yields*, pages 260–261			

* Note: 2 g dry yeast is 1/2 teaspoon, leveled. That's about one-third of one (7g) packet. Use any type of dry yeast.

** Note: see 100% Spelt Bread Formula, pages 191–192.

Ancient Grain Hearth Bread with Barley Levain and Spelt

Procedure, Main Dough

1	**Mise en Place**	H$_2$O @ 92° ; Levain @ 70°	ddt°= 78°
2	**Ingredient Mixing**	Add Yeast to Levain and Water	*Autolyse*
3	**Development**	Speed #2, 2 m; + Rest 5 m; + **Add (optional) Spelt Berries** + Speed #1, 2 m	*Improved* **Add (optional) Spelt Berries after 5 m rest period.**
4A	**Floor Fermentation**	45 m @ 78° (70% hum); + Degas and Fold; + 45 m @ 78° (70% hum)	
4B	**Cool Fermentation**	No Cool Fermentation required; see *Understanding*	Move directly to *Shaping*
5	**Shaping**	Scale @ 2# 4 oz piece; Form as gentle round; Bench rest 20 m; Final Form as Round or Boulot	
6	**Proofing**	1h 00 @ 78° (70% hum), covered; + 30 to 45 m more, uncovered	
7	**Décor & Baking**	Score; See **Baking Chart**	

Ancient Grain Hearth Bread with Barley Levain and Spelt

Baking Chart

Ancient Grain Hearth Bread with Barley Levain and Spelt
@ 2# to 2# 4 oz

Oven	Stage I	¿Steam?	Vent @	Stage II	Duration	Int. temp°
Deck	500° (9.9.1) [3.3.1]	10 secs	8 m	435° (6.6.0) [2.2.0]	+ 8 m •••••••••• check*/rotate + 8 to 10 m more	200°
Rack (w/ convection + oven stone)	440°	10 secs	8 m	390°	+ 8 m •••••••••• check*/rotate + 8 to 10 m more	200°

@ 1# to 1# 4 oz

Oven	Stage I	¿Steam?	Vent @	Stage II	Duration	Int. temp°
Deck	450° (8.8.1) [3.3.1]	15 secs	6 m	450° (8.8.0) [2.2.0]	+ 6 m •••••••••• check*/rotate + 6 to 8 m more	200°

Check means inspect bottom crust. If it is browning more than the top crust and appears it would burn with additional baking, elevate the loaves onto the back of an inverted sheet pan placed directly on the hearth.
Rotate loaves only if necessary.

Apple Walnut Farmhouse Bread

This farmhouse style bread is an imperfectly round shape with caramelized pieces of fruit and nuts poking through the surface. Inside there's a medium-sized crumb with a seductive purple hue from the walnuts. Enhance the exterior appearance by lining your proofing baskets with a combination of rice flour and wheat bran.

UNDERSTANDING

Apples

Whether store-bought or house-made, condition the dried apple pieces before adding them to the dough.

- Cut them into pieces no longer than 3/4-inch. Use a chef's knife or a pair of foodsafe kitchen scissors.
- Soak the apples in the apple juice for just 15 minutes. Toss occasionally so the pieces evenly absorb the juice. If some pieces stick together, pull them apart.
- After 15 minutes, place the apples on a parchment-lined sheet tray. Don't squeeze excess juice from them. Any liquid left behind can be used for another project.
- Let the apples sit uncovered and at ambient temperature for one hour, absorbing whatever juice clings to them. Toss them once or twice while they sit.

The main dough formula calls for additional apple juice. Use new apple juice for this, don't use the soaking liquid. The soaking juice has more flavor, but the added sugar absorbed from the apples interferes with the dough's fermentation.

When distributing the apple pieces, don't overwork the dough. When you degas and fold the dough midway through the *Fermentation* phase, you can gently redistribute the apple slices once again.

Walnuts

Toast the walnuts at 350° for 3 to 4 minutes. Don't use a sauté pan because it draws oil from the nuts and gives the bread a greasy mouth feel. Bite into a walnut that you think is done. You will feel a slight snap as the nut breaks under your tooth. If it feels gummy, it needs more toasting.

When you chew the walnut, you will feel a butter-like sensation on your palate. If the walnut feels gritty, it needs more toasting.

Either way, don't give them a toasted brown appearance. The object is to draw out the natural oil in the nut, not to brown the exterior.

Cool them on a parchment-lined sheet tray. Use a chef's knife to rough cut the pieces.

Lightly salt the walnuts after they are prepped. They steal salt from the dough if they don't have enough of their own and your bread tastes flat.

Apple Walnut Farmhouse Bread

Walnuts have a pigment—anthocyanin—the same one that's in red cabbage. In the presence of acid, the pigment turns reddish purple. To encourage this color for your bread's interior, separate about 10% of the walnuts and finely mince them under the knife. Mix them with the larger pieces.

PRODUCTION

Handle this dough gently. Like all doughs with solid inclusions—raisins, chocolate chips, chunks of hard cheeses—this dough resists being molded and rounded.

- Divide pieces of dough and mold them like a round of potter's clay. Gently pat the dough and tuck the corners underneath to round the dough. Don't try to make it perfect.
- Dust your bench with flour. With both hands, gently scoop up the rounded dough and drop it onto the floured bench from a height of about 3 or 4 inches. From that height, gravity provides enough pressure to close the bottom edges.
- Bench Rest the rounds for 20 minutes, draping them with plastic.
- Prepare the bannetons first with rice flour and then a thin layer of bran. Wheat Bran is more appropriate for this formula but Oat Bran can be used if it's on hand. Set the bannetons aside.
- For the Final Form, sprinkle a layer of Bran on your bench. Use a metal bench scraper to scoop up the dough rounds and transfer them—seam-side still facing down—onto the layer of bran. Roll them around slightly so a layer of bran sticks to the bottom of the dough and comes about a half-inch up the sides.
- Transfer them into the prepared bannetons, bran coating still face-down in the baskets.
- When the breads are proofed and ready for scoring, dust your loading peel with additional Bran and a light layer of bread flour. Invert the loaves onto the peel so the seams are finally face-up.
- Let the dough rounds rest about 5 minutes on the peel. The loaves will start to open up along their seams. During the *Oven Spring*, the breads open even more. You'll end up with attractive, irregular looking breads, with pieces of fruit and nuts poking out here and there. (If the seams don't open by themselves before loading, you can score the breads with a serrated knife.)

SPECIFICATION

Once again, wipe your oven deck with a damp rag about 5 minutes before loading your breads. Collect an empty sheet tray nearby to slide between the loaves and the deck surface during the last stage of baking.

When scoring, use a serrated bread knife. Exposed apples respond better to a serrated blade than to the baker's lame.

Make the score marks about 1/2-inch deep, slightly deeper than your other breads. When a dough has solid garnishes in it, like Apples and Walnuts, the breads need a lot of oven spring. A deeper score helps.

Apple Walnut Farmhouse Bread

Finally, load your breads with the oven's bottom element set to "1", as indicated in the baking schedule. But lower the setting to "0" once the breads are loaded. Steam the breads as usual.

Solids and the sugar from the apples make the crust take color quickly. Don't hesitate to lower your oven temperature 25 to 50 degrees if the breads are getting too dark for your preference.

Watch the bottom crust! Take special care to monitor the amount of heat from the deck surface.

Bake the bread to an internal temperature of 200°F. Always use an instant-read thermometer to test a bread with fruit inclusions. The interior bakes unevenly, so test the internal temperature at two different spots.

Formula, Whole Wheat Levain

| Ingredient | BP% | 4-1/2 or 6 Qt | | 8 Qt | 20 Qt |
		Ounces	Grams		
Water	50%	1 oz	25 g	35 g	75 g
Starter Culture, ripe	100%	1-1/2 oz	50 g	70 g	150 g
Whole Wheat Flour	100%	1-1/2 oz	50 g	70 g	150 g
Yields		4 oz	125 g	175 g	375 g
enough to make main dough @		2# 8 oz or 1,200 g main dough		1,900 g main dough	4,900 g main dough

Procedure, Whole Wheat Levain

		8-hour shift ddt°= 70°F	5-hour shift ddt°= 76°F
1	Mise en Place	H2O @ **70°**; Starter Culture @ 70°	H2O @ **84°**; Starter Culture @ 70°
2	Ingredient Mixing	Combine Water & Starter Culture; add Whole Wheat Flour	same
3	Development	Stir until blended	none
4A	Fermentation *On the Floor*	**5h 00 @ 70°** (70% hum)	**2h 00 @ 76°** (70% hum)
4B	Fermentation *RFG*	+ stir for 10 seconds + 16 to 24h 00 in RFG	+ stir for 10 seconds + 20 to 28h 00 in RFG

Apple Walnut Farmhouse Bread

Formula, Main Dough

Hybrid Levain

Ingredient	BP%	4-1/2 or 6 Qt Ounces	4-1/2 or 6 Qt Grams	8 Qt	20 Qt
Levain (from above)	17%	3 oz	85 g	135 g	340 g
Water	57%	10 oz	285 g	455 g	1,140 g
Additional Apple Juice (@ 80°F)	17%	3 oz	85 g	135 g	335 g
Dry Yeast	0.4%	2 g	2 g	3.25 g	9 g
Whole Wheat Flour	9%	1-1/2 oz	45 g	70 g	175 g
Bread Flour	91%	1 #	450 g	720 g	1,800 g
Salt	2.7%	13.5 g	13.5 g	22 g	54 g
Dried Apples	22%	4 oz	110 g	175 g	450 g
Organic Apple Juice*	28%	5 oz	140 g	225 g	565 g
Walnuts	17%	3 oz	85 g	135 g	340 g
Yields**		**2# 8 oz**	**1,200 g**	**1,900 g**	**4,900 g**
Number of pieces		See *About Formula Yields,* pages 260–261			

*Not all of the Apple Juice is absorbed by the Dried Apples. Only half the weight of the Apple Juice is included in the total formula yield.
** Note: The yields for this formula are approximately 10% higher than the other breads in this section. Larger loaves accentuate the Apples and Walnuts.

Apple Walnut Farmhouse Bread

Procedure, Main Dough

1	**Mise en Place**	H$_2$O @ 92°; Levain @ 70°	ddt°= 78° Recondition Apple pieces; Toast Walnuts See *Understanding*
2	**Ingredient Mixing**	Add yeast to Levain and Water	*Autolyse*
3	**Development**	Speed #2, 2 m; + Rest 5 m; + **add Apple pieces and Walnuts* (see note)** + Speed #1, 2 m	*Improved* + **add Apple pieces and Walnuts* after 5 m rest**
4A	**Floor Fermentation**	45 m @ 78° (70% hum); + Degas and Fold + 45 m @ 78° (70% hum)	
4B	**Cool Fermentation**	No Cool Fermentation required	Proceed to *Shaping*
5	**Shaping**	Scale @ 2# 4 oz Form as gentle round Bench rest 15 m Final Form as Round	
6	**Proofing**	1h 30 @ 78° (70% hum), covered; + about 45 minutes more, uncovered	
7	**Décor & Baking**	Score See **Baking Chart**	

*Note: Add the solids by hand if you are using the 4-1/2 Qt mixer.

Apple Walnut Farmhouse Bread

Baking Chart

Apple Walnut Wild Yeast Bread
@ 1# to 1# 4 oz

Oven	Stage I	¿Steam?	Vent @	Stage II	Duration	Stage III	Duration	Int. Temp°
Deck	460° (8.8.1)	15 secs	6 m	460° (8.8.0)	+ 6 m •••••• check* (+ insert one sheet tray)	460° (8.8.0)	+ 6 to 9 m more	200°

@ 2# to 2# 4 oz

Oven	Stage I	¿Steam?	Vent @	Stage II	Duration	Stage III	Duration	Int. Temp°
Deck	500° (9.9.1) [3.3.1]	10 secs	8 m	425° (6.6.0) [2.2.0]	+ 8 m •••••• check*/ rotate	400° (6.6.0)	+ 8 to 12 m more	200°
Rack (w/ convection + oven stone)	440°	10 secs	8 m	390°	+ 8 m •••••• check*/ rotate	340°	+ 8 to 10 m more	200°

*Check: Watch bottom crusts. You may need to slide an inverted sheet tray between the breads and the surface of the hearth.

When a wild yeast bread has a high percent of solids, like the Apples and Walnuts in this bread, a *3-Stage Bake* is preferred.

- **Stage I** (a high temperature setting) allows for maximum Oven Spring,

- **Stage II** (about a 10% temperature reduction) initiates crust color and heats the bread's interior, and

- **Stage III** (another 10% reduction) deepens crust color and allows heat to penetrate, thoroughly baking the interior of the bread.

Hybrid Levain

Wild Yeast Dough + Commercial Yeast

As the sun rose on the early 1900's, it brought to light a mise en place of technological change, namely the invention of electricity, a mechanical method for developing dough, and a new commercial ingredient for bread. The new product was *baker's yeast*—the concentrated form of a wild yeast starter—easier to care for and longer-lasting.

The tradition of the boulanger, virtually the same since Man made his first leavened breads, was set to embrace these innovations.

Introduction

A hybrid method for bread baking evolved in Paris in the 1930's. Just a small amount of this new commercial yeast accelerated dough fermentation. Boulangers saved time in production, especially during cold months when fermentation is slower.

The baker's name for this method is ***Levain de Pâte***. In this book, we'll use the term ***Hybrid Levain***.

A Hybrid Levain bread has a less tangy flavor profile than one made without the addition of commercial yeast. On the other hand, a Hybrid Levain bread delivers more flavor from fermented flour and grain.

French guidelines specify that commercial yeast is *never* used in either the Wild Yeast Culture or the Basic Levain itself. It's only the Main Dough that can include what has come to be called a *spike* of commercial yeast.

Levain de Pâte (luh **vanh** duh **pott**) French term for a wild yeast bread with a small percent of commercial yeast added. Fresh yeast or any form of dry yeast can be used.

By French regulation, the maximum Baker's Percent (BP%) of Dry Yeast that can be added to a wild yeast dough is 0.10% (one-tenth of one percent).

Scheduling Advantages

The Fermentation Phase is reduced by 33%

If a wild yeast dough normally ferments for *1 hour 30 minutes at 78°*, changing to the Hybrid Levain method reduces the total fermentation time to *1 hour at 78°*. The dough still receives its Degas & Fold halfway through the Fermentation Phase.

Time saved: 30 minutes

The Proofing Phase is reduced by 25%

If the bread normally requires a *2-hour proofing* time, the Hybrid Levain version can be expected to *proof in 1 hour 30 minutes*.

Time saved: 30 minutes more

Total time saved: 1 hour

When do I add the Commercial Yeast?

The first step of the Ingredient Mixing Phase for all wild yeast doughs is combining the Water with the Basic Levain. Once you've done that, sprinkle the commercial yeast over the water. Allow 3 to 5 minutes for the yeast to hydrate, then swirl it through the mixture with a plastic scraper or your fingers. Fresh Yeast or any form of Dry Yeast can be used.

Production Tip

Assuming your Basic Levain was made and fermented yesterday, you'll have enough time to make and bake a Hybrid Levain version of the main dough in a 5-hour shift.

Do I need to modify other Phases of Bread?

No. The *Development*, *Shaping*, *Bench Rest*, and *Baking Phases* stay the same whether or not the main dough is a Hybrid Levain.

What about the Temperature and Humidity for the Fermentation and Proofing Phases?

The times are shorter, but the Temperature and Humidity settings stay the same.

Baker's Tip

Counter to logic, a wild yeast Baguette has a slower oven spring than a boule of the same weight. There's less surface tension in the shape of the Baguette compared to the round boule. As it proofs, the Baguette flattens outward instead of rising upward. The crumb tends to be dense.

If you want a more open crumb in your wild yeast Baguettes, use the Hybrid Levain method.

Doing the Math

How do I change a wild yeast dough formula into a Hybrid Levain?

Based on the total weight of the flour(s) in the main dough,
the baker adds **one-tenth of one percent Dry Yeast** to the main dough.

What does a Baker's Percent = 0.10% look like?

To see how much *one-tenth of one percent* really is, visualize one dollar's worth of pennies. One hundred pennies.

Move a single penny away from the pile and set it by itself. That single penny is *one percent*, one of the 100 cents you started with.

Now, cut that penny into ten equal pieces. One of those single pieces is *one-tenth of one percent*. Not very much, considering the pile of pennies you started with.

How do you calculate a BP% = 0.10%?

First, find the weight of the total flour in the **main dough**. For this example, don't worry about the weight of any flour(s) used to make the Levain. Only calculate the weight of the flour(s) that haven't yet had the chance to get wet.

Multiply that total flour weight by **0.001** on your calculator.

The very small number you get for an answer is one-tenth of one percent of the flour. That's how much dry yeast you add to the Water and Levain mixture.

If the amount of yeast seems too small to be true, check your math...

Multiply the number by 1,000 (one thousand, yes).

If all the correct numbers were pressed, the answer you get will be the same as the total weight of dry flour that you started with.

Example

Let's say your main dough formula calls for 500 grams of flour.   BP% = 100%

One percent of 500 grams is 5 grams.   BP% = 1%

To continue,
One-tenth of 5 grams is 0.5 grams   BP% = 0.10%

That's one-half of one gram.

One-half of one gram of Dry Yeast measures *1/8th teaspoon*.

Hold that up against the 500 grams of flour you started with and see how small that really is. With practice, you will quickly develop the ability to approximate just how little Dry Yeast you need for every pound of flour in the main dough.

Note: Fresh Cake Yeast can be used, too.
You'll need twice as much as Dry.

For more information about the Levain de Pâte method, read **The Taste of Bread** by Raymond Calvel, Aspen Publishers, 2001.

Bridgetown Craft Bread

DESCRIPTION

This bread is named in honor of Portland, Oregon and the city's thriving craft baking scene. A trip to Bridgetown, as it is nicknamed, is incomplete until you visit at least two or three bakeries. *Grand Central Baking Company* and *Pearl Bakery* first brought artisan baking to Portland. A second generation includes *Essential Baking Company, Ken's Artisan Bakery,* and *Little T American Bakery. Little T*'s baker is Tim Healea, former U.S. Breadbaking World Cup medalist.

UNDERSTANDING

There's a *house blend* of grain flavors in this bread. The flour types include White Flours (both Bread and All-purpose), Whole Wheat and Rye. The creamy-chewy texture of this bread comes from the 60% Bread Flour. All-Purpose Flour creates a light interior. The dough ferments and proofs quicker than the Pain au Levain because of the additional wild yeast found in the Whole Wheat and Rye Flours.

In the oven, give this bread a few more minutes once it looks done. Make the crust color dark reddish-brown, almost black. Think of the basic taste contrast between the sweet creamy custard of a *crème brûlée* and its bitter, dark crust. That's the target.

The color and crispness of the crust comes from the Malt Syrup in the formula.

If you use Malt Powder instead, substitute it in equal weight for the Malt Syrup in the formula. When using Malt Powder, blend it with the varietal flours (Whole Wheat and Rye) and then add this combination all at once after the Levain and Water have been blended.

Malt Syrups are available in a variety of colors, or roasts, like coffee beans. Light, medium, and dark. Each brings a unique nuttiness, caramel flavor and color to the bread. The malt sugars caramelize as part of the Maillard Reaction when the crust browns (Appendix 1). Experiment with different malt syrups. Discover which flavor profile you and your customers prefer.

Dark malt syrup has high flavor intensity. Use half the indicated amount the first time you make this formula. It's easier to evaluate its flavor contribution when you use less. Next time, increase the amount if you prefer.

PRODUCTION

Loaves can be scaled according to your preference. For loaves scaled at 1# to 1# 4 ounces, the oven temperature and element settings are higher. Larger loaves, scaled at 2# to 2# 8 ounces, are baked at a lower temperature and for a longer time at each separate stage of the bake. The oven element settings are lower for larger loaves, too.

Watch that the bottoms don't burn. The malt encourages a darker crust color and, with the extended baking times for these loaves, the bottoms darken quickly. (See page 637 for managing the effects of direct heat on the bottom crusts.)

Like all breads in this section, these breads follow the 2-Stage Baking Sequence. Even if you trust your ovens implicitly, don't overlook the *check/rotate* step halfway through Stage II of the bake. Have a full-sized sheet tray and a baking buddy nearby in case you need to insulate the loaves from the direct heat of the oven floor.

As always, refer to the *Baking Schedule* for oven temperatures, times, and element settings.

Definition: *Provenance*

Within the art world, as in any area of specialization, there is a vocabulary used to describe artists, their works of art, and the influences on them. Take the word *provenance.*

Provenance (**PRO** ven ance) tells the story of how a particular painting found its way from one collector to the next. *Who first owned this painting? Why did they sell it? How'd it end up on the wall in this particular museum?* Art dealers and connoisseurs are respected for knowing the answers to these questions of ownership.

Bread baking is an art. A loaf of bread is not a painting though, and happily so. As a work of art, its life is a handful of hours at most.

The provenance of the Baguette I'm eating as I write is my friend's wood-fired oven a bike ride away. This isn't really news-worthy.

Bread baking, like painting, is also a craft. A painter, like a bread baker, copies the works of other artists he admires to learn principles of composition, color, and a host of other elements. Especially in their early works, artists reveal the influence of their masters.

I suppose *influence* would be a more accurate term when speaking of a bread baker's style, but I'd rather borrow from the meaning of *provenance.*

Where did this style of bread baking come from? Who else practiced it along the way? These questions speak less to ownership than to how bakers carry out our craft. Bakers have a philosophy based on sharing, transferring skills, and continuing our tradition.

As a word, *provenance* speaks without judgment. It embraces the idea that a technique or style of bread baking is not owned by a single baker. Instead, it is learned from our predecessors, modified, and passed on once again.

Bridgetown Craft Bread

Provenance of the *Bridgetown Craft Bread*

From the first bite this bread haunted me. Crackling thin, reddish-brown crust surrounded a creamy texture and tender chew. The contrast brought to mind a *crème brûlée*, the creamy custard with its crunchy caramel topping. It was the closest I had come in the U.S. to the hearth breads I had learned during my French apprenticeship.

This and other breads had found their way into my backpack at a farmers' market in Portland, Oregon. Unfortunately, there were too many to remember which bakery stand each had come from, let alone who had baked them.

Back in San Francisco, I spent the next month recreating the bread. Of its three characteristics—the crust, the interior texture, and the flavor—I could capture only two at a time. Never all three at once. I put the project aside, hoping to be successful another time.

Enter Maggie Glezer and her groundbreaking **Artisan Baking Across America**, the first cookbook to explore the country's *Artisan Bread Revolution*, as it was called at the end of the twentieth century. Randomly opening the book, I was surprised to see the dark-crusted bread that had enchanted me months before.

There it was in full color. A rustic French loaf with dark caramel crust and open, tender crumb. There was its formula too, on the facing page. I had found it.

Essential's Columbia was the bread's name, designed by George DePasquale at *Essential Bakery*. The fact that the shop was located in Seattle and not Portland was disconcerting, so I decided to use the formula as a starting point in finalizing my own bread.

I added some Whole Pumpernickel Meal to satisfy my personal preference for an open crumb with a slightly coarse feel. To make the procedure fit a classroom schedule, I included an overnight, cool fermentation. Those are the only changes I made to the original formula.

This bread represents an important stage in my development as a craft baker and is now one of the more versatile breads in my repertoire. Heartfelt thanks to George DePasquale for developing such a haunting bread and to Maggie Glezer for her wisdom to include it in her book.

Bridgetown Craft Bread

For more contrast between the Crust and Crumb, shape the loaves as long Bâtards. Each piece has a full ring of crust when the loaves are sliced.

To proof this shape, bakers use a sheet of linen that can be pleated to a variety of widths. This is called a *couche*, based on the French word meaning *to sleep*.

COUCHE

pronounced *koosh*

A *couche* is a length of linen cloth
used to hold breads during the Proofing Phase.
When there are two or more couches, there's an "s" at the end of the word.
But the pronunciation stays the same—*koosh*.

Viewed from the side, a layer of proofing breads nestle together, as if asleep for the night, snug in a pleated blanket. As it proofs, each bread pushes against the fold in the cloth. Meanwhile, its neighbor is pushing with equal pressure against the cloth from the other side.

With this back and forth pressure, the breads virtually shape themselves. A batch of Baguettes proofed in couches have more uniformity than ones proofed in individual molds or forms.

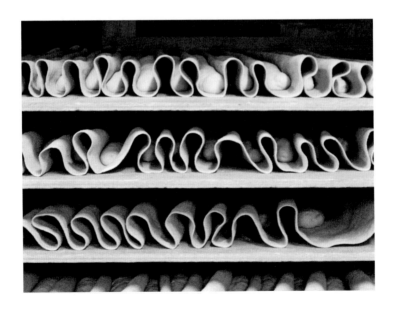

Bridgetown Craft Bread

All About *Couches*

A standard *couche* is 24 inches wide. That's the *length* of a full-sized sheet tray or bread board, so one of those is often used to support the *couche*.

Professional grade *couche* are heavy, giving them durability over years of baking. They are available at bakery or restaurant supply stores. Lighter grade linen can be purchased at fabric stores. A frugal baker can cut these to any length and keep them from fraying by stitching a hem.

Linen wicks moisture from bread as it proofs. The surface dries to create a silky skin so the bread better holds its shape. Decorating breads that proof in couche takes less pressure from the baker's lame or scoring tool than breads proofed in other kinds of molds.

Once it's *broken in* through several uses, linen is a non-stick surface for breads. At the start, it must be seasoned.

To do this, lay the couche flat on the bench. Cast a light layer of either bread flour or rice flour, brown or white, over the material. With a flat and open hand, use broad back and forth gestures to work the flour into the material.

Couche doesn't need to be washed. It does need to be shaken free of surface flour and other debris once it has been used, though. Hand-sweeping the couche on a wooden bench with a firm-bristle brush is routine practice in a production bakery.

Thoroughly dry the linen before storing it. If a damp couche is rolled and stored, it develops mold. Moldy couches must be discarded.

Baker's Tip

Tea towels, or side towels as they are often called in restaurants, can also be used. Don't use material with nubs or pieces of cloth that come free and can stick to the bread. Tea towels or side towels work better if you rub a layer of bread or rice flour into the material first.

Getting Bread into a *Couche*

Spread out the couche and cast an even layer of bread or rice flour over its entire length. Rub it into the cloth gently with an open hand.

Drape the couche over a wooden bread board or a full-sized sheet tray. Position the couche at right angles to the board or sheet tray.

To make it easier to remove the proofed breads, invert the sheet tray so the walls of the tray don't interfere. Be careful with this method and move an inverted sheet tray cautiously. Once the couche is loaded with breads, it won't have the support from the walls of the sheet tray to keep the breads in place.

Photo Gallery #18

Couche (Linen Proofing Cloth)

Bridgetown Craft Bread

With the loaves nestled in the couche, fold the excess material over the top of the loaves to cover them. Pull the material snug so the loaf on the end has support.

Do the same with the excess from the other end. If the material is new, put a bench scraper or two on top of the material to hold things in place.

Carefully move the loaded couche to a safe, warm area for the proofing phase. Select a part of the bakeshop with an ambient temperature of 78° to 82°F, away from foot traffic.

If there's a draft, drape a piece of plastic wrap over any exposed breads.

Proofing in *Couche*

The total proof time for a bread does not change when it's proofed in couches.

Recall that breads proofed in bannetons spend the last 20 to 30 minutes uncovered. This dries the surface of the dough, makes it easier to slide the bread from the loading peel, and prevents it from sticking to the deck surface.

When breads proof in couche, they develop a slight skin. There's no need to uncover the breads in this case. The total proofing time stays the same, the baker just saves a step in unwrapping them.

Unloading *Couches*

Breads that proof in couche usually bake directly on the hearth, the stone floor of the oven.

You'll need what's called a **transfer peel**. It's a thin, light piece of sturdy material, usually wood. The edges are beveled so breads can roll sideways, on and off the board, as they are transferred. A standard size for a *transfer peel* is 26" long by 6" to 8" wide, though they can be any width necessary to securely transfer breads in their tender, proofed state.

Transfer peels, also called *flipping boards*, are available at bakery supply stores. In a pinch, I've taken an empty box of baking parchment and cut it lengthwise into 9-inch wide strips.

When it's time to decorate and load the breads, transfer the *loaded couche and sheet tray assembly* to a workbench. If you are **right-handed**, grab the *transfer peel* with your *left hand*. This leaves your dominant hand to do the actual work and control the couche.

Unload the breads from the couche starting at the right hand side and working toward the left hand side. Here's how:

1. Gather some of the free material with your right hand.

2. Gently pull the material toward the right, using a zig-zag motion.

3. Stop when the first pleat in the material flattens out.

4. Place the long side of the transfer peel on the material, to the left of the first bread. Don't put the flipper directly against the side of the bread. Leave a 1-inch space or so.

5. Angle the transfer peel about 20 degrees to the workbench. Press down so the transfer peel anchors the couche onto the bench, preventing it from slipping.

6. With your right hand, draw the couche up and toward your left hand, moving the material over the top of the first bread. With a quick tug, literally flip the bread onto the peel in the process. With the bread now on the transfer peel, draw the couche back to the right and then release it.

7. From here, transfer the bread onto a loading tool such as an oven peel or bread board. Transfer one or two more breads if you have enough space on your loading tool.

8. Arrange your breads evenly on the loading peel and score them.

9. Load them into the oven using the same procedure described for round boules on page 124.

Photo Gallery #19   From the Couche to the Loading Peel

Caring for *Couches*

When done with the couche, gently shake it over a compost bin. The couche must be completely dried before it is stored. In a production bakery, there are sometimes a series of wooden dowels or towel rods affixed to one wall in the bakeshop for this purpose. For infrequent use, drape the couche over a rolling rack while it air dries.

The dried couche can be folded or rolled. In this shape, 6 to 8 couches are easily stored on a full sheet tray in the equipment box. In a classroom bakeshop, this system works well:

1. Lay the dried couche flat on the bench,

2. fold it so it's half as long,

3. starting at the folded edge, roll the couche into a cylinder, like a yoga mat.

Bridgetown Craft Bread

Formula, Levain

Ingredient	BP%	4-1/2 or 6 Qt Ounces	4-1/2 or 6 Qt Grams	8 Qt	20 Qt
Water	50%	1-1/2 oz	50 g	65 g	175 g
Starter Culture, ripe	150%	4-1/2 oz	150 g	200 g	525 g
Bread Flour	100%	3 oz	100 g	130 g	350 g
Yields		9 oz	300 g	395 g	1,050 g
enough to make main dough @		2# 4 oz or 1,000 g main dough		1,750 g main dough	5,000 g main dough

Procedure, Levain

		8-hour shift ddt°= 70°F	5-hour shift ddt°= 76°F
1	Mise en Place	H2O @ **70°**; Starter Culture @ 70°	H2O @ **84°**; Starter Culture @ 70°
2	Ingredient Mixing	Combine Water & Starter Culture; add Flour	same
3	Development	Stir until blended	same
4A	Fermentation *On the Floor*	**5h 00 @ 70°** (70% hum)	**2h 00 @ 76°** (70% hum)
	Fermentation *RFG*	+ stir for 10 seconds + 16 to 24h 00 in RFG	+ stir for 10 seconds + 20 to 28h 00 in RFG

Bridgetown Craft Bread

Formula, Main Dough

| Ingredient | BP% | 4-1/2 or 6 Qt | | 8 Qt | 20 Qt |
		Ounces	Grams		
Levain (from above)	41%	7 oz	210 g	360 g	1,010 g
Water	65%	12 oz	335 g	570 g	1,600 g
Malt Syrup	2%	1/3 oz	10 g	16 g	45 g
Whole Wheat Flour*	8%	1-1/2 oz	40 g	65 g	190 g
Pumpernickel Meal*	2%	1/2 oz	10 g	20 g	50 g
Toasted Wheat Germ*	3%	1/2 oz	15 g	25 g	70 g
All-Purpose Flour	29%	5 oz	150 g	255 g	720 g
Bread Flour	58%	11 oz	300 g	510 g	1,440 g
Salt	2.9%	1/2 oz	15 g	25 g	72 g
Yields		**2# 4 oz**	**1,000 g**	**1,750 g**	**5,000 g**
Number of pieces		See *About Formula Yields,* pages 260–261			

*Note: Combine Varietal Flours with Wheat Germ

Bridgetown Craft Bread

Procedure, Main Dough

1	**Mise en Place**	H$_2$O @ 92°; Levain @ 70° Combine Varietal Flours with Wheat Germ	ddt°= 78°
2	**Ingredient Mixing**	Add Malt to Levain and Water	Autolyse
3	**Development**	Speed #2, 2 m; + Rest 5 m; + Speed #1, 2 m	*Improved*
4A	**Floor Fermentation**	1h 30 m @ 78° (70% hum); + Degas and Fold; + 1h 30 @ 78° (70% hum)	
4B	**Cool Fermentation**	18 to 24h 00 @ 50° (70% hum)	
5	**Shaping**	Temper dough 1h 00 *on the floor* Scale @ 2# 4 oz or @ 1# 2 oz Form as gentle round Bench rest 20 m Final Form as Bâtards (smaller pieces) or Boulot (larger piece, formed into same shape)	
6	**Proofing**	2h 00 @ 78° (70% hum); Proof in *couche*	
7	**Décor & Baking**	Score; See **Baking Chart**	

Photo Gallery #17   Forming the Bâtard Shape

Bridgetown Craft Bread

Baking Chart

Bridgetown Craft Bread
@ 1# to 1# 4 oz

Oven	Stage I	¿Steam?	Vent @	Stage II	Duration	Int. temp°
Deck	500° (9.9.1) [3.3.1]	10 secs	6 m	435° (9.9.0) [2.2.0]	+ 6 m ·········· check*/rotate + 8 to 10 m more	200°
Rack (w/ convection + oven stone)	500°	10 secs	6 m	425°	+ 6 m ·········· check*/rotate + 8 to 10 m more	200°

@ 2# to 2# 8 oz

Oven	Stage I	¿Steam?	Vent @	Stage II	Duration	Int. Temp°
Deck	490° (8.8.1) [3.3.1]	10 secs	8 m	425° (8.8.0) [2.2.0]	+ 8 m ·········· check*/rotate + 11 to 13 m more	200°
Rack (w/ convection + oven stone)	430°	10 secs	8 m	380°	+ 8 m ·········· check*/rotate + 10 to 12 m more	200°

*Check means inspect bottom crust. If it is browning more than the top crust and appears it would burn with additional baking, elevate the loaves onto the back of an inverted sheet pan placed directly on the hearth.
Rotate loaves only if necessary.

Honey Rye Hearth Bread

DESCRIPTION

Rye breads have a sweet grain flavor. In American bakeries, the sweetness is not always evident when the breads are garnished with seeds like caraway, fennel, or even anise.

This formula expands your repertoire to include a rye hearth bread. Use its moderately assertive flavors to broaden your tastes and your product line.

Honey highlights the natural sweetness of rye flour. Its mouth-coating texture complements the slight coarseness of the whole pumpernickel meal.

UNDERSTANDING

Whether it's light, medium, or whole grain (like Pumpernickel or Rye Meal), Rye Flour* ferments quicker than white flour. It brings a low level of bitterness to the main dough, along with its sweetness.

This Honey Rye formula blends 40% Rye Flour with 60% white bread flour. The larger percent of bread flour in the main dough formula develops a sturdy hearth bread with good volume and a more open crumb structure. The flavor profile is intensified by pre-fermenting additional Rye Flour in the Levain.

> *Rye Flours and Pumpernickel Meals can be labeled with confusing terms. Appendix 1 explains these terms and helps you make an informed choice.*

PRODUCTION

Honey accelerates the *Fermentation* and *Proofing Phases* of this dough. The procedure doesn't require overnight cool fermentation so this bread can be mixed and baked in one day. You can also follow the 2-stage fermentation (*on the floor* for a while, plus overnight in the refrigerator), if this fits your schedule.

When loading proofed loaves onto the oven peel, place the seam-side facing up. If the loaves were gently formed, the seam might open naturally and gently.

Take advantage of this situation. Don't score the breads. Instead, let the Oven Spring force the loaves to open along their natural seams. Each loaf will have its own personality and surface. Sometimes the seam gets dark brown, almost black. This brings a hand-crafted appearance and more flavor contrast and complexity to the humble-looking breads.

We taste first with our eyes.

Use this mantra to reinforce the earthy notes of Rye's flavor profile. Line your proofing forms with a combination of dark rye flour, pumpernickel meal and/or rice flour for a rustic look to your breads.

Rye breads are tacky and stick to proofing molds. Line your bannetons or proofing molds first with rice flour, its fine grind fills the crevices in the proofing mold. Then, dust the mold with coarse Rye Flour or Pumpernickel Meal.

Honey Rye Hearth Bread

Rye Breads have a unique baking schedule compared to other wild yeast breads:

- They bake with more steam and for a longer time in Stage I;

- The oven temperature is reduced for Stage II;

- And it's reduced once more for Stage III.

- The internal temperature for the finished breads is 200°F—and even more importantly, the sides of the loaves are hard when flicked with a fingertip or rapped with the back of a spoon.

Once baked, the loaves need at least 4 to 5 hours for the flavor and the texture to ripen.

If you can schedule an overnight rest for these breads, wrap each cooled bread first in parchment. Then, loaves can be wrapped in plastic.

SPECIFICATION

Shape boules for bannetons, or shape boulots for proofing in linen couches.
For boulots, scale the dough at 20-ounce pieces.

Form these into gentle rounds and allow them a ten-minute bench rest, covered. If the dough seems slightly sticky, leave the rounds uncovered on the bench while they rest, so they can air-dry.

Baker's Tip

If your hand pressure is gentle, you can proceed from *Dividing* directly to *Final Forming*. No *First Form* and *Bench Rest* is necessary.

But—

you must use no more flour than necessary on your hands or on the dough. And you've got to combine gentle pressure with a firm touch when shaping.

For the final shape, lightly flour the dough pieces and use a bench scraper to invert them onto a clean part of your bench. Gently form them into cylinders. Apply just enough pressure to prevent air gaps between the folds of dough as you roll.

Don't try to seal each roll of the dough, as for Baguettes or Bagels. You don't even need to pinch together the seam once the dough is completely rolled. The weight of the dough, its moisture, and the natural adhesion of a rye dough will close the seam. Keep the seams down when proofing.

If you're using linen couches for the proofing phase, prepare them now by coating them with a light dusting of rice flour and set them aside. Then, sift a light layer

Honey Rye Hearth Bread

of rice flour onto your bench. Use a scraper to lift the dough cylinder and transfer it onto the rice-floured bench.

Roll the bread side to side, along its length, so the flour comes about one-half inch up the sides. Immediately move it to the prepared couche, placing the seam-side down. (See pages 155–157 for using *couches*.)

When it's time to bake, place the proofed loaves seam-side (still facing down) on the loading peel. Score the dough in the more traditional rye pattern of *sausage cuts* and load onto the deck. For a semi-gloss surface, apply an optional starch wash to the breads once they have been transferred to the loading peel and before they are scored (see below).

Meteil (meh **tay**) **v. Seigle** (**say** gleh)

In the repertoire of French boulangeries, there are two styles of Rye Breads. It depends on how much rye flour is used in the formula.

A bread with lots of rye flour, (usually a Baker's Percent above 60%) is called a *Pain de Seigle*. This is a descriptive menu term and appears on bakeshop signage and in display cases.

When the Baker's Percent of rye flour is less than 50%, the style of bread is called a *Meteil* in France. *Meteil* is a technical term used in the back-of-the-house. For customers, these breads are usually labeled *avec farine de seigle* (*with rye flour*).

Starch Wash
(enough for 3 loaves)

1 egg white
1 oz water
1 teaspoon red wine vinegar
pinch of salt
3 Tablespoons bread flour, or enough to make a thin paste

Use a fork to blend together egg white, water, vinegar, and salt.
Gradually add enough of the flour to make a paste the thickness of paint.
Store at ambient temperature, covered.
Thin with water as necessary.

Honey Rye Hearth Bread

Formula, Rye Levain

Ingredient	BP%	4-1/2 or 6 Qt		8 Qt	20 Qt
		Ounces	Grams		
Water	100%	4 oz	120 g	200 g	480 g
Starter Culture, ripe	50%	2 oz	60 g	100 g	240 g
Whole Rye Flour*	100%	4 oz	120 g	200 g	480 g
Yields		10 oz	300 g	500 g	1,200 g
enough to make main dough @		2# 6 oz or 1,000 g main dough		1,850 g main dough	4,800 g main dough

*Finely ground preferred

Procedure, Rye Levain

		8-hour shift ddt°= 70°F	5-hour shift ddt°= 76°F
1	Mise en Place	H2O @ 70°; Starter Culture @ 70°	H2O @ 84°; Starter Culture @ 70°
2	**Ingredient Mixing**	Combine H2O & Starter Culture; add Flour	same
3	**Development**	Stir until blended	none
4A	**Fermentation** *On the Floor*	**5h 00 @ 70°** (70% hum)	**2h 00 @ 76°** (70% hum)
4B	**Fermentation** *RFG*	+ stir for 10 seconds + 16 to 24h 00 in RFG	+ stir for 10 seconds + 20 to 28h 00 in RFG

Honey Rye Hearth Bread

Formula, Main Dough

Ingredient	BP%	4-1/2 or 6 Qt		8 Qt	20 Qt
		Ounces	Grams		
Rye Levain (from above)	50%	9 oz	250 g	450 g	1,150 g
Water	60%	10-1/2 oz	300 g	540 g	1,380 g
Dry Yeast	0.4%	2 g	2 g	2.5 g	9 g
Honey	8%	1-1/2 oz	40 g	72 g	185 g
Rye Flour (*Light* or *Medium*)	30%	6 oz	150 g	270 g	690 g
Whole Rye Meal (coarsely ground)	10%	2 oz	50 g	90 g	230 g
Bread Flour	60%	10 oz	300 g	540 g	1,380 g
Salt	2.5%	1/2 oz (scant)	12.5 g	22.5 g	58 g
Yields		**2# 6 oz**	**1,000 g**	**1,850 g**	**4,800 g**
Number of pieces		See *About Formula Yields,* pages 260–261			

Honey Rye Hearth Bread

Procedure, Main Dough

1	**Mise en Place**	H_2O @ 94° ; Levain @ 70°	ddt°= 82°*
2	**Ingredient Mixing**	Autolyse	
3	**Development**	Speed #2, 3 m; + Rest 5 m; + Speed #1, 3 m	*Improved*
4A	**Floor Fermentation**	1h 30 m @ 82° (70% hum); 1 X Degas and Fold	
4B	**Cool Fermentation**	No Cool Fermentation	Proceed directly to *Shaping*
5	**Shaping**	Scale @ 2# 4 oz piece; Form as gentle round; Bench rest 20 m; Final Form as Round or Boulot	See *Specification* notes
6	**Proofing**	1h 00 @ 80° (70% hum), covered; + 15 to 30 m more, uncovered	For *Proofing* Rye Breads, see HTBB, page 357.
7	**Décor & Baking**	Score; See **Baking Chart**	See *Specification* notes

*Note: The ddt° for Rye Breads is higher than breads made with white or whole wheat flour(s). (Appendix 1)

Honey Rye Hearth Bread

Baking Chart

Honey Rye Hearth Bread
@ 2# 2 oz

Oven	Stage I	¿Steam?	Vent @	Stage II	Duration	Stage III	Duration	Int. Temp°
Deck	460° (8.8.1) [2.2.1]	20 secs	10 m	** 425° (7.7.0) [2.2.0]	+ 8 m	** 390° (7.7.0) [2.2.0]	+ 8 to 10 m	200° plus very firm sides
Rack (w/ convection + oven stone)	375°	20 secs	10 m	340°	+ 8 m	320°	+ 8 to 10 m	200° plus very firm sides

@ 1# to 1# 4 oz

Oven	Stage I	¿Steam?	Vent @	Stage II	Duration	Stage III	Duration	Int. Temp°
Rotating Deck (w/ convection)	420°	20 secs	10 m	** 380°	+ 8 m	** 340°	+ 6 m	200° plus very firm sides

** Rye Breads have 3 Baking Stages.

Stage I is high heat with lots of steam.
Moisture keeps crust starches malleable, helping with Oven Spring.

Vent the oven for Stage II.
Reduce the oven setting by approximately ten percent.

For Stage III, reduce the oven temperature a second time.
As usual, once the oven has been vented to eliminate steam,
keep the vent open for the duration of the bake.

Pumpernickel Sandwich Bread

This sandwich bread is slightly sweet with a tender crumb, more in the American tradition of dark rye than in the German one. The bread gets its deep color from coffee and a small percent of unsweetened cocoa powder. Molasses gives it sweetness and Vegetable Oil delivers a tender crumb. None of these ingredients is found in an Old World German Pumpernickel.

This bread is better suited for sandwiches. It's essential for a Grilled Reuben Sandwich, the New York City deli combination of corned beef, Swiss cheese, sauerkraut, and Russian dressing.

The American Pumpernickel bread evolved in the early 1900's along with another foodservice innovation—the delicatessen. Urban growth brought skyscrapers to the New York City skyline and an influx of Europeans to its urban workforce. By necessity, the mid-day meal period had to be quick as well as wholesome—large portions, easily eaten and easy to hold. The German delicatessen with its cheeses and cured meats suspended from the ceiling was quick to re-invent itself, providing sit-down service and quick meals, especially lunch. The modern deli was born.

The originally dense and dark Old World German loaf evolved into a lighter, more flexible, and easily sliced sandwich bread. The American Pumpernickel took its place as an innovative component of the quickly expanding foodservice industry of the era.

Old World German Pumpernickel is sliced thin, spread with sweet butter, and served with cured meats and strong cheeses. It's a time-consuming project that involves gentle mixing, slow rising, and often incorporates loaves of older, unsold Pumpernickel that are soaked in water and then added to a new main dough.

This **soaker** technique allows enzymes in the bread to reactivate and digest longer chains of starches in the bread. The process releases small molecules of sugar in the dough, what baker's call *fermentable sugars*. When fermentable sugars come from bread that's already been baked, they create more complex flavors in the second bread.

When these second-generation sugars caramelize on the bread's surface, the crust becomes thinner and its color gets deeper. This makes the crust more crisp and causes small surface cracks as the loaves cool. Each succeeding generation of breads made this way becomes darker. These are some of the reasons that dark pumpernickel has a cult following in the U.S.

Once you bake this Pumpernickel Sandwich Bread, you might find yourself drawn to dense, Old World German Ryes. For more information and foolproof ways to make them, refer to Jeffrey Hamelman's ***Bread: A Baker's Book of Techniques and Recipes***, John Wiley & Sons, 2012.

Pumpernickel Sandwich Bread

About the Coffee

Use brewed coffee or instant granules diluted according to the manufacturer's directions. Don't use coffee extract.

Coffee encourages a dark crumb color and its bitterness rounds the flavor profile of the bread. Select a coffee with light to medium body, like Mocha Java. Strong-bodied coffees like French or Italian roast are assertive and distort the flavor profile. If you have only strong coffee on hand, dilute it with an equal part of water and then measure what you need.

About the Cocoa Powder

Cocoa powder for baking comes in two styles—*Dutch* process, also called *Dutched*, and *natural*. Select either type for this formula but not one that's intended for instant hot cocoa drinks.

The choice of cocoa powder affects the flavor profile, color, and texture of your bread. *Dutched Cocoa* brings a dark brown color to the dough and a low bitterness that balances the flavor profile of the dough itself. *Natural Cocoa* has a more assertive flavor. Its acidity strengthens the protein network, increasing the bread's chewiness but not making it tough.

Sensory

Natural Cocoa has an acidic and bitter taste profile. It has what's called a *quick attack* on the palate, enhancing flavor recognition. In this Pumpernickel Sandwich Bread, cocoa intensifies the fermentation notes in the bread's interior and the dried fruit and roasted notes of the crust.

Technique

Natural Cocoa has a pH of 5.0 to 5.4 (neutral pH is 7.0 and Lemon Juice is 2.0 to 2.3). Natural cocoa tends to form clumps, making it hard to dissolve in pastry batters and bread doughs.

There are mechanical ways around natural cocoa's tendency to clump. Dispersing it in a dry ingredient first, such as granulated sugar or some of the flour in a recipe, is a go-to technique for baked goods like Devil's Food Cake or extra dark Brownies.

When dissolving natural cocoa in liquid, like warm milk or boiling water, a small bit of the liquid is first blended with the dry powder to form a paste. More liquid is gradually added while stirring continues.

Pumpernickel and Rye breads need steam when baking. Use lots of it and trap it in the oven chamber for a greater percent of the total baking time. The baking strategy for rye breads has 3 Stages. For more specifics, see Appendix 1.

Pumpernickel Sandwich Bread

These breads need a firm crust but the tenderizers in this formula (molasses, cocoa powder, brown sugar) retain moisture in the crust longer. Reduced oven temp and a few more minutes in the oven is not unusual to get a thorough bake.

Don't space loaves close together. Circulating air develops a firmer crust on the sides of the loaves. Three-inch spacing between loaves is a rule of thumb.

When you flick your finger on the crust of a fully baked American Pumpernickel—or tap it with the back of a spoon—you will hear a clicking or similar sound. Sometimes the crust even cracks—and then you know for sure you've got a full bake.

Once its internal temperature reads 195 degrees, give the bread a few more minutes in the oven to solidify the crust. If the crust color is too dark to sustain further baking, lower the oven temp by 40 degrees and leave the oven door ajar. The handle of a wooden spoon is a good tool for this job.

Check the bottom of your bread. The tenderizers increase the chances of burning the bottom crust. If needed, place an inverted sheet tray directly on the hearth. Transfer the bread onto the back of the sheet tray for the duration of its bake. If you're baking on a tray in a convection oven, carefully remove the bread to a safe spot on the bench. Place another tray (a cool one) on top of the hot one. Return the bread to the oven to finish baking.

In the production bakeshop, our Pumpernickels are the last bake of the day. This gives us the chance to reset the oven temp as low as 325 degrees, prop the oven door open, and encourage a solid crust.

SPECIFICATION

If you're fortunate to have access to a steam-injected convection oven, bake the loaves there. A well-steamed convection oven delivers a thin corona (the thickness of the crust line) about 1/8th of an inch thick. Bread performs better for sandwiches when the corona is thinner and slices easily. If the sandwich is grilled or pressed like a *panini*, the bread toasts evenly and has better color when the crust is thinner.

Baked in a deck oven or most home ovens, the bread's corona is thicker, about 1/4- to 1/3- inch. The bite and chew of a thicker crust bring additional textural elements, making the hearth-baked version better for the dinner table or thinly sliced to accompany a platter of cured meats, fermented vegetables, or cheeses.

Pumpernickel Sandwich Bread

Formula, Rye Levain

Ingredient	BP%	4-1/2 or 6 Qt Ounces	4-1/2 or 6 Qt Grams	8 Qt	20 Qt
Water	58%	**2.25 oz**	70 g	85 g	210 g
Starter Culture, ripe	70%	3 oz	85 g	100 g	255 g
Rye Flour	100%	4 oz	120 g	145 g	360 g
Yields		9.25 oz	275 g	330 g	825 g
enough to make main dough @ (optional Walnuts or Raisins not included)		3# or 1,350 g main dough		1,750 g main dough	4,000 g main dough

Procedure, Levain

		8-hour shift ddt°= 76°F	5-hour shift ddt°= 76°F
1	Mise en Place	H2O @ **84°**; Starter Culture @ 70°	same
2	Ingredient Mixing	Combine Water & Starter Culture; add Flour	same
3	Development	Stir until blended	same
4A	Fermentation	**2h 00 @ 76°** (70% hum) (see note)	same
4B	Fermentation	+ stir for 10 seconds + 20 to 28h 00 in RFG	same

Rye flour ferments more quickly than white flour. After a Floor Time of two hours @ 76°F, the Rye Levain is active enough to be refrigerated.

Pumpernickel Sandwich Bread

Formula, Main Dough

Ingredient	BP%	4-1/2 or 6 Qt		8 Qt	20 Qt
		Ounces	Grams		
Rye Levain (from above)	36%	7 oz	210 g	280 g	630 g
Water	82%	1# 1 oz	483 g	645 g	1,450 g
Dry Yeast	1.1%	1/4 oz	7 g	9 g	20 g
*Varietal Flours**					
Whole Wheat Flour	7%	1-1/2 oz	42 g	56 g	125 g
Rye Flour	11%	2-1/2 oz	63 g	84 g	190 g
Pumpernickel Meal	11%	2 oz	63 g	84 g	190 g
*Varietal flours may be scaled together in a single container.					
*Tenderizers***					
Cocoa Powder	1%	1/4 oz	6 g	8 g	18 g
Coffee	7%	1-1/3 oz	42 g	56 g	126 g
Dark Brown Sugar	5%	1 oz	31 g	40 g	93 g
Vegetable Oil	1.7%	1/3 oz	10 g	14 g	30 g
Molasses	5%	1 oz	31 g	40 g	93 g
**Tenderizers may be scaled together in a single container.					
Bread Flour	71%	15 oz	420 g	560 g	1,260 g
Salt	3.1%	2/3 oz	18.5 g	27 g	56 g
Yields		3#	1,350 g	1,750 g	4,000 g
Number of pieces (optional Walnuts or Raisins not included)		3 Bâtards @ 420 g (14 oz)		4 Bâtards	9 Bâtards
Optional					
Dark Raisins	11%	2 oz	65 g	90 g	200 g
Walnut pieces, lightly toasted	9%	1-3/4 oz	50 g	75 g	150 g
-or-					
Caraway seeds, lightly toasted	2.7%	1/2 oz	16 g	24 g	50 g

Rye Flours and Pumpernickel Meals can be labeled with confusing terms. *HTBB*, page 352 explains these terms and helps you make an informed choice.

Pumpernickel Sandwich Bread

Procedure, Main Dough

1	**Mise en Place**	H$_2$O @ 94°; Rye Levain @ 70°; Combine Varietal Flours; Combine Tenderizers	**ddt°= 82°***
2	**Ingredient Mixing**	Water and Yeast; + Levain; + add Varietal Flours (hydrate 5 m); + add Tenderizers; + add Bread Flour & Salt	Modified Mixing Sequence
3	**Development**	Speed #2, 2m + Rest 5m; **+ add optional Walnuts and Raisins, or Caraway Seeds;** + Speed #1, 2m	Improved + add optional solids after 5 m rest
4A	**Floor Fermentation**	45 m @ 84° (70% hum); + 1 X Degas and Fold; + 45 m @ 84° (70% hum)	
4B	**Cool Fermentation**	No Cool Fermentation required	Proceed to *Shaping*
5	**Shaping**	Scale 3 pieces @ 420**g; Form as gentle rounds; Bench rest 15 m; Final form as Boulots	
6	**Proofing**	45-50m @ 80° (70% hum), covered	See *Specification*
7	**Decor & Baking**	Brush with 1 egg white + 1 TBSP H2O Score	or, use Starch Wash (page 164)

*Note: The ddt° for Rye Breads is higher than breads made with white or whole wheat flour(s) (Appendix 1).
**420 g weight is for main dough only; pieces will weigh more if optional Walnuts or Raisins are incorporated into dough.

Pumpernickel Sandwich Bread

Baking Chart

Pumpernickel Sandwich Bread
@ 420 g pieces

Oven	Stage I	¿Steam?	Vent @	Stage II	Duration	Stage III	Duration	Int. Temp°
Deck	450° (8.8.1) [3.3.1]	20 secs	10 m	375° (6.6.0) [2.2.0]	+ 10 m ****** check*	360° (6.6.0) [2.2.0]	+ 8 to 12 m	195° plus very firm sides
Rack (w/ oven stone)	360°	20 secs	10 m	320°	+ 10 m ****** check*	300°	+ 8 to 12 m	195° plus very firm sides

*Check: Watch bottom crust. You may need to slide an inverted sheet tray between the breads and the surface of the hearth.

Rye Breads have 3 Baking Stages.
See page 168.

Rosemary Raisin Bread

DESCRIPTION

Of all Italian cities, Venice was more strategically located on the spice trading routes during the Middle Ages. In the 1200's, the city was the hub of western exports—herbs, spices and foods from the rest of Italy and several European countries. At the same time, it was the primary import center for herbs and spices from exotic eastern places like North Africa, China and India. With the wealth of fragrances mingling in the air, the cuisine of Venice and the surrounding Veneto region became known for its blending of east-west flavors and ingredients.

This bread pays respect to that culinary heritage. **Sweet Golden Raisins** blend with Rosemary's perfume. Semolina brings a slight chewiness to the bread and a grain-like sweetness that supports the sweet and savory profile.

UNDERSTANDING

In the main dough, the raisins slowly rehydrate, drawing moisture from their surroundings. This helps them develop a starch bond with the dough. They suspend sturdily and are easy to distribute during the Shaping Phase.

Unless the raisins are so dry that they are covered with sugar crystals, don't soak them before incorporating them into the dough. Raisins that first sit in water release that moisture later, in the dough. When the bread is sliced, you'll see raisins surrounded by white, soggy circles of dough.

PRODUCTION

Capture the Venetian mystery of flavors better with Golden Raisins. Use them whole. Don't chop or mince them.

For the Rosemary, make sure there are no stems or woody bits. You can gently bruise the rosemary needles in a mortar and pestle just before adding them to the dough.

SPECIFICATION

This bread makes for haunting sandwiches—particularly with cured meats. Serve thin slices of bread as a complement to charcuterie or a platter of salume.

For table service, shape this dough as three-ounce rolls. The varied flavor profile wakes up the palate when the rolls are torn apart and eaten in small pieces. A sweet bite, a tangy bite, a savory one.

Mist the rolls with water and sprinkle with coarse sea salt before baking to emphasize their savory flavors. Or, sprinkle them with coarse sugar for a brunch buffet.

Baking Considerations

The bottom crust of these loaves can brown quickly. Follow the guidelines found on page 127 to monitor the deck's surface temperature.

Rosemary Raisin Bread

SENSORY

The basic formula calls for 4 grams of fresh rosemary needles. How you prepare the rosemary changes the aroma and flavor profile of your bread. The finer an herb is cut, the higher its flavor intensity.

In this formula, the rosemary needles are left whole. They release a subtle and delicate flavor. When toasted slices are served for breakfast, the slight herbal intensity brings a lively, wake-me-up experience to the bread.

Chopped rosemary is better-suited with a table bread, dinner rolls, or sandwich slices. Especially with roast pork, Provolone cheese and roasted red peppers.

Don't mince the rosemary finely. The aroma dominates, overriding the delicate flavor profile of the bread itself.

Rosemary Raisin Bread

Formula, Levain

Ingredient	BP%	4-1/2 or 6 Qt Ounces	Grams	8 Qt	20 Qt
Water	125%	3-3/4 oz	100 g	150 g	375 g
Starter Culture, ripe	150%	4-1/2 oz	120 g	180 g	450 g
Bread Flour	100%	3 oz	80 g	120 g	300 g
Yields		11 oz	300 g	450 g	1,125 g
enough to make main dough @		2# 4 oz or 1,050 g main dough		1,900 g main dough	5,000 g main dough

Procedure, Levain

		8-hour shift ddt°= 70°F	5-hour shift ddt°= 76°F
1	Mise en Place	H2O @ **70°**; Starter Culture @ 70°	H2O @ **84°**; Starter Culture @ 70°
2	Ingredient Mixing	Combine Water & Starter Culture; add Flour	same
3	Development	Stir until blended	same
4A	Fermentation *On the Floor*	**5h 00 @ 70°** (70% hum)	**2h 00 @ 76°** (70% hum)
4B	Fermentation *RFG*	+ stir for 10 seconds + 16 to 24h 00 in RFG	+ stir for 10 seconds + 20 to 28h 00 in RFG

Rosemary Raisin Bread

Formula, Main Dough

Ingredient	BP%	4-1/2 or 6 Qt		8 Qt	20 Qt
		Ounces	Grams		
Levain (from above)	42%	7-1/2 oz	210 g	380 g	1,000 g
Water	50%	9 oz	250 g	450 g	1,200 g
Semolina	8%	2 oz	40 g	75 g	200 g
Honey	2.5%	1/2 oz	13 g	24 g	60 g
Bread Flour	92%	1 #	460 g	825 g	2,200 g
Salt	2.1%	1/3 oz	10.5 g	19 g	50 g
Raisins	15%	3 oz	75 g	135 g	350 g
Rosemary, fresh (see *Sensory, page 000*)	0.4%	1/2 tsp	2 g	3.5 g	8 g
Yields		2# 4 oz	1,050 g	1,900 g	5,000 g
Number of pieces		See *About Formula Yields,* pages 260–261			

Rosemary Raisin Bread

Procedure, Main Dough

1	Mise en Place	H_2O @ 92°; Levain @ 70°	ddt°= 78°
2	Ingredient Mixing	Autolyse	
3	Development	Speed #2, 2 m; + Rest 5 m; + **Add Raisins and Rosemary** + Speed #1, 2 m	*Improved* **Add Raisins and Rosemary** **after 5 m rest period.**
4A	Floor Fermentation	1h 00 m @ 78° (70% hum); + Degas and Fold; + 1 h 00 @ 78° (70% hum)	
4B	Cool Fermentation	18 to 24h 00 @ 50° (70% hum)	
5	Shaping	Temper dough 1h 00 on the floor Scale @ 2# 4 oz piece Form as gentle round Bench rest 20 m Final Form as Round or Boulot	
6	Proofing	2h 00 @ 78° (70% hum), covered; + 30 m more, uncovered	
7	Décor & Baking	Score; See **Baking Chart**	

Rosemary Raisin Bread

Baking Chart

Rosemary Raisin Bread
@ 2# to 2# 2 oz

Oven	Stage I	¿Steam?	Vent @	Stage II	Duration	Int. temp°
Deck	500° (9.9.1) [3.3.1]	10 secs	8 m	435° (6.6.0) [2.2.0]	+ 8 m • • • • • • • • • • check*/rotate + 8 to 10 m more	200°
Rack (w/ convection + oven stone)	440°	10 secs	8 m	390°	+ 8 m • • • • • • • • • • check*/rotate + 8 to 10 m more	200°

@ 1# to 1# 4 oz

Oven	Stage I	¿Steam?	Vent @	Stage II	Duration	Int. temp°
Deck	450° (8.8.1)	15 secs	6 m	450° (8.8.0)	+ 6 m • • • • • • • • • • check*/rotate + 6 to 9 m more	200°

*__Check__ means inspect bottom crust. If it is browning more than the top crust and appears it would burn with additional bak-
ing, elevate the loaves onto the back of an inverted sheet pan placed directly on the hearth.
__Rotate__ loaves only if necessary.

Seedy Bâtards

DESCRIPTION

Craftsy, an online teaching platform with studios in Denver, Colorado, produces competency-based lessons for students of cooking, baking, and many other crafts. They're one of the most professional content production companies I've had the pleasure to work with during my career as a teacher. While collaborating on the program **Secrets of Whole Grain Bread Baking**, my producer Denise Michelson asked if I could include a multi-seed bread in the menu. *Of course I will, no problem*. But I knew it *would* be a little bit of a problem and I'd have a lot of baking and research ahead of me before I had a bread I liked.

Adding dry ingredients like seeds to a dough can make the bread dry, coarse, or crumbly. I started soaking seeds overnight before adding them to the main dough. Too much water made the main dough difficult to handle and shape. Not enough water and the seeds clumped together. Many loaves later, I discovered a reliable ratio of water to seeds. I present it here, in what I call **The Seedy Soaker.**

The name is mine, the original idea is not. I was inspired by Peter Reinhart's **Whole Grain Breads**, Ten Speed Press, 2007. This ground-breaking book has struck a path for modern craft bakers seeking to use more whole grains and whole grain flours.

Whereas Peter's formulas are based almost exclusively on whole wheat flour for the main dough, I selected white flour for this version. The bread's flavor is less earthy but white flour makes the loaves perform well for sandwiches. White flour makes the slices more tender and easy to slice, well-suited for spreads like hummus, roasted eggplant, or peanut butter and jelly.

UNDERSTANDING

Adding pre-soaked seeds to a main dough provides several benefits for the baker. From a textural perspective, hydrated seeds are more tender. Stored moisture in the seeds gives a longer shelf life to the bread. Wrapped in parchment and then sealed in a plastic bag, this bread can be stored at ambient temperature for a week.

When activated in water, natural enzymes break down the starches in the seeds. This makes them easier to digest and increases their nutritional availability. To further enhance the nutty character of soaked seeds, there's Walnut Oil in the main dough, a lesson learned from Carol Field in **The Italian Baker**, originally Harper Collins, 1985; republished by Ten Speed Press, 2011.

The Seedy Soaker gives the dough a sticky surface, so don't add additional flour during the Development Phase. Instead, adjust for this during the Shaping Phase.

Once the dough is divided and formed into its first shape, let the pieces rest uncovered on your workspace. The surface of the dough dries, making the final shapes easier to form. Conversely, if the first shapes don't feel sticky, drape a piece of plastic over them for the bench rest so they don't develop a dry surface.

Seedy Bâtards

PRODUCTION

You can bake the bread the same day you mix the main dough or you can cold ferment it overnight. If you want to bake the same day you mix, add the optional commercial yeast. The bread has a lighter texture and slightly larger crumb in this case.

For 1-pound bâtards, 4-ounce burger buns, or 3-ounce slider rolls, include the optional commercial yeast in the main dough. Breads and rolls this size hold their shape better when mixed, proofed, and baked in one day.

If you cold ferment the dough overnight, omit the optional commercial yeast. Temper, Shape, Proof, and Bake the next day. The bread will be slightly denser and its air cells are smaller. Serve thin slices with cured meats, pâtés, grilled sausages, and a selection of mustards.

SPECIFICATION

This formula is designed to make bâtards—the long loaf shape tapering to pointed ends (see Photo Gallery #17). Scale bâtards at 420 g (14 ounces). If you prefer the boule shape, scale them at 630 g (21 ounces).

The interior of the bread is done when it registers 200° on an instant-read thermometer. But the moisture in the Seedy Soaker slows the crust development, especially on the sides of the loaves.

Continue baking this bread until the crust is evenly dark and the sides are firm. If the interior is done but the crust needs more time, reduce the oven temperature to 375° (deck oven) or 360° (convection oven). Bake until the crust suits your preference, about 4 to 7 minutes more.

No need to use a thermometer on 3- or 4-ounce rolls. Bake them so the crust is firm, the color rich and dark, and the caramelized aroma notes fill your kitchen.

Seedy Bâtards

Formula, Seedy Soaker

| Ingredient | BP% | 4-1/2 or 6 Qt | | 8 Qt | 20 Qt |
		Ounces	Grams		
Water	133%	7-1/2 oz	220 g	330 g	750 g
Salt	0.6%	1/4 tsp	1 g	**1.5 g**	**3.5 g**
Flax seeds, any color	18%	1 oz	30 g	45 g	100 g
Sunflower seeds, raw & unsalted	18%	1 oz	30 g	45 g	100 g
Sesame seeds, black preferred	9%	1/2 oz	15 g	25 g	50 g
Pumpkin seeds, raw, hulled, & unsalted	18%	1 oz	30 g	45 g	100 g
Meal or Flour from seeds, like pumpkin, flax, or sunflower	37%	2 oz	60 g	90 g	210 g
Yields		13 oz	385 g	580 g	1,300 g
enough to make main dough @		2# 10 oz or 1,200 g main dough		2,000 g main dough	4,500 g main dough

BP% calculations for *Seedy Soaker* are based on total weight of seeds and meal. (In the Basic Formula, that total is 165 g).

Procedure, Seedy Soaker

		8-hour shift ddt°= 76°F	5-hour shift ddt°= 76°F
1	Mise en Place	H2O @ 60°F	H2O @ 60°F
2	Ingredient Mixing	Combine Water & Salt; add remaining ingredients	same
3	Soaking Time (see note)	5h 00 @ 70° (70% hum); + 16 to 24h 00 in RFG	2h 00 @ 78° (70% hum); + 20 to 28h 00 in RFG

Note: If the ambient temp° of your bakery overnight is 65° or lower, there's no need to refrigerate the Seedy Soaker. Instead, leave it covered on the floor for the time indicated. If you refrigerate the Seedy Soaker, temper it to 75° before adding it to the main dough.

Seedy Bâtards

Formula, Levain

Ingredient	BP%	4-1/2 or 6 Qt		8 Qt	20 Qt
		Ounces	Grams		
Water	50%	2 oz	50 g	80 g	200 g
Starter Culture, ripe	150%	6 oz	150 g	240 g	600 g
Bread Flour	100%	4 oz	100 g	160 g	400 g
Yields		12 oz	300 g	480 g	1,200 g
enough to make main dough @		2# 10 oz or 1,200 g main dough		2,000 g main dough	4,500 g main dough

Procedure, Levain

		8-hour shift ddt°= 70°F	5-hour shift ddt°= 76°F
1	Mise en Place	H2O @ 70°; Starter Culture @ 70°	H2O @ 84°; Starter Culture @ 70°
2	Ingredient Mixing	Combine Water & Starter; add Flour	same
3	Development	Stir until blended	same
4A	Fermentation *On the Floor*	**5h 00 @ 70°** (70% hum)	**2h 00 @ 76°** (70% hum)
4B	Fermentation *RFG*	+ stir for 10 seconds + 16 to 24h 00 in RFG	+ stir for 10 seconds + 20 to 28h 00 in RFG

Seedy Bâtards

Formula, Main Dough

Ingredient	BP%	4-1/2 or 6 Qt Ounces	4-1/2 or 6 Qt Grams	8 Qt	20 Qt
Levain (from above)	55%	9 oz	250 g	415 g	930 g
Water	34%	5 oz	155 g	255 g	575 g
Dry Yeast*	0.4%	2 g	2 g	3 g	7 g
Seedy Soaker (from above)	77%	12 oz	385 g	580 g	1,300 g
Agave Syrup (Amber preferred)	7.5%	1-1/4 oz	35 g	55 g	120 g
Walnut Oil (or Canola)	5.5%	7/8 oz	25 g	40 g	90 g
Bread Flour	100%	1 #	455 g	760 g	1,710 g
Salt	3.5%	1/2 oz plus a pinch	16 g	27 g	62 g
Yields		**2# 10 oz**	**1,200 g**	**2,000 g**	**4,500 g**
Number of pieces		3 Bâtards @ 420 g (14 oz) or 2 Boules @ 630 g (21 oz)		5 Bâtards @ 400 g	10 Bâtards @ 450 g

*Note: 2 g dry yeast is 1/2 teaspoon, leveled.

Seedy Bâtards

Procedure, Main Dough

1	Mise en Place	H_2O @ 92°; Levain @ 70° Seedy Soaker @ 70°	ddt°= 78°
2	Ingredient Mixing	Autolyse	H_2O + yeast; + Levain; + Seedy Soaker; + Tenderizers & Salt; + Flour
3	Development	Speed #2, 2m + Rest 5m; + Speed #1, 2m	Improved (Dip hands in H_2O for easier handling)
4A	Floor Fermentation	45 m @ 78° (70% hum) + 1 X Degas and Fold + 45 m @ 78° (70% hum) + 1 X Degas & Fold + 30 m @ 78° (70° hum)	same

		Next-day Bake	**Same-day Bake**
4B	Cool Fermentation	18 to 24h 00 @ **50°** (70% hum)	No Cool Fermentation required. Proceed directly to *Shaping*
5	Shaping	Temper dough 1h 00 *on the floor* prior to shaping	Scale 3 pcs @ 420 g (for Bâtards) or 2 pcs @ 630 g (for Boules); Form as gentle round; Bench rest 20 m; Final Form as Boules or Bâtards
6	Proofing	same	*Bâtards (in couche)* 1h 30 m @ 78° (70% hum) *Boules (in bannetons)* 1 h 30 m @ 78° (70% hum), covered; + 30 m more, uncovered
7	Decor & Baking	Score; See Note for **Next-day Bake** on Baking Chart	Score; See **Baking Chart**

Seedy Bâtards

Baking Chart (same day)

Seedy Bâtards
@ 420 g pieces

Oven	Stage I	¿Steam?	Vent @	Stage II	Duration	Int. temp°
Deck	500° (9.9.1) [3.3.1]	10 secs	8 m	435° (9.9.0) [2.2.0]	+ 8 m •••••••••• check*/rotate + 7 to 9 m more •••••••••• *For Next-day Bake, see Note**	200°
Rack (w/ convection + oven stone)	460°	10 secs	8 m	425°	+ 8 m •••••••••• check*/rotate + 7 to 9 m more •••••••••• *For Next-day Bake, see Note**	200°

*Check means inspect bottom crust. If it is browning more than the top crust and appears it would burn with additional baking, elevate the loaves onto the back of an inverted sheet pan placed directly on the hearth. Rotate loaves only if necessary.

**Next-day Bake: If your breads have cold fermented overnight, add 5 to 8 minutes more to the total baking time.

Seedy Bâtards

Baking Chart (same day)

Seedy Bâtards
@ 630 g pieces

Oven	Stage I	¿Steam?	Vent @	Stage II	Duration	Int. temp°
Deck	490° (8.8.1) [3.3.1]	10 secs	8 m	435° (8.8.0) [2.2.0]	+ 8 m •••••••••• check*/rotate + 10 to 12 m more •••••••••• *For Next-day Bake, see Note** *	200°
Rack (w/ convection + oven stone)	430°	10 secs	8 m	390°	+ 8 m •••••••••• check*/rotate + 9 to 11 m more •••••••••• *For Next-day Bake, see Note** *	200°

*Check means inspect bottom crust. If it is browning more than the top crust and appears it would burn with additional baking, elevate the loaves onto the back of an inverted sheet pan placed directly on the hearth. Rotate loaves only if necessary.

**Next-day Bake: If your breads have cold fermented overnight, add 5 to 8 minutes more to the total baking time.

100% Spelt Bread w/Whole Berries

Spelt is a species of wheat, a variety that pre-dates the modern wheat that gives us Bread, All-Purpose and Cake flours. With a pedigree dating from 4,000 BCE, Spelt takes its rightful place among a category of cereals called *Ancient Grains*. This group includes *Kamut (*Ka **moot***)*, *Barley,* and *Quinoa* (**Keen** wa).

In its whole form, grains of Spelt are called Spelt Berries. Grind Whole Spelt Berries and you get Spelt Flour. Compared to Bread Flour, Spelt Flour has slightly less carbohydrates and can sometimes have as much as 20% more protein. Most Spelt Flour is made from the whole berry for more nutritional benefit.

Spelt is sometimes better tolerated by people with gluten sensitivity. Spelt Flour can be substituted on a one-to-one basis for Bread Flour in many preparations. An earthy, sweet note is added to breads by substituting Spelt Flour for some of the Bread Flour in the main dough.

A ratio of 40% Spelt Flour to 60% Bread Flour is common when experimenting with Spelt Flour in your repertoire. Substituted at more than 50%, Spelt Flour changes the dough's behavior. The baker needs to adapt his techniques and schedule (see *Understanding*).

UNDERSTANDING

As far as Protein goes, Spelt Flour contains more *gliadin* amino acids than *glutenin* amino acids (Appendix 1). In a bread dough, this means more *extensibility* and less *elasticity*. The more spelt flour is used as a substitute for bread flour in a dough, the more extensible the dough becomes. Like many things, this is a mixed blessing for the baker.

In breads where uniformity is required, like sandwich loaves, too much spelt flour makes the dough slack. A pan loaf with spelt flour will proof more quickly than the 100% bread-flour version. You can recognize this quick proofing if your baked loaf has a flat or sunken top crust and a dense, compressed layer of dough along the bottom of the loaf. Adjust proofing times downward by about 10% when using Spelt Flour in your experiments.

In hearth breads, substituting spelt flour in a bread formula brings a slightly relaxed-looking boule. Adding visual character with a free-form appearance, the bread spreads outward as it bakes more than it rises upward.

PRODUCTION

When scheduled to mix and bake the same day, a two-hour fermentation for this dough delivers slight nuttiness and sweetness. An earthy note and slight sourness round the flavor profile. The interior texture is similar to the Pain au Levain, just softer. It's tender to bite and moderately chewy. Because the interior is soft, sweet, and light, the bread provides contrasting textures when you bake the crust slightly darker than other breads.

A cold fermentation overnight changes the flavor profile. The nutty grain flavor increases and the sweetness is replaced with a lemon or citrus sourness. Thin slices of this version make a peanut butter and jelly sandwich into a complex sensory experience.

Whole Grain Soakers

Whole Spelt Berries can be added to the main dough, bringing textural contrast to the bread. And because they are a solid addition, they make the dough easier to handle, proof a little slower, and hold its shape better.

To soften whole grains before adding them to a main dough, the baker prepares what is called a *Soaker*. There are dozens of variables when making a Soaker. Generally, cool water is used so the grains swell uniformly. Hot water can be used if the grains are needed in a hurry. In this case, watch that they don't get water-logged.

When a whole grain absorbs water, its natural enzymes are activated. These enzymes break down the starch in the grain, releasing sugar and flavor compounds.

When a soaked grain is added to the main dough, the yeast in the main dough can feast not only on the sugars in the bread flour, but also on the buffet of fermentable sugars found in the soaked grain.

(For details about natural enzymes in grains, read *Nature's Instant Bread Dough* on page 14.)

When a formula calls for both a Levain and a Whole Grain Soaker, prepare both on Day One. Let them stand *on the floor* for the specified times and then move them into the refrigerator. Keep them on the same schedule. It's easier to keep track of them.

To control the spontaneous fermentation of the whole grains, a tiny amount of salt is added to a whole grain soaker. Helpful in warm bakeshops or during summer months, salt retards the natural yeast activity in the grains.

Once they are soaked and drained, salt the grains to taste. Just as you would lightly salt sautéed mushrooms before using them to top a Focaccia, always season soaked grains with salt.

Once incorporated into a main dough, unsalted grains rob salt from their environment. As a result, the overall saltiness of the bread is lowered and the bread tastes flat.

Cooked Grain Soakers

You must soak whole grains before adding them to a bread dough. There's not enough moisture in the dough for them to hydrate properly. But you don't have to stop there. You can cook them, too.

When soaked grains are also cooked, your breads have better texture, more flavor, and extended shelf life. Prepping whole grains is a 2-step cooking process, similar to the method used for dried beans and legumes, like favas, red beans, and black-eyed peas.

Here are some guidelines for soaking and cooking Whole Spelt Berries. For more information, especially about other ancient grains, read Maria Speck's award-winning book *Ancient Grains for Modern Meals* (Ten Speed Press, 2011).

Soak Spelt Berries in 1-1/2 times as much water overnight. (If the ambient temp° is higher than 70°F, move the grains to the refrigerator after they've soaked for 4 hours.)

The next day, drain the Spelt Berries. The soaker water is nutrient-rich, so use it in your garden.

To cook Spelt Berries, use 1-1/2 times fresh water to the soaked berries (**by volume**, as you'd cook Long Grain White Rice). Combine them in a small sauce-pot with a pinch of salt.

Bring to the boil and reduce to a simmer. Cook, with the lid off, until the berries are *al dente*, about 45 to 55 minutes.

Depending on how dry the berries are initially, they may need more or less water during the cooking phase. Don't worry if the whole thing looks a little soupy, and don't worry about adding a little more water if the mixture looks dry. You can stir the berries once or twice during the process for even cooking.

Drain the berries, discard the water, and cool the berries on a sheet tray lined with parchment paper or a Silpat®.

If you cook Spelt Berries ahead, cool them and store them in a plastic bag in the refrigerator for 2 or 3 days. Or freeze them for 1 month. In either case, temper them to 70°F before adding them to your dough.

Prep more than you need. Cooked Spelt berries can be added to salads, re-heated and served in a soup or stew, or dressed with a vinaigrette and served as a side dish.

To prepare Spelt Berries for the smallest formula yield for this bread:

1. Soak 2 ounces of Spelt Berries in 3 ounces of Water with a pinch of salt.
2. The next day, drain the Berries.
3. Combine them with 1 cup of fresh water and another pinch of salt.
4. Simmer them stovetop for 45–55 minutes, uncovered.
5. Drain them, cool them, and salt them to taste.
6. Weigh the required amount for your formula.

100% Spelt Bread w/Whole Berries

Formula, Spelt Berry Soaker

Ingredient	BP%	4-1/2 or 6 Qt		8 Qt	20 Qt
		Ounces	Grams		
Water	100%	2 oz	60 g	100 g	250 g
Salt	n/a	pinch	pinch	pinch	1/8 tsp
Whole Spelt Berries	100%	2 oz	60 g	100 g	250 g
Yields		4 oz	120 g	200 g	500 g
enough to make main dough @		2# 5 oz or 1,050 g main dough		1,900 g main dough	4,900 g main dough

Procedure, Spelt Berry Soaker

		8-hour shift ddt°= 70°F	5-hour shift ddt°= 70°F
1	Mise en Place	H2O @ **60°**	H2O @ **60°**
2	Ingredient Mixing	Combine Water & Salt; add Spelt Berries	same
3	Development	none	none
4A	Fermentation *On the Floor*	5h 00 @ 70°	2h 00 @ 70°
4B	Fermentation *RFG*	+ 16 to 24h 00 in RFG	+ 20 to 26h 00 in RFG

100% Spelt Bread w/Whole Berries

Formula, Spelt Flour Levain

| Ingredient | BP% | 4-1/2 or 6 Qt | | 8 Qt | 20 Qt |
		Ounces	Grams		
Water	67%	2-1/3 oz	65 g	120 g	265 g
Starter Culture, ripe	100%	3-1/2 oz	100 g	180 g	400 g
Spelt Flour	100%	3-1/2 oz	100 g	180 g	400 g
Yields		9 oz	265 g	480 g	1,065 g
enough to make main dough @		2# 5 oz or 1,050 g main dough		1,900 g main dough	4,900 g main dough

Procedure, Spelt Flour Levain

		8-hour shift ddt°= 70°F	5-hour shift ddt°= 76°F
1	**Mise en Place**	H2O @ **70°**; Starter Culture @ 70°	H2O @ **84°**; Starter Culture @ 70°
2	**Ingredient Mixing**	Combine Water & Starter; add Spelt Flour	same
3	**Development**	Stir until blended	same
4A	**Fermentation** *On the Floor*	**5h 00 @ 70°** (70% hum)	**2h 00 @ 76°** (70% hum)
4B	**Fermentation** *RFG*	+ stir for 10 seconds + 16 to 24h 00 in RFG	+ stir for 10 seconds + 20 to 28h 00 in RFG

100% Spelt Bread w/Whole Berries

Formula, Main Dough

Hybrid Levain

Ingredient	BP%	4-1/2 or 6 Qt Ounces	4-1/2 or 6 Qt Grams	8 Qt	20 Qt
Water	70%	11 oz	315 g	560 g	1,400 g
Spelt Flour Levain (from above)	50%	8 oz	225 g	400 g	1,000 g
Dry Yeast*	0.4%	2 g	2 g	3.5 g	8 g
Spelt Flour	100%	1 #	450 g	800 g	2,000 g
Salt	2.8%	13 g	13 g	22 g	56 g
Soaked or Cooked Spelt Berries** (optional)	25%	4 oz	115 g	200 g	500 g
Yields		**2# 5 oz**	**1,050 g**	**1,900 g**	**4,900 g**
Number of pieces		See *About Formula Yields,* pages 260–261			

*Note: 2 g dry yeast is 1/2 teaspoon, leveled.

100% Spelt Bread w/Whole Berries

Procedure, Main Dough

1	Mise en Place	H$_2$O @ 92°; Spelt Levain @ 70°; Spelt Berries @ 70°	ddt°= 78°
2	Ingredient Mixing	Dissolve Yeast in Water; Add Levain	*Autolyse*
3	Development	Speed #2, 2 m; + Rest 5 m; **+ Add Spelt Berries** + Speed #1, 2 m	*Improved* **Add Spelt Berries after 5 m rest period.**
4A	Floor Fermentation	1h 00 m @ 78° (70% hum); + Degas and Fold; + 1h 00 @ 78° (70% hum)	
4B	Cool Fermentation	No Cool Fermentation required	
5	Shaping	Scale @ 2# 4 oz piece; Form as gentle round; Bench rest 20 m; Final Form as Round or Boulot	
6	Proofing	1h 30 @ 78° (70% hum), covered; + 30 m more, uncovered	
7	Décor & Baking	Score; See **Baking Chart**	

100% Spelt Bread w/Whole Berries

Baking Chart

100% Spelt Bread with Whole Spelt Berries
@ 2# to 2# 4 oz

Oven	Stage I	¿Steam?	Vent @	Stage II	Duration	Int. temp°
Deck	500° (9.9.1) [3.3.1]	10 secs	8 m	435° (6.6.0) [2.2.0]	+ 8 m •••••••••• check*/rotate + 8 to 10 m more	200°
Rack (w/ convection + oven stone)	440°	10 secs	8 m	390°	+ 8 m •••••••••• check*/rotate + 8 to 10 m more	200°

*Check means inspect bottom crust. If it is browning more than the top crust and appears it would burn with additional baking, elevate the loaves onto the back of an inverted sheet pan placed directly on the hearth.`
Rotate loaves only if necessary.

Classic Breads

Pain au Levain

This is the Representative for the Family of Wild Yeast Breads. See the detailed instructions on pages 73–132.

Formula, Basic Levain

Ingredient	BP%	4-1/2 or 6 Qt Ounces	4-1/2 or 6 Qt Grams	8 Qt	20 Qt
Water	50%	1 oz	25 g	50 g	90 g
Starter Culture, ripe	150%	3 oz	75 g	150 g	270 g
Bread Flour	100%	2 oz	50 g	100 g	180 g
Yields		6 oz	150 g	300 g	540 g
enough to make main dough @		2# 2 oz or 950 g main dough		1,800 g main dough	4,100 g main dough

Procedure, Basic Levain

		8-hour shift ddt°= 70°F	5-hour shift ddt°= 76°F
1	Mise en Place	H2O @ **70°**; Starter Culture @ 70°	H2O @ **84°**; Starter Culture @ 70°
2	Ingredient Mixing	Combine Water & Starter Culture; add Flour	same
3	Development	Stir until blended	same
4A	Fermentation *On the Floor*	**5h 00 @ 70°** (70% hum)	**2h 00 @ 76°** (70% hum)
4B	Fermentation *RFG*	+ stir for 10 seconds + 16 to 24h 00 in RFG	+ stir for 10 seconds + 20 to 28h 00 in RFG

Pain au Levain

Formula, Main Dough

Ingredient	BP%	4-1/2 or 6 Qt		8 Qt	20 Qt
		Ounces	Grams		
Basic Levain (from above)	20%	4 oz	120 g	240 g	500 g
Water	70%	14 oz	400 g	800 g	1,725 g
Whole Wheat Flour	20%	4 oz	120 g	240 g	500 g
Bread Flour	80%	1 #	450 g	900 g	2,000 g
Salt	2.5%	1/2 oz	14 g	30 g	64 g
Yields		**2# 2 oz**	**950 g**	**1,800 g**	**4,100 g**
Number of pieces		See *About Formula Yields,* pages 260–261			

Pain au Levain

Procedure, Main Dough

1	**Mise en Place**	H$_2$O @ 92° ; Levain @ 70°	ddt°= 78°
2	**Ingredient Mixing**	Autolyse	
3	**Development**	Speed #2, 2 m; + Rest 5 m; + Speed #1, 2 m	*Improved*
4A	**Floor Fermentation**	1h 00 m @ 78° (70% hum); + Degas and Fold; 1h 00 @ 78° (70% hum)	
4B	**Cool Fermentation**	18 to 24 h 00 @ 50° (70% hum)	
5	**Shaping**	Temper dough 1h 00 *on the floor* Scale @ 2# 2 oz piece Form as gentle round Bench rest 20 m Final Form as Round or Boulot	
6	**Proofing**	1h 30 @ 78° (70% hum), covered; + 30 m more, uncovered	
7	**Décor & Baking**	Score; See **Baking Chart**	

Pain au Levain

Baking Chart

Pain au Levain
@ 2# to 2# 2 oz

Oven	Stage I	¿Steam?	Vent @	Stage II	Duration	Int. temp°
Deck	500° (9.9.1) [3.3.1]	10 secs	8 m	435° (6.6.0) [2.2.0]	+ 8 m •••••••••• check*/rotate + 8 to 10 m more	200°
Rack (w/ convection + oven stone)	440°	10 secs	8 m	390°	+ 8 m •••••••••• check*/rotate + 8 to 10 m more	200°

*__Check__ means inspect bottom crust. If it is browning more than the top crust and appears it would burn with additional baking, elevate the loaves onto the back of an inverted sheet pan placed directly on the hearth.
__Rotate__ loaves only if necessary.

One-Build Sourdough Bread

DESCRIPTION

This is an old school sourdough from San Francisco. It gets more tangy the longer you chew. This classic bread makes great dinner rolls (scaled at 2-1/2 ounces). As a hearth bread, thin slices make a firm sandwich bread for avocado, local tomatoes and roasted turkey breast. Small rounds of dough (scaled at 6 ounces) can be proofed, baked, and then hollowed out. Like the ones on *Fisherman's Wharf* that are used to serve Cioppino, the Italian-American seafood stew that originated in San Francisco.

UNDERSTANDING

Allow a full proof for these breads before they are baked. Sometimes, this translates to an hour more proofing time than other wild yeast doughs. Shape these breads first thing in your production day. Let them sit in their bannetons and come to full proof while you're busy with other projects.

Viewed from the side, a white flour sourdough like this has a flat profile when fully proofed. It loses the domed looked that the other wild yeast yeast doughs have when they are proofed.

The center of the dough appears to be sinking. The pressure pushes the dough outward, making the shoulders of the dough rise higher (see *Proofing*, pages 101–103).

PRODUCTION

When a main dough uses only white flour, like the High Gluten or Bread Flour in this formula, the dough has a slower fermentation rate. If it's one of several projects being produced within the same shift, this dough will be the laggard. Make sure you start this project before other breads.

Another remedy, especially if the ambient temperature in the bakery is less than 80°, is to *spike* the dough with a small amount of dry yeast. A pinch is all that is needed and it does the trick in helping this dough keep up with the pace of the other wild yeast breads in this section.

To add a *yeast spike*, sprinkle any type of commercial yeast (fresh or dry) onto the Water and Levain mixture at the start of the *Ingredient Mixing Sequence*. Strategies for using commercial yeast in a wild yeast dough are in *Hybrid Levain*, pages 148–150.

SPECIFICATION

The *1-Build Levain* formula in this formula yields enough to make the *One-Build Sourdough Bread* and the *Two-Build Sourdough Bread* (page 212).

To make only the One-Build Sourdough Bread, make half of the 1-Build Levain formula on page 206.

One-Build Sourdough Bread

Formula, 1-Build Levain*

Ingredient	BP%	4-1/2 or 6 Qt		8 Qt	20 Qt
		Ounces	Grams		
Water	50%	2 oz	55 g	105 g	255 g
Starter Culture, ripe	80%	3-1/4 oz	90 g	170 g	410 g
Bread Flour	100%	4 oz	110 g	210 g	510 g
Yields		9-1/4 oz	255 g	485 g	1,175 g
enough to make main dough @		2# 2 oz or 950 g main dough		1,950 g main dough	4,700 g main dough

* Note: The *1-Build Levain* is thicker than the other Levain formulas in this book.

If it looks too thick, just weigh the whole Levain mixture. It's total weight will be close to the formula yield listed, give or take about 20 grams (there's always some stuck to a spoon, somewhere).
If the weight of your Levain is incorrect, compost it. Check your scale to make sure the batteries aren't running low, then make another *1-Build Levain*.

Procedure, 1-Build Levain

		8-hour shift ddt°= 70°F	5-hour shift ddt°= 76°F
1	Mise en Place	H2O @ **70°**; Starter Culture @ 70°	H2O @ **84°**; Starter Culture @ 70°
2	Ingredient Mixing	Combine Water & Starter Culture; add Flour	same
3	Development	Stir until blended	same
4A	Fermentation *On the Floor*	5h 00 @ 70° (70% hum)	3h* 00 @ 76° (70% hum)
4B	Fermentation *RFG*	+ stir for 10 seconds + 16 to 24h 00 in RFG	+ stir for 10 seconds + 20 to 28h 00 in RFG

*Note the extended Floor Time for 1-Build Levain.
White Flour Levains ferment slowly and need longer floor fermentation.

One-Build Sourdough Bread

Formula, Main Dough

Ingredient	BP%	4-1/2 or 6 Qt Ounces	4-1/2 or 6 Qt Grams	8 Qt	20 Qt
1-Build Levain (from above)	50%	8 oz	225 g	450 g	1,100 g
Water	70%	11 oz	315 g	630 g	1,540 g
Dry Yeast	0.4%	2 g	2 g	4 g	9 g
Bread Flour	100%	1#	450 g	900 g	2,200 g
Salt	2.7%	1/2 oz (scant)	**12.5 g**	25 g	60 g
Yields		**2# 2 oz**	**950 g**	**1,950 g**	**4,700 g**

Number of pieces   See *About Formula Yields,* pages 260–261

One-Build Sourdough Bread

Procedure, Main Dough

1	Mise en Place	H2O @ 92°; Levain @ 70°	ddt° = 78°F
2	Ingredient Mixing	Autolyse *only* H2O and Flour; + Add Levain and then Salt; + Speed #1, 1 m to combine ingredients to *Take Up*	**Baker's Tip:** When adding a *stiff* Levain, like the one in this formula, it's easier to add it *after* the H2O and Flour complete the 15-minute *Autolyse.*
3	Development	Speed #2m 2m; + Rest 5m * (see *note*, below); + Speed #1, 2 m	*Improved*
4A	Floor Fermentation	1h 30 @ 78° (70% hum); + Degas and Fold; + 1 h 00 @ 78° (70% hum)	**Baker's Tip:** Add 30 m more *Floor Fermentation* if time allows
4B	Cool Fermentation	18 to 24h 00 @ 50° (70% hum)	
5	Shaping	Temper dough 1 h 00 *on the floor* Scale @ 2# 4 oz piece Form as gentle round Bench rest 20 m Final Form as Round or Boulot	
6	Proofing	2h 00 min @ 78° (70% hum), covered; + 30 m more, uncovered	**Baker's Tip:** Extend total proofing time by **1h 00** if dough is cooler than 78°
7	Décor & Baking	Score; See **Baking Chart**	

*Note: If using a machine mixer, invert dough midway in the Development Phase (Appendix 1).

One-Build Sourdough Bread

Baking Chart

One-Build Sourdough Bread
@ 2# to 2# 2 oz

Oven	Stage I	¿Steam?	Vent @	Stage II	Duration	Int. temp°
Deck	500° (9.9.1) [3.3.1]	10 secs	8 m	435° (6.6.0) [2.2.0]	+ 8 m •••••••••• check*/rotate + 8 to 10 m more	200°
Rack (w/ convection + oven stone)	440°	10 secs	8 m	390°	+ 8 m •••••••••• check*/rotate + 8 to 10 m more	200°

* *Check* means inspect bottom crust. If it is browning more than the top crust and appears it would burn with additional baking, elevate the loaves onto the back of an inverted sheet pan placed directly on the hearth.
Rotate loaves only if necessary.

Palate Development for Bread

A developed palate is one of the best resources in a baker's toolkit. Take every opportunity to hone yours.

Use it to track customer preference, for example. Do they prefer a lactic or an acetic acid flavor profile? Which breads pair better with the heavy fare of winter—braises, root vegetables, and game meats? Which flavors and textures do they prefer for summer's quickly-cooked foods like juicy vegetables, seafoods, and light proteins?

A baker uses these discoveries to keep his product line innovative and maintain customer loyalty.

HOW TO TASTE BREAD

Step One

Mindfully chew a piece of the **Mie**, the interior part of the bread. Pay attention to the basic tastes—Salt, Sweet, Sour, and Bitter. In what sequence do the tastes reveal themselves? Do they work in balance, like the bitterness from whole wheat flour as it plays back and forth with the saltiness in the bread. Is the antagonism a friendly one? Or do they fight for attention, the saltiness making the bitterness seem harsh, and vice versa.

Did you notice that we are talking about the inside of the bread—not the **Crust**? In bread tasting protocol, start on the inside. The *Mie* reveals the bread's true flavor and texture. It's where you learn about the dough's *Fermentation* and how it was handled during *Development, Shaping,* and *Proofing.*

The *Crust* is saved for later. It's a completely different product from the interior of the bread. Like the hard sugar shell on a *crème brûlée* or the charred, crispy end cuts from a Standing Rib Roast.

Step Two

Focus on the Sour Taste in isolation. Use your focus to *lift out* (i.e. to *ignore*), the Salt, Sweet, and Bitter. Take another bite of the bread. Chew it at least 10 or 12 times and let your saliva blend with the bread so the sourness can spread evenly in your mouth.

Chew with your mouth open, aerate the flavor profile as you chew. Much to the dismay of Moms everywhere, you get more flavor from your food if there's more air in your mouth when you chew it.

Can you identify the style of sourness in the bread? Does it have a yogurt, chewy type of character? Does it have a sharp, vinegar character?

Make notes on your formula pages about what style of sourness the bread delivers. This is your key to unlocking your customer preferences.

Comparative Tasting

The One-Build and Two-Build Sourdough Breads are a good starting point for palate development. Both are made from White Flour only. They are made with the same procedures.

There's only one difference between the two breads:

The Levain for the One-Build Sourdough is built from the Wild Yeast Culture. The Levain for the Two-Build Sourdough is built from fermented 1-Build Levain.

Here's the strategy so you can prepare both breads for a comparative tasting:

1 Make the One-Build Sourdough Bread. Bake it, cool it, and wrap it in a piece of parchment. Then, wrap that in plastic. Store it at ambient temperature overnight and continue with the Two-Build Sourdough project.

2 When the Two-Build Sourdough bread is baked, cool it and wrap it with parchment only. You don't have to let the second bread sit overnight but the flavors do need to ripen for at least 2 to 3 hours before tasting.

3 Compare the two breads side by side. They look similar but their aroma and flavor profiles differ. Evaluating these two breads together is the best way to understand how additional fermentation of the dough, especially cool fermentation, builds more flavor in your bread.

btw, when you're done, it's OK to eat the crust!

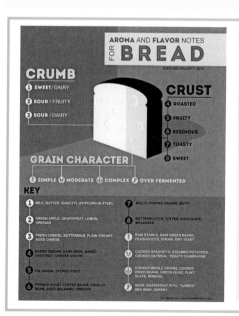

Tasting bread involves three different groups of aromas and flavors—the Crust, the Crumb, and the bread's overall level of Fermentation.

This chart identifies the more common notes, especially those found in wild yeast breads.

See Photo Gallery #21

Two-Build Sourdough Bread

DESCRIPTION

Recall that the 1-Build Levain from the previous project was divided into two portions. One portion was used to make the One-Build Sourdough Bread and the other portion was set aside.

Use this reserved portion to make the 2-Build Levain for this project. The procedure is the same as for the Basic Levain. Namely, thin the 1-Build Levain with Water and then thicken it with Flour. Ferment it *on the floor* and then transfer it to the refrigerator overnight.

What's the advantage? Flavor.

The LAB colonies in the 1-Build Levain get a second feeding of Fresh Flour and Water. They enjoy another overnight and develop even more flavor acids. Because it's based on an already-fermented Levain, the second one is called a *2-Build Levain*. A second generation Levain.

UNDERSTANDING

Making a Two-Build Sourdough Bread takes commitment. Technically, it's no more challenging, but it requires yet one more day and a mindful baker willing to monitor the additional steps. If you're making this project in a bakery classroom, you'll need to start the 1-Build Levain two days prior to the first class meeting for the week. If you lack refrigeration space or the necessary time outside the class schedule, better to save this bread until you have the time.

PRODUCTION

This is a 100% White Flour dough. To speed its *Proofing* phase, add a spike of commercial yeast to the main dough. (See *Production* from the One-Build Sourdough Bread.)

SPECIFICATION

Visual differences in your product line are important for your customers. When different breads sit side-by-side on a retail shelf, change the scoring pattern for each kind of bread. One slash for the One-Build Sourdough Bread, two slashes for the Two-Build Sourdough Bread. It's an easy way for your customers to tell the loaves apart.

Two-Build Sourdough Bread

Formula, 2-Build Levain*

| Ingredient | BP% | 4-1/2 or 6 Qt | | 8 Qt | 20 Qt |
		Ounces	Grams		
Water	50%	3 oz	80 g	150 g	375 g
1-Build Levain, ripe (see One-Build Sourdough Bread Formula)	80%	5 oz	130 g	240 g	600 g
Rye Flour	5%	1/2 oz	10 g	20 g	40 g
Bread Flour	95%	5-1/2 oz	150 g	280 g	710 g
Yields		14 oz	370 g	690 g	1,725 g
enough to make main dough @		2# 2 oz or 1,000 g main dough		2,000 g main dough	5,000 g main dough

*Note: The 2-Build Levain is thicker than the other Levain formulas in this book.

Baker's Tip

Separately scale each of the four ingredients in the 2-Build Levain. Check the weights once more before mixing them together. There may not be enough 1-Build Levain reserved from the first project if there's a scaling mishap. If you do run short, just make up the difference with more Ripe Starter Culture.

The main dough will be slightly more slack as a result. But if you've decided to make this formula, then your confidence level is high enough to handle a dough that's a little more hydrated.

Two-Build Sourdough Bread

Procedure, 2-Build Levain

		8-hour shift ddt°= 70°F	5-hour shift ddt°= 76°F
1	**Mise en Place**	H2O @ **70°**; 1-Build Levain @ 70°	H2O @ **84°**; Starter Culture @ 70°
2	**Ingredient Mixing**	Combine Water & 1-Build Levain; add Rye and Bread Flours	same
3	**Development**	Stir until blended	none
4A	**Fermentation** *On the Floor*	5h 00 @ 70° (70% hum)	3h* 00 @ 76° (70% hum)
4B	**Fermentation** *RFG*	+ stir for 10 seconds + 16 to 24h 00 in RFG	+ stir for 10 seconds + 20 to 28h 00 in RFG

*Note the extended time for this Levain.
White Flour Levains ferment slowly and need longer floor fermentation.

Formula, Main Dough

Ingredient	BP%	4-1/2 or 6 Qt		8 Qt	20 Qt
		Ounces	Grams		
2-Build Levain (from above)	80%	11-1/4 oz	320 g	640 g	1,600 g
Water	70%	10 oz	280 g	560 g	1,400 g
Dry Yeast	0.4%	2 g	2 g	4 g	10 g
Bread Flour	100%	14 oz	400 g	800 g	2,000 g
Salt	2.8%	2/5 oz	11 g	22 g	56 g
Yields		**2# 2 oz**	**1,000 g**	**2,000 g**	**5,000 g**
Number of pieces		See *About Formula Yields,* pages 260–261			

Two-Build Sourdough Bread

Procedure, Main Dough

1	Mise en Place	H2O @ 92°; 2-Build Levain @ 70°	ddt° = 78°F
2	Ingredient Mixing	Autolyse *only* H2O and Flour; + Add Levain and then Salt; + Speed #1, 1 m to combine ingredients to *Take Up*	**Baker's Tip:** When adding a *Stiff Levain*, like the one in this formula, it's easier to add it *after* the H2O and Flour complete the 15-minute *Autolyse.*
3	Development	Speed #2m 2m; + Rest 5m *(see *note*, below); + Speed #1, 2 m	*Improved*
4A	Floor Fermentation	1h 00 @ 78° (70% hum); + Degas and Fold; + 1 h 00 @ 78° (70% hum)	**Baker's Tip:** Add 30 m more *Floor Fermentation* if time allows
4B	Cool Fermentation	18 to 24h 00 @ 50° (70% hum)	
5	Shaping	Temper dough 1 h 00 *on the floor* Scale @ 2# 4 oz piece Form as gentle round Bench rest 20 m Final Form as Round or Boulot	
6	Proofing (note longer time for this dough)	2h 00 min @ 78° (70% hum), covered; + 30 m more, uncovered	**Baker's Tip:** Extend total proofing time by **1 h 00** if dough is cooler than 78°
7	Décor & Baking	Score; See **Baking Chart**	

*Note: If using a machine mixer, invert dough midway in the Development Phase (Appendix 1).

Two-Build Sourdough Bread

Baking Chart

Two-Build Sourdough Bread
@ 2# to 2# 2 oz

Oven	Stage I	¿Steam?	Vent @	Stage II	Duration	Int. temp°
Deck	500° (9.9.1) [3.3.1]	10 secs	7 m	435° (6.6.0) [2.2.0]	+ 7 m •••••••••• check*/rotate + 7 to 9 m more	200°
Rack (w/ convection + oven stone)	440°	10 secs	8 m	390°	+ 7 m •••••••••• check*/rotate + 7 to 9 m more	200°

Check means inspect bottom crust. If it is browning more than the top crust and appears it would burn with additional baking, elevate the loaves onto the back of an inverted sheet pan placed directly on the hearth.
Rotate loaves only if necessary.

Porridge Breads

About Porridge Breads

A *Porridge Bread* is made by layering a fermenting dough, like the Pain au Levain dough, with a cooked and seasoned grain called a *porridge*. To visualize the process, think of a pastry dough such as Croissant or Puff Pastry.

To make a *laminated* dough, as these pastry doughs are called, a baker needs two preparations. On one hand there's a mass of dough which may be yeasted or not. Croissant yes, Puff Pastry no. On the other hand, there's a high baker's percent of fat, the frequent choice being Butter.

The baker extends the dough with a rolling pin, then spreads malleable butter over two-thirds of it. The next step is folding the assembly upon itself to make a sort of club sandwich with alternating layers of dough-butter-dough-butter-dough.

Sensory

A Porridge Bread delivers the textural contrast of a Crème Brûlée.

There's a thin, crisp, crackling exterior that's dark brown, almost reddish, caramel color by the end of the bake.

The interior has a pillow-like quality with an open and irregular structure and the crumb is moist, pearlescent, and shiny.

The tender grain adds a smooth, creamy texture to the crumb.

With more rollings and foldings, the number of alternating layers increases and their thickness decreases. This creates the stratified appearance of a baked Croissant or Puff Pastry dessert. Depending on how many folds and who's doing the arithmetic, the number of layers in the finished dough ranges from 80 to 100 for a yeasted dough like Croissant. In Classic Puff Pastry the range is 800 to 1,000 plus.

A porridge bread is developed with a similar technique. Though the bread doesn't retain the layered look of a Croissant or Danish pastry, the rolling and folding procedure is a useful mechanical analogy so you can visualize the process.

The Porridge

Cook the porridge separately. You can cook it once your main dough starts the Fermentation Phase or prepare it ahead and keep it refrigerated.

Soak the grains overnight to soften them and shorten the cooking time. Soaking activates enzymes which digest the starches and produce sugar molecules and flavor compounds. Soaked grains are easier to digest and have more flavor.

For more information, see *How to Cook Creamy Grains for Porridge Bread*, pages 234–238.

Mixing and Developing the Main Dough

The desired dough temperature for a porridge bread is 82° compared to a ddt° of 78° for Pain au Levain. Other than that, the Ingredient Mixing Sequence and Development Phases for the main dough are the same as the Pain au Levain's.

The Stretch & Fold Technique

During the Fermentation Phase, replace the standard *De-Gas & Fold* Technique with a **Stretch & Fold**. The techniques are similar, but in the latter, the baker wants to retain the CO_2 bubbles in the dough as it is gently stretched. This creates a more open and irregular crumb structure in the bread compared to the Pain au Levain's crumb.

For a *Stretch & Fold,* flour the dough and the bench. Flour the top of the dough once you invert it onto the bench. Stretch the right hand edge of the dough farther to the right, lift it, fold it back over the center of the dough, and then release it. Stretch, lift, and fold the left hand edge. Do the same with the top and bottom edges. Invert the dough and return it to its fermentation container with the seam facing down.

Each time the dough is stretched and folded back on itself in this way, the protein network develops its ability to stretch without breaking. This characteristic of gluten is called *extensibility.*

Chad Robertson & Tartine Bakery, San Francisco

Chad Robertson perfected the porridge bread technique during his journeys through Sweden, Germany, and Austria.

Chad is our craft bread renegade, artist, and technician. *Tartine* is the shop where he and his wife showcase their formidable talents. His with bread, hers with pastries.

They've collected several James Beard awards for their bakery, restaurants, and books. In a town known for its food fanaticism, their reputations are indomitable.

Your can read a lot more about his technique for porridge breads in **Tartine Book No. 3,** Chronicle Books, 2013.

The structure that results is not uniform. Some cells are large while others are small. By gradually manipulating the dough over a period of two hours or sometimes more, the baker encourages this organic structure.

One student suggested the *Stretch & Fold* technique is like doing a series of ab crunches. Slowly, and with a rest between each crunch. This strengthens and firms the ab muscles without making them tough. Working out in this way you get muscle tone, not definition. For a porridge bread, this method of gluten development is preferred.

By contrast, visualize the tight, even crumb of a Baguette, Honey Whole Wheat Loaf, or other bread from *HTBB*. Many doughs from *HTBB* use *Intensive Development* characterized by rhythmic rolling, folding, and turning either by hand or on a machine. This organizes the protein network so the doughs perform well as pan loaves, dinner rolls, and other shapes that require uniformity. With a porridge bread, less focus is given to uniformity. Building the protein network is not an intensive activity, it's more organic.

Use Your Oven as a Fermentation Tank

These porridge bread formulas are designed to be cold fermented overnight and baked the next day. If you're not otherwise using your oven on Day 1 when you're making the bread, turn it into a controlled environment to ferment the dough.

But don't preheat the oven. Above 120°, yeast activity slows. At 140° it stops altogether. With pre-heating, the oven walls and the wire racks become too hot before the air in the oven chamber reaches an 84° to 90° target range.

Humidity is a quicker way to increase the air temperature without overheating the oven walls. Place an oven thermometer in the center part of the oven. You can use an instant-read thermometer if the oven isn't turned on. On the lowest shelf in your oven, place an empty baking tray or shallow pan for water. Wider is better, encouraging more steam to fill the oven chamber. Boil some water on the stove top. Use a liquid measuring cup to carefully pour it into the empty pan and shut the door.

After 15 minutes, empty the tray and replenish with more boiling water. Depending on the size of your oven and its starting temperature, repeating this process two or three times creates a warm, humid environment for your dough. For a dough with a ddt° of 82°, use this method to warm your oven to 90°.

Once you place the dough in the oven to ferment, turn your attention away from the oven's temperature and focus on the dough's. Use your insta-read thermometer to monitor the dough's temperature so it hovers near its 82° target.

Adding the Porridge to the Main Dough

A Porridge Bread Gets Four *Stretch & Fold's*. The first two *Stretch & Fold's* occur during the Fermentation Phase and involve only the main dough. They build the extensibility of the gluten network and start capturing large, uneven air cells in the dough. The third and fourth *Stretch & Fold's* occur during the Shaping Phase.

Baker's Tip

It's easier to distribute the grains if you have smaller rounds of the main dough when time comes to add the porridge.

Before the 2nd Stretch & Fold, divide the dough into two pieces (or more, according to the formula's yield). On a lightly floured bench, use a Stretch & Fold to round each piece of dough individually.

Place the dough rounds on a lightly oiled surface such as a Silpat® or cutting board. Cover with a piece of lightly oiled plastic. Continue to ferment the dough as directed. For the formulas in this book, that's 30 minutes.

Meanwhile, divide the porridge mixture into two equal batches (or more, according to the formula's yield). When each dough round has a pre-measured amount of porridge set aside for it, your final breads are more consistent.

For the third Stretch & Fold, you spread the porridge mixture over the dough during the process. The fourth Stretch & Fold further distributes the porridge mixture through the main dough while you also form the dough into its final shape as a boule (round).

Third Stretch & Fold

When it's time for the 3rd Stretch & Fold, combine each dough piece with its pre-measured porridge using this process:

- Stretch one dough piece into a larger disc. Take the porridge assigned to it (including any solids such as raisins or goat cheese) and spread HALF of it over the dough. Use a plastic scraper to lift one side of the dough and fold the dough in half.
- Spread half the remaining (pre-measured) porridge mixture over the dough. Now fold the dough in half again.
- Finally, spread the rest of the (pre-measured) porridge mixture over the dough. Fold the dough in half one last time.
- Invert the dough and let it rest with the seam facing down for the remaining fermentation time, 30 minutes for the breads in this book.

- Repeat the process with the other dough piece(s) and their pre-measured porridge(s).

Fourth Stretch & Fold

The 4th Stretch & Fold also gives the final form to the dough. Invert it using a plastic scraper. Stretch the right side of the dough and fold it over the center. Repeat with the other three sides.

As a final step, invert the dough onto a floured bench and let it rest un-

Photo Gallery #20   Porridge Bread—
Adding the Porridge

covered with the seam facing down for 5 minutes. When you transfer the dough into the banneton, place the seam facing up.

Tips for Final Shaping

The high hydration and the added moisture from the porridge calls for the baker's close attention when shaping a porridge bread. Here are two tips for handling shaped breads before and after transferring them to their proofing baskets.

Tip #1

Lightly dust a portion of your workspace with flour such as rice, whole wheat, or bench flour. Transfer the final round onto the floured bench with the seam facing down for 5 minutes. Dust the top of the round with flour, too. This closes the seam.

Tip #2

Once the boule is covered and in its banneton, give it a 10- to 15-minute rest before moving it to the refrigerator. This is called *floor time*. The protein network relaxes and the dough settles into the proofing basket. When baked, the bread has a rounder shape.

Extend the *floor time* to an hour when your schedule allows. As it rises in the proofing basket, the dough's interior becomes less dense. It chills more evenly in the refrigerator and, when removed and tempered the next day, warms more quickly.

Linen Proofing Baskets

A porridge bread becomes more slack as it proofs. The surface becomes sticky, making it difficult to unmold, score, and load into the oven.

Linen-lined proofing baskets are preferred for higher hydration doughs like porridge breads. The linen is cut to size, its edges are folded for durability, and the cloth is stitched onto the banneton. Professionally lined baskets can be found online or in specialty cookware stores. (See photo on page 97.)

To make your own, line your banneton with a piece of linen. Thoroughly rub rice flour or a rice flour/whole wheat blend into the linen before placing it in the banneton. Pleat or fold the linen so that it fits as smoothly as possible.

Light-weight linen is preferred. Lacking that, any dye-free cloth that's tightly woven and has a smooth feel can be used. The cloth's flexibility is more important than what it's made of. Stiff linen forces the proofing dough into awkward shapes that are difficult to unmold for baking.

At home, I have a set of plain white table napkins I bought at a discount housewares store. Mine are a tightly-woven cotton and poly blend, not linen. They mold easily to the bannetons and I can shake them out and hang them to dry. Several times I've scrubbed dried dough and rice flour from them with a bottle brush, also from the housewares store. And they've never been washed, except before their first use. I store them on a wooden hanger with plastic clips on the inside of the pantry door.

Scoring

Turn the proofed breads onto the loading peel at least five minutes prior to loading. This gives the bread opportunity to relax, stretching its protein strands and enlarging the air cells.

When you score the porridge bread, it relaxes even further, looking almost as if it's deflating. Don't worry. In the hot, steam-filled oven the bread springs to life, demonstrating what's called *Oven Spring*. Air cells expand, moisture inside the dough turns to steam, air cells expand even more.

Scoring the bread is optional. Without it, the dough finds a weak spot in the crust and ruptures to release pressure during the Oven Spring stage. This gives a unique look to each loaf and is part of the style of porridge breads.

Baking Porridge Breads

Instead of using internal temperature to judge when a porridge bread is properly baked, focus on the crust color. The darker the better.

During the bake, the crust color changes from golden to tan and then to brown. The first time you bake one, a porridge bread may look done when its crust is evenly brown. It's not done, the interior is very moist. Keep baking.

The next color stage is a deep brown. A few charred spots is a good sign. Continue baking and you'll see a reddish glow to the crust. Aim for this deep brown color with rich red tones.

Baker's Tip

Score and Bake on a Sheet Tray
If the idea of transferring a proofed porridge bread onto a loading peel—and then into an oven—seems daunting, omit the oven peel altogether. Try this procedure:

At home, I unmold porridge breads directly onto a single sheet pan lined with a Silpat® (not parchment). Dust the silicone mat with bench or whole wheat flour first. This set-up makes it easier to rotate the bread when baking.

If the bottom crust is becoming too dark, sandwich two trays and create a layer of air between them to cushion the bottom crust from the oven heat. Experiment with your oven until you get the arrangement you prefer.

These color changes correspond to steps of the *Maillard Reaction*—the caramelization of sugar-amino acids as the crust browns. The Maillard Reaction is responsible for the roasted, sweet, and fruity aroma notes in the crust. As the bread cools, these volatile aroma compounds permeate the bread. They condense inside the air cells, bringing complexity to the bread's flavor profile.

Read more about *Aroma & Flavor Notes for Bread* at
www.MichaelKalanty.com

Photo Gallery #21   Bread Tasting Guide

Cooling & Ripening

Before slicing, cool the bread on a rack to firm the structure and ripen the flavor profile. The added liquid from the porridge gives the bread a moist interior and this concentrates toward the center of the bread while it's baking.

Just as you'd let a roasted turkey rest before carving, letting the moisture of the bread redistribute itself makes slicing easier and reduces ripping.

When warm, the loaf is better hand-torn, revealing steamy grains scattered through the landscape of the bread.

Schedule your work over 3 days

The schedule for a Porridge Bread is similar to the Pain au Levain's. The elapsed time might seem to be a lot but your hands-on time is under three hours. Here's the schedule:

Day	Activity	Elapsed Time	Hands-On Time
2 days ago	Soak Grain overnight;	20 m	10 m
	Prepare Levain		10 m
Yesterday	Cook & Cool Porridge;	2 h 40	30 to 40 m
	Mix, Develop, &		
	Ferment Main Dough;		30 m
	Add Porridge, Shape Loaves;		30 m
	Cold Proofing	18 to 24 h	——
Today	Temper Shaped Loaves;	3 hours	——
	Score & Bake Bread	35 to 45 m	35 to 45 m
TOTAL			**2 h 45 m**

Conclusion

This book includes two formulas for porridge breads based on the Pain au Levain. The *Oatmeal Raisin Bread* has a low sweetness and is good for breakfast. The *Grits and Goat Cheese Bread* suits the dinner table and also makes an assertive sandwich bread.

The procedure is the same for both breads so you quickly learn a straight-forward approach to this style of baking. With confidence, you will soon be folding new ingredients into your own porridge breads.

Though I've reduced the hydration of the main dough from *Tartine's* much higher percent, I'm indebted to Chad Robertson's technique. The result is a less open crumb than Tartine's signature breads, but the lower hydration makes this technique easier to master.

Once your hands are confident, you can increase the hydration of the main dough. At first, use a 5% increase in water based on the total flour in

Grits and Goat Cheese Bread

DESCRIPTION

The Grits are sweet, the Goat Cheese is tangy. Together they give this wild yeast bread a complex flavor profile and tender, moist interior.

UNDERSTANDING

When the grits are cooked and cooled, season them with salt as needed. During formula development, it was normal to add 1/8 to 1/4 teaspoon additional salt to the cooked grits to bring our their natural sweetness and to reduce any bitterness that can accompany whole ground grains.

PRODUCTION

Don't add the cheese to the grits while they're still warm. The cheese blends well but when cooled, it's difficult to spread the porridge over the main dough.

If you want a different cheese, select one that melts and blends evenly with other ingredients. Something from the Cheddar or Swiss families is preferred.

Stringy cheeses like Mozzarella don't blend well with the gluten structure of the bread. Fresh cheeses, like Ricotta or Farmer's Cheese, bring more water to the dough and make handling a challenge. Grating cheeses, like Parmigiano and Asiago, overpower the delicate acidity of the main dough. Better results are achieved with White Cheddar, Colby, and Monterey Jack.

The Grits and Goat Cheese bread takes longer to proof than the Oatmeal Raisin. When cheese is added to bread dough, lactic acid in the cheese tightens the protein network of the main dough. During formulation, we recorded a 3- to 3-1/2-hour tempering time once the proofed breads were removed from the refrigerator after their night of cold proofing.

SPECIFICATION

Select yellow grits that deliver a sweet natural corn flavor with that stoney note you find in mineral water. Coarse grits provide a stronger visual when this bread is sliced, but any grind can be used. Quick-cooking grits may be used but don't use Instant Grits—these deliver little flavor of the true product and bring a pasty texture to the bread.

The coarseness of the grind affects the total amount of water the grits need and their corresponding time on the stove. When in doubt about cooking ratios and times, follow the directions on the purveyor's packaging.

Plan to soak the grits overnight. For the bread formula yielding 2,000 grams, measure 125 grams of raw grits and transfer it to a stainless bowl. Cover it with about 2 inches of cool water. Swish the grain with your hand once or twice, then let it settle. After 5 minutes, skim and discard the small particles that float to the top. Cover the assembly and set in a cool place, away from foot traffic.

The next day, strain the grits. Reserve the water and measure 250 grams of it for

ANSON MILLS®

With a vision more in common with seed cultivators and farmers from the 19th century, Glenn Roberts founded Anson Mills in Columbia, South Carolina in 1998. He shares the farmer's code of breeding for flavor—not for transport, not for visual appeal, not for shelf life. Glenn seeks to maximize the benefit of terroir in his grains. In this tradition, *Anson Mills* continues to reintroduce diverse and flavorful foods of the Old South.

Some elements of modern technology have been incorporated into his processing, particularly in the area of flavor cryogenics. His grains are cold-milled, packed in carbon dioxide-filled vacuum bags, and then stored at minus 10°F. He explains that "Plant flavor cryogenics keeps enzymes and volatile oils from changing once the grains have been ground."

He started small. A handful of ingredient-conscious chefs across the country used his products and promoted them to their customers and colleagues. Today, his crop productions are larger but still small by industry standards. His circle of influence has widened and American chefs do friendly battle to be part of the distribution system at *Anson Mills*.

"Grits with the Flavor of the Old South"

These are not your everyday grits. Procurement, storage, and cooking instructions recall historical foodways of the South when time and attention were common ingredients for the plantation dinner table. When my breads have a high-profile engagement, such as the *American Culinary Federation's* Annual Conference Dinner, *Anson Mills* is my go-to resource.

Grits and Goat Cheese Bread

cooking the grain. Pour the grits and 250 g soaking water into a small pot. On medium heat, stir the mixture occasionally until the grain absorbs the soaking water.

Add an additional 30 grams water and reduce the heat so the mixture barely simmers. Place a lid slightly ajar and allow the grain time to absorb the water.

If you soak the grits overnight, the total cooking process takes 10 to 12 minutes. Unsoaked, the grits need almost twice as much time.

Formula, Levain

Note: The weights in these two columns are intentionally the same.

Ingredient	BP%	4-1/2 or 6 Qt Ounces	Grams	8 Qt	20 Qt
Water	50%	1 oz	30 g	30 g	100 g
Starter Culture, ripe	150%	3 oz	90 g	90 g	300 g
Bread Flour	100%	2 oz	60 g	60 g	200 g
Yields (see note)		6 oz	180 g	180 g	600 g
enough to make main dough @		2# 8 oz or 1,250 g main dough		1,900 g main dough	6,800 g main dough

Note: The formulas yield slightly more Levain than is needed. Unused Levain can be composted or discarded.

Procedure, Levain

		8-hour shift ddt°= 70°F	5-hour shift ddt°= 78°F
1	Mise en Place	H2O @ **70°**; Starter Culture @ 70°	H2O @ **84°**; Starter Culture @ 70°
2	Ingredient Mixing	Combine Water & Starter Culture; add Flour	same
3	Development	Stir until blended	none
4A	Fermentation *On the Floor*	5h 00 @ 70° (70% hum)	2h 00 @ 76° (70% hum)
4B	Fermentation *RFG*	+ stir for 10 seconds + 16 to 24h 00 in RFG	+ stir for 10 seconds + 20 to 28h 00 in RFG

Grits and Goat Cheese Bread

Formula, Grits Porridge

| Ingredient | BP% | 4-1/2 or 6 Qt | | 8 Qt | 20 Qt |
		Ounces	Grams		
Water	200%	9 oz	250 g	350 g	1,150 g
Whole Ground Grits	100%	4-1/2 oz	125 g	175 g	575 g
Salt	1.2%	scant 1/2 tsp	1.5 g	2 g	6.5 g
Additional Water (for cooking)	25%	1 oz or more, as needed	30 g or more, as needed	45 g or more, as needed	150 g or more, as needed
Yields (see note)		12 oz	350 g	500 g	1,700 g
enough for		2 boules @ 625 g		1,900 g main dough	6,800 g main dough

Note: The formulas yield slightly more Porridge than is needed.

Procedure, Grits Porridge

		8-hour shift ddt°= 60°F	5-hour shift ddt°= 60°F
1	Mise en Place	H2O @ 60°;	same
2	Ingredient Mixing	Combine Water & Grits	same
3	Fermentation/ Soaking	16 to 24h 00 @ 60° (covered)	same
4A	Cooking	See *Specification* See *How to Cook Creamy Grains*, pages 234–238	same
4B	Cooling	Can be prepared ahead and refrigerated. Temper before adding to dough.	same

Grits and Goat Cheese Bread

Formula, Main Dough

Ingredient	BP%	4-1/2 or 6 Qt		8 Qt	20 Qt
		Ounces	Grams		
Levain (from above)	21%	3 oz	90 g	130 g	500 g
Water	70%	10-1/2 oz	300 g	450 g	1,650 g
Dark Rye Flour or Pumpernickel Meal	13%	2 oz	50 g	75 g	275 g
Bread Flour	87%	13 oz	380 g	570 g	2,100 g
Salt	3.2%	1/2 oz	14 g	21 g	70 g
Olive oil or cold press Corn oil	2.3%	1/3 oz	10 g	15 g	50 g
Goat Cheese	46%	7 oz	200 g	300 g	1,000 g
Grits Porridge (scaled from above)	70%	10 oz	300 g	450 g	1,600 g
Salt (for Grits)	n/a	pinch	pinch	1/8 tsp	1/3 tsp
for Grits plus Cheese mix		1/8 tsp or more, to taste	1/8 tsp or more, to taste	1/8 tsp or more, to taste	1/8 tsp or more, to taste
Yields		**2# 8 oz**	**1,250 g**	**1,900 g**	**6,800 g**
Number of pieces		2 boules @ 625 g		3 boules	10 boules

Grits and Goat Cheese Bread

Procedure, Main Dough

1	Mise en Place	H$_2$O @ 94°; Levain @ 70°	**ddt° = 82°**
2	Ingredient Mixing	Autolyse	
3	Development	Speed #2, 2m + Rest 5m + Speed #1, 2m	*Improved*
4A	Floor Fermentation **(2h 00)**	**45m @ 82°** (70% hum)	Coat fermentation container with panspray or oil.
		+ Stretch & Fold (#1) **+ 45m @ 82°** (70% hum)	
		+ Divide dough into 2 pieces + Stretch & Fold (#2) **+ 30 m @ 82°** (70% hum)	Stretch & Fold each dough piece separately Transfer dough rounds onto inverted baking tray lined with an oiled Silpat® or an oiled cutting board. Let rest for 30 min. *See Photo Gallery #20 (Image 1)* Porridge @ 70°
	Adding Porridge Stretch & Fold (#3)	Turn dough onto floured bench. Stretch into larger round. Spread porridge mixture over top. Spread cheese over porridge. Encase porridge between the folds of the dough. Invert rounded dough.	*See Photo Gallery #20 (Images 2 through 10)*
	Floor Fermentation (continued) **(30 m)**	**+ 30m @ 82°** (70% hum)	Covered
4B	Cool Fermentation	Not required. Proceed directly to **Shaping**.	

Grits and Goat Cheese Bread

5	Shaping	Stretch & Fold each dough piece to form the final round. *See Photo Gallery #20 (Images 13 through 16)*	Place final rounds seam facing down on floured bench for 5 minutes to close the seams.
	Stretch & Fold (#4)		
	Into the Banneton	Invert boule round into banneton, seam facing up. Cover. *See Photo Gallery #20 (Images 15 & 16)*	Meanwhile, dust the top face of the boules. Use rice/wheat/ flour or a blend
6	*Cold* Proofing	18 to 24h 00 @ **40° to 50°** (70% hum)	
7	Décor & Baking	Temper; Score; See **Baking Chart**	2h 00 to 2h 30 m *on the floor*, covered.

Baking Chart

Oven	Stage I	¿Steam?	Vent @	Stage II	Duration	Int. temp°
Deck	500° (10.10.1) [3.3.1]	15 secs	8 m	425° (10.10.0) [2.2.0]	+ 8 m •••••••••• check*/rotate + 8 m more ••••••••• check* + 6 to 8 m more	200°F plus dark crust + firm sides

*Check: Watch bottom crust. You may need to slide an inverted sheet tray between the breads and the surface of the hearth.

**"You don't really *cook* grains.
You let them soften and swell by slowly *absorbing water*."**

Cooking grains is an exercise in ratios. For example, a rule of thumb for long grain white rice is 2 parts water to 1 part rice.

From there, you can use more or less water depending on how firm you prefer your rice. The 2 cups of water can vary from 1-1/2 cups for firmer rice up to 2-1/2 cups for softer. Whether serving rice as a starchy side or adding to stuffing or soups, the firmness of the grain is an important choice for the cook.

But what if you want the grains to be ***creamy***? That smooth, silky feel that supports and carries the grains on your palate, making them seem like a liquid food as well as a solid one. Visualize a creamy, steamy bowl of oatmeal on a cold morning.

Unnecessary cooking water is sometimes added to grains to give them this smooth, homogeneous texture. But the extra water doesn't make the grains creamy so much as it makes them soupy, saucy, or just plain loose. A Grain Porridge cooked to this texture weighs down the main dough, yielding a dense bread that spreads out as it bakes instead of springing upward.

Creamy grains are better for porridge breads. Neither firm nor soft, but tender to the bite. Changing the ratio of water to grain is not how to achieve this texture. It's all about technique.

When in doubt, always refer to the package directions for the amount of water to grain. Note that most sources don't give ratios in weight, they use cup measurement for both grains and water.

Be Gentle

To cook creamy grains without adding unnecessary water, look to the method for cooking arborio rice, the Italian short-grain white rice that, under a watchful hand, transforms into the creamy rice dish Risotto. The technique consists of slow cooking, adding warm liquid in increments, and alternating between times of stirring balanced with slow, undisturbed simmering.

In general, you bring two-thirds of the total water called for to a boil in a medium-sized pot. When the water boils, add the grain and turn the heat to moderate. Separately, bring the remaining water called for in the formula to a simmer. When it's added to the pot later, warm water swells cooking grains more evenly than cold water.

On medium heat, continue cooking the grains until they absorb their first measure of water. Use a wooden or heat-proof plastic spoon and stir occasionally.

Draw the spoon through the grain and if this leaves a trail, the mixture's thick enough for more water. Add about one third of the reserved simmering water and continue cooking. Stir occasionally until this liquid is absorbed and the mixture again leaves a trail when a spoon is dragged through it.

Add the rest of the water in two additions, each time letting the mixture become thick enough so the spoon leaves a trail in its wake.

Baker's Tip
Use low heat to cook grains.

A boiling pot causes water to evaporate instead of letting grains absorb it. High bottom heat can scorch the grains and they won't absorb water evenly.

More About Grains

Ancient grains are especially suited for a porridge bread. Their flavor, texture, and nutritional value complement the home-style comfort these breads deliver. For more information and ideas for other grains you can use in porridge breads, get a copy of **Simply Ancient Grains** (Ten Speed Press, 2015) or **Ancient Grains for Modern Meals** (Ten Speed Press, 2011), both by Maria Speck. Her books are filled with reliable instructions and well-crafted recipes, some of the reasons why she won the Julia Child Cookbook Award.

Cook with the *Lid On* or *Lid Off?*

For porridge breads, cook grains with the lid off.

Under a tight-fitting lid, steam condenses and returns to the grains. This gives them a soft exterior. The grains stick together and pack densely when scooped onto a serving spoon or ladle. If you plan to purée or even smash them against the side of the pot to thicken a soup, lid-on cooking is the better choice for your grains.

Cooked with the lid off, grains tend to stay separate from one another. In a salad, stuffing, or other preparation where individuality of the ingredients is desired, this characteristic is preferred. You can still purée or smash them in a soup, but they deliver a less smooth feeling to your palate that's better-suited for rustic preparations.

In a porridge bread, grains cooked lid-off are easier to spread on the main dough. Inside the dough, the grains resist clumping. They adhere to the gluten network and rise with the dough instead of weighing it down.

Cooling the Porridge

While the grains are simmering, line a half sheet tray with a Silpat. Lacking those tools, take a large dinner plate and coat it with a light-flavored oil such as Vegetable or Safflower. When the grains are done, cool them slightly and then pour them from the pot directly onto the prepared surface and level them with your cooking spoon.

SAFE FOOD HANDLING

Don't wrap hot food. Grains and starches like rice, potatoes, and even pasta are more susceptible to micro-organism growth when held in the *temperature danger zone (approx. 40° to 140°)* for more than two hours.

Cool the grains to ambient temperature. Then cover them with a piece of plastic wrap, piercing the plastic with the tip of a paring knife in a few places.

You can keep the porridge at ambient temperature for up to two hours. Refrigerate it after that. If you prepare the porridge a day in advance, keep it refrigerated. Temper it to 80° before you add it to the main dough.

Benefits of Pre-Soaking

Soaked grains taste sweeter and are easier to digest. They cook more quickly, too. In about half the time.

Overnight soaking activates enzymes which break down starch in the grains and release sugar molecules.

When the cooked grains are cooled and spread over the dough, the yeast in the main dough feeds on these sugars. The porridge ferments and the intensity of the grain flavor increases.

This is the essence of a porridge bread. The baker isn't just folding in a savory garnish such as walnuts, olives, or roasted garlic. The baker is complementing the flavor profile of the main dough with fermentation notes from the grits, oats, or other grain used to make the porridge.

The Best Pot for Cooking Grains

Designate one of your pots in which to cook grains and use it consistently for this job. You'll quickly learn which grains need more or less water, which ones cook faster or slower. The intuitive information you collect is invaluable in developing your kitchen instincts.

Pot diameter is important. The wider the pot, the more water evaporates instead of being absorbed by the grain. Wider, shallow pots can scorch the grains on the bottom, too.

My designated grain pot is 8 inches in diameter and 3-1/2 inches deep. It happens to be stainless steel but that's coincidental. It's 1/4- to 1/3-inch thick, so its heat is gentle and even.

Seasoning Cooked Grains

A principle of cooking is that whenever two (or more) separate preparations will be combined later, season each one separately so their taste profiles are in balance. In this case, balance the salt intensity of the cooled porridge with that of the main dough.

Try this sensory technique when salting the porridge:

Take a pinch from the main dough and taste it, spreading it around your palate. Properly salted dough *tastes* slightly salty. Focus on the tip of your tongue and take a mental note of how much tingling or saltiness you feel there.

Take a drink of water. Now taste some of the cooled porridge, spreading it around your palate in a similar fashion. Do you feel that same level of saltiness on the tip of your tongue that you found in the main dough?

If not, add more salt to the porridge. Toss it through the grain and give it time to dissolve. Toss it once more, then taste it.

Ask yourself if the added salt helps you perceive the flavor of the grain more quickly. And is that perception moving forward on your tongue, toward the tip. Repeat this technique as needed. So long as the grains don't taste salty, you can continue to add a pinch at a time, stir, and re-taste.

This calibration technique helps you bring the taste profiles of the two separate preparations into balance. When combined, each retains its identity and enhances the other.

The Sensory Science behind *Creamy* Oatmeal and Grits

When referring to the ingredients of a food, the word *creamy* tells you the dish includes a milk fat or dairy component, such as heavy cream or melted cheese. But as a sensory word, *creamy* describes a sensation on the palate. It refers to the texture of the cooked grains, it doesn't mean that a dairy product is present. Here's the distinction:

Visualize two pots of rice. In the first, cook the rice stove–top over a **high heat.** Most likely, the grains at the bottom of the pot will be hard on the outside. In the middle of the pot, the grains will be mushy or a little gummy. The top layer of grains will have an al dente texture—tender on the outside and soft inside.

Stirred together and scooped onto your dinner plate, this rice delivers a variety of textures on your tongue. As you bite and chew, you're aware of the individual grains and the different textures they have. Words will come to mind to describe this rice, but *creamy* won't be one of them.

Let's cook a second pot of rice. Slowly, over **low heat.** In fact, let's turn off the heat for five minutes halfway through cooking yet keep the timer running. The rice continues to swell and soften even if the heat is momentarily turned off.

Imagine eating a spoonful of this rice. The grains are uniformly swollen. They're tender to bite and not gummy when chewed.

As a sensory experience, this rice feels smooth and homogeneous. The grains have similar textures and fewer of them are recognized as separate grains on your palate. In the Language of Sensory Science, we use the word *creamy* to describe the sensation of a soft, homogeneous texture like this on the palate.

A non-dairy fruit smoothie that includes fresh whole strawberries will not have a creamy texture. As you spread the smoothie over your tongue, the seeds interfere with its smoothness. Substitute slices of peeled, ripe peach for the strawberries in the same smoothie, and the texture changes.

Though there's no dairy component present, the peach version is described as *creamy.* Next time you hear something described as *smooth and creamy*, use your sensory skills to visualize this texture.

Oatmeal Raisin Porridge Bread

This long-keeping bread is a breakfast table favorite. If you're hurrying out the door to work, grab a thick slice to pair with your thermos of coffee. For a savory version that yields an enviable sandwich bread, omit the raisins.

UNDERSTANDING

Salt the cooked porridge to taste before adding the honey and dark raisins. Once you add these to the oats, taste the porridge mixture again.

Do you notice that the salt intensity of the porridge is diminished when honey is added? Sweeteners make the grains themselves taste dull. A pinch of salt revives their flavor intensity.

The Oat/Raisin mixture can sit, covered, up to two hours at ambient temperature before you add it to the main dough or you can make the mixture much earlier. It can be refrigerated up to 72 hours, covered. In this case, temper the porridge to 80 degrees before adding it to your dough.

PRODUCTION

Shaped and in its proofing basket, this bread is easier to handle when it cold proofs overnight. Chilling firms its structure and the bread is easier to unmold, score, and bake the next day.

SPECIFICATION

Rolls made from a porridge bread stand up to messy proteins like pot roasts and slow-cooked meats. To make sandwich rolls, mix the dough as directed. Prepare the porridge but omit the raisins and honey.

Ferment the main dough for two hours as directed, but don't divide it into smaller pieces. When it's time to add the porridge, do this all at once, stretching the dough as much as possible. Layer the porridge as usual, fold the dough, and ferment it for 30 minutes, as the schedule indicates. Without shaping it, cold ferment the dough overnight.

Scale the fermented dough at 120 g (4 ounces) the next day, while it's still cold. Round the dough pieces and place them 3 x 3 on a parchment-lined half sheet tray or baking sheet.

Proof the rolls 1h 30 to 2h 00. For a simple finish, dust them with whole wheat flour before baking. For a heartier look, brush the proofed rolls with egg wash and press rolled oats (not steel cut) onto their tops.

Follow the baking schedule as listed, but keep the oven temp at 450 degrees throughout. The bake time for rolls is a little more than half the time specified for the loaves. They're done when they are dark brown. Cool thoroughly on a rack before slicing or storing.

Oatmeal Raisin Porridge Bread

Formula, Levain

Note: The weights in these two columns are intentionally the same.

| Ingredient | BP% | 4-1/2 or 6 Qt | | 8 Qt | 20 Qt |
		Ounces	Grams		
Water	50%	1 oz	30 g	30 g	100 g
Starter Culture, ripe	150%	3 oz	90 g	90 g	300 g
Bread Flour	100%	2 oz	60 g	60 g	200 g
Yields (see note)		6 oz	180 g	180 g	600 g
enough to make main dough @		2# 8 oz or 1,100 g main dough		1,725 g main dough	6,400 g main dough

Note: The formulas yield slightly more Levain than is needed. Unused Levain can be composted or discarded.

Procedure, Levain

		8-hour shift ddt°= 70°F	5-hour shift ddt°= 78°F
1	Mise en Place	H2O @ **70°**; Starter Culture @ 70°	H2O @ **84°**; Starter Culture @ 70°
2	Ingredient Mixing	Combine Water & Starter Culture; add Flour	same
3	Development	Stir until blended	same
4A	Fermentation *On the Floor*	5h 00 @ 70° (70% hum)	2h 00 @ 76° (70% hum)
4B	Fermentation *RFG*	+ stir for 10 seconds + 16 to 24h 00 in RFG	+ stir for 10 seconds + 20 to 28h 00 in RFG

Oatmeal Raisin Porridge Bread

Formula, Oatmeal Porridge

Ingredient	BP%	4-1/2 or 6 Qt		8 Qt	20 Qt
		Ounces	Grams		
Water	200%	6 oz	200 g	300 g	1,000 g
Starter Culture, ripe	5%	5 g*	5 g	8 g	25 g
Steel Cut Oats	100%	3 oz	100 g	150 g	500 g
Salt	1.5%	1/3 tsp	1.5 g	2 g	7 g
Additional Water (for cooking)	120%	3-2/3 oz or more, as needed	120 g or more, as needed	180 g or more, as needed	600 g or more, as needed
Yields (see note)		10 oz	300 g	450 g	1,500 g
enough for		2 boules @ 550 g		1,725 g main dough	6,400 g main dough

* estimate 1/2 Tablespoon
Note: The formulas yield slightly more Porridge than is needed.

Procedure, Oatmeal Porridge

		8-hour shift ddt°= 60°F	5-hour shift ddt°= 60°F
1	Mise en Place	H2O @ **60°**; Starter Culture @ 60°	same
2	Ingredient Mixing	Combine Water & Starter; add Oats	same
3	Fermentation/ Soaking	**16 to 24h 00 @ 60°** (covered)	same
4A	Cooking	See *How To Cook Creamy Grains,* page 234–238	same
4B	Cooling	Can be prepared ahead and refrigerated. Temper before adding to dough.	same

Oatmeal Raisin Porridge Bread

Formula, Main Dough

Ingredient	BP%	4-1/2 or 6 Qt Ounces	4-1/2 or 6 Qt Grams	8 Qt	20 Qt
Levain (from above)	21%	3 oz	90 g	130 g	500 g
Water	70%	10-1/2 oz	300 g	450 g	1,650 g
Pumpernickel Meal or Whole Wheat Flour	13%	2 oz	50 g	75 g	275 g
Bread Flour	87%	13 oz	380 g	570 g	2,100 g
Salt	3%	1/2 oz (scant)	13 g	20 g	70 g
Honey (for Main Dough)	5%	3/4 oz	22 g	33 g	120 g
Raisins, dark	23%	3-1/2 oz	100 g	150 g	500 g
Oatmeal Porridge (from above)	58%	9 oz	250 g	375 g	1,400 g
Salt	n/a	a pinch	a pinch	1/8 tsp	1/3 tsp
Honey (for Porridge)	6%	7/8 oz	25 g	35 g	130 g
Yields		**2# 8 oz**	**1,100 g**	**1,725 g**	**6,400 g**
Number of pieces		2 boules @ 550 g		3 boules	10 boules

Oatmeal Raisin Porridge Bread

Procedure, Main Dough

1	Mise en Place	H₂O @ 94°; Levain @ 70°	**ddt° = 82°**
2	Ingredient Mixing	Autolyse	Combined cooled Oat Porridge with Raisins and Honey; Season with salt; Cover and set aside.
3	Development	Speed #2, 2m + Rest 5m + Speed #1, 2m	*Improved*
4A	Floor Fermentation (2h 00)	**45m @ 82°** (70% hum)	Coat fermentation container with panspray or oil.
		+ Stretch & Fold (#1) **+ 45m @ 82°** (70% hum)	
		+ Divide dough into 2 pieces + Stretch & Fold (#2) **+ 30 m @ 82°** (70% hum)	Stretch & Fold each dough piece separately Transfer dough rounds onto inverted baking tray lined with an oiled Silpat® or an oiled cutting board. Let rest for 30 min. *See Photo Gallery #20 (Image 1)* Porridge @ 70°
	Adding Porridge Stretch & Fold (#3)	Turn dough onto floured bench. Stretch into larger round. Spread porridge mixture over top. Encase porridge between the folds of the dough. Invert rounded dough.	*See Photo Gallery #20 (Images 2 through 10)*
	Floor Fermentation (continued) (30 m)	**+ 30m @ 82°** (70% hum)	Covered
4B	Cool Fermentation	Not required. Proceed directly to **Shaping**.	

Oatmeal Raisin Porridge Bread

5	**Shaping**	Stretch & Fold each dough piece to form the final round. *See Photo Gallery #20 (Images 13 through 16)*	Place final rounds seam facing down on floured bench for 5 minutes to close the seams.
	Stretch & Fold (#4)		
	Into the Banneton	Invert boule round into banneton, seam facing up. Cover. *See Photo Gallery #20 (Images 15 & 16)*	Meanwhile, dust the top face of the boules. Use rice/wheat/ flour or a blend
6	*Cold* **Proofing**	18 to 24h 00 @ **40° to 50°** (70% hum)	
7	**Décor & Baking**	Temper; Score; See **Baking Chart**	2h 00 to 2h 30 m *on the floor*, covered.

Note: The Oat/Raisin mixture can sit, covered, up to two hours at ambient temperature, waiting to be incorporated into the main dough. The mixture can also be refrigerated up to 72 hours, covered. Temper to 80 degrees before adding to your dough.

Baking Chart

Oven	Stage I	¿Steam?	Vent @	Stage II	Duration	Int. temp°
Deck	500° (10.10.1) [3.3.1]	15 secs	8 m	425° (10.10.0) [2.2.0]	+ 8 m • • • • • • • • • • check*/rotate + 8 m more • • • • • • • • • • check* + 4 m more	200°F plus dark crust + firm sides

*Check: Watch bottom crust. You may need to slide an inverted sheet tray between the breads and the surface of the hearth.

Appendices

Appendix 1

References from
How To Bake Bread:
The Five Families of Bread®

by Michael Kalanty

Red Seal Books, 2011

In the spirit of developing your skills, this book builds on concepts and techniques established in the first book in this series, **How To Bake Bread.** When something from **HTBB** is introduced, it is summarized within the text itself or in a nearby pull-out or sidebar.

More detail about the strategy, procedure, or concept in question can be found in this appendix. Each entry includes a notation, such as **HTBB, p 57–62,** indicating where the material was initially discussed in **How To Bake Bread: The Five Families of Bread.**

Page 569   Baker's Percent—BP%

Bakers have a unique understanding of the concept of percentages. We rarely consider the ratio between a single ingredient, like Sugar, and the weight of an entire batch of dough.

Nutritionists need to calculate these individual ratios for ingredient panels on packaged foods. Product developers need to think this way too because each ingredient changes production cost.

Bakers consider only the weight of the sugar compared to the weight of flour in the formula. Say a formula calls for one hundred pounds of flour. If it's a formula for a soft dough like Burger Buns, it has on average five pounds of sugar. Dividing 5 by 100, the Baker's Percent of Sugar in the formula is 5%. Sugar, divided by Flour.

Increasing the weight of sugar to 12 pounds and keeping everything else the same, we'd have a Sweet Bun dough, suitable for making Cinnamon Buns, for example. Since we still have 100 pounds of flour, the Bakers Percent of Sugar in this dough is 12%.

This is the essence—and the beauty—of Baker's Percent. Before we even scale an ingredient, knowing its BP% gives us insight into how a dough formula will look and feel, and how it will behave in the oven.

Sugar is a tenderizing agent in bread dough. By comparing the percent of Sugar in the two bread formulas, a baker can expect to get a softer, stickier dough from the one with 12% sugar. Accordingly, buns made from it will brown more quickly, so the oven temperature would be lower. (*HTBB*, p 57–62)

Page 581   *Sponge plus Main Dough* **Ingredient Mixing Sequence**

This refers to a two-stage mixing process for combining ingredients. Its primary benefit is improved aroma and flavor.

In the first stage, some of the flour in the formula is mixed with water. Adding a small percent of commercial yeast initiates fermentation. At the conclusion of this (preliminary) fermentation, the mixture is called a *pre-ferment*. The pre-ferment is the starting point when incorporating the rest of the ingredients in the formula. This includes the rest of the water, yeast, and flour. And now the salt.

The Focaccia in *HTBB* introduces this technique, using 40% of the formula's flour with a comparatively short fermentation of 45 minutes. This quick style of pre-ferment is called a *Sponge*. The main dough for Focaccia is then assembled, incorporating the remaining ingredients. The entire process is called the *Sponge plus Main Dough Sequence*.

For each of the breads in this book, the pre-ferment is a Levain made from your Wild Yeast Culture. The two-stage mixing sequence for a Wild Yeast dough is similar to the Focacia's. (*HTBB*, p 260–1)

Page 593   **Controlling Dough Temperature**

The flavor profile of each bread is determined by its Fermentation Schedule. This specifies how long the dough is fermented and at what temperature it is maintained.

The Pain au Levain's fermentation schedule is 2 hours @ 78° plus 18 to 24 hours @ 50°.

A baker uses the fermentation schedule as a guide, conditions are rarely perfect. A small variation in temperature—2 to 3 degrees higher or lower—is addressed by adjusting the corresponding fermentation time. In this case, 10 to 15 minutes shorter or longer.

Greater variations from the schedule affect the bread's flavor profile. When the dough is too cool or not given enough time, the bread develops less flavor. Too warm or too much time, the bread's flavor becomes tainted with over-fermented notes, like milk or beer left open on the kitchen counter. Controlling the dough temperature is the baker's best way to achieve consistent flavor in breads.

The dough's temperature is analogous to a car's speed on the highway. For example, let's head down the interstate at 78 mph. (This is the desired dough temperature of the Pain au Levain. It makes a reasonable reference here, though a poor example for safe driving.) Using basic calculations, in one hour we'll be at Point X. The mall, for example, in plenty of time to make the movie.

If I lose my attention in our conversation and start driving quickly (analogous to the dough's temperature being 5 or 10 degrees higher), in one hour we'll have passed our exit. If we're moving slowly because there's more traffic than anticipated (colder dough, continuing the bread analogy), the one hour travel time will put us short of the mall and we'll likely miss the film. (*HTBB*, p 106–111)

Page 603 Balancing *plasticity* and *elasticity* in dough

Bakers use the terms *plastic* and *elastic* gluten. Dough that is easy to stretch and form into loaves is said to be *plastic*. On the other hand, a dough that retracts after being stretched or shaped is said to be *elastic*. Together, a dough displaying a balance of *plastic* and *elastic* properties is said to have **high quality gluten**. (*HTBB*, p 93–5)

Page 605 The *Fishtail Technique*

Named for the back and forth motion of a fish's tail, this technique is used to develop a slack dough directly on the baker's bench. With a metal scraper drawn through the dough in a gentle zig-zag gesture, the protein network develops without ripping. With a plastic scraper in your other hand, it's easy to manage the dough and keep it from sticking to your hands. (*HTBB*, p 266–7)

Page 617 *Poker Chip Gesture*

You're sitting at a table of *Texas Hold'em*, showing the highest hand. You stretch your arms over the pile of chips, clasp your hands, and draw the winnings toward you. Moving slowly, you keep your hands and forearms in contact with the felt table. If you don't, some of those chips get left behind. That's the visualization for this dough-rounding technique. (*HTBB*, **p 135**)

Page 623 *Rare-Medium-Well* **test**

How does a hotline chef judge the doneness of a steak without slicing it? He joins his index finger to his thumb and then presses on the pad of flesh just below the thumb. That's what a *Rare* steak feels like. He presses on the steak as it's grilling to see how much longer he's got to cook it.

Joining his middle finger and thumb, he can simulate what a *Medium* steak feels like. The ring finger to thumb connection produces more tightness in the pad under his thumb—this is *Well Done*. (*HTBB*, **p 354–56**)

Page 640 **Ripening Bread and its Effects**

When you make one of the tomato gravies that South Philadelphia is famous for, you have to chill it and store it in the refrigerator overnight so that, in the vernacular, the *flavors can marry*. And though you should not store a wild yeast bread in the refrigerator, the idea of an extended rest period after baking brings out the bread's flavor profile in a similar way.

It's taken a long time to build the flavor profile of your Culture. When you elaborate on that flavor by building a Levain, and then building a main dough, you're using time to create complexity in the bread's flavor profile. Once it's baked, cool your bread fully and then give it additional time so its flavor can emerge.

Unwrapped and at ambient temperature, two or three hours ripening time is sufficient. Wrapped in parchment paper and then plastic wrap, 16 to 20 hours ripening brings fuller, rounder flavor.

The crust will soften during this phase as it absorbs humidity from the environment. Re-crisping the bread in a preheated 375°F oven takes 5 to 8 minutes. (*HTBB*, **p 170–3**)

Page 668   **Maillard Reaction**

Named for a French chemist, this refers to the caramelization of proteins and sugars which in turn bring color, aroma, and flavor notes to food like a grilled steak or crusty bread. In baking, the surface of the dough exposes sugars, broken proteins and amino acids, and the flavor acids that the baker develops through fermentation. Depending on the random combinations these molecules form, the caramelization process creates a variety of color, aroma, and flavor notes. (*HTBB*, p 165)

For more about the sensory aspects of bread and a chart of crust browning notes, see "Aroma & Flavor Notes for Bread" at www.MichaelKalanty.com.   Photo Gallery #21

Pages 682
& 689   **Inverting Dough between Initial and Final Developments**

This procedure applies when you're using a vertical mixer, such as a 6- or 8-quart tabletop model or a 12- or 20-quart stand mixer. For dough developed by hand on the bench, this instruction does not apply.

Vertical mixers like these need the baker's assistance to evenly distribute ingredients and to develop a uniform gluten network in a dough. Developed entirely by machine, the bottom and the top portions of the dough become more elastic because they are agitated more vigorously by the dough hook. The middle portion of the dough receives less manipulation and is less elastic by comparison.

When the Initial Development is completed, turn the machine off. Activate any safety devices (such as moving the safety screen aside on the 20-quart stand mixer) and lower the mixing bowl using the mechanical arm. Remove the bowl from the machine, turn the dough onto a floured bench, and flour the top of the dough.

Fold the dough by gathering the side farthest from you, stretching it upward and then toward yourself. Release it so the part you're holding falls over the center of the mound of dough. Repeat with the other three sides of the dough.

Invert the dough and return it to its bowl. Return the bowl to the machine and continue to develop it according to the schedule you're following. In most cases, this resumes with a 5-minute rest followed by the Final Development stage. (*HTBB*, p 198–9)

Page 691   Baking with Rye Flour

Compared to breads based on white flour milled solely from the part of the wheat kernel called the endosperm (ex., *Bread* or *All-purpose Flour*), breads made with Rye flour are handled differently at several phases of bread baking:

- The ddt° is higher.
- The Development speed is slower, the time is shorter.
- Shaping requires a gentler touch.
- Proofing temperature is warmer and Proofing time often shorter.

The reasons for these adjustments include:

- Rye flour contains a type of starch called a *pentosan* which, when not taken into account, causes a gummy texture in the bread.
- The lower protein content of rye flour makes loaves less able to keep their shape while proofing.
- Reduced protein calls for a gentler touch, especially during the Development Phase. (*HTBB*, p 350–60)

Page 691   Rye Flours and Meals

Whole kernels are called *Rye Berries*. Berries can be ground to a *Rye Meal*, its texture can be coarse or medium. In some markets these products are labeled as *Pumpernickel Meal*. When rye berries are **finely** ground, the result is called *Rye Flour*. And since we're still talking about the entire kernel in this case, it's often identified as *Whole Rye Flour*.

All these meals and flours are versions of the whole grain, breads made from these are flavorful and nutritious. The various degrees of coarseness determine the uniformity of the crumb structure. *Whole Rye Flour* for more uniformity, *Coarse Rye Meal* for less.

The rye berry can be stripped of its bran and germ, leaving only the portion of the grain called the endosperm. Often finely ground, this product is sold as *Medium* or *Light Rye Flour*. Rye Flour is analogous to white flour (like *Bread* or *All-purpose*). Breads made from these rye flours have less flavor and nutrition than ones using rye meal.

Medium and *Light Rye* flour bring a fine texture to a rye bread. They are handled similarly to white flour, so these products give beginning bakers more confidence when exploring these breads. The rye breads in **HTBB** use Medium and Light Rye flours. As you develop your baker's touch, you can substitute some of the rye flour in a formula with rye meal. Start with fine to medium ground meals and work your way to coarse ground as your skill develops.

*The term **Pumpernickel Flour** has conflicting standards of identity that vary according to manufacturer. Most often the term refers to whole rye berries, finely ground.* (**HTBB, p 352**)

Page 693   Scoring Rye Breads

Scoring proofed breads before baking gives them designated areas in which to release steam and CO2 during oven spring. As in most crafts, a functional technique like this provides the craftsperson opportunity to display personal style.

For example and compared to the French versions, German Ryes have more score marks. They are spaced closer together and generally form a 25-degree angle to the horizontal. French score marks, as seen on a Baguette, are more acute and form a 75-degree angle. (**HTBB, p 358–9**)

Page 693   Starch Wash for Rye Breads

American rye breads often have a high percent of white flour and do not include a Levain or Wild Yeast Culture in the dough. These breads develop small tears in their surface when proofing and can lose their shape in the oven. As a precaution, a rice flour and water paste is often painted over the proofed breads. The starch seals these tears and helps the tender crust resist splitting during the oven spring stage of baking. As it bakes, the starch paste forms a shiny crust.

The rye breads in this book are based on a Levain. The acidity of the Levain strengthens the protein structure of dough. This gives them improved resilience during Oven Spring.

Applying a starch wash to these rye breads is done more for appearance sake. It's the baker's option. **(HTBB, p 358)**

Page 696   Increased dough temperature for Rye Breads

A Rye Bread performs better when its dough temperature is two degrees higher than a bread made with white flour. A higher dough temperature is a strategy to control the pentosans in rye flour, the sugar molecules that cause gumminess in rye bread.

A higher dough temperature means the breads proof in a shorter time than breads made entirely with white flour. Keep an eye on your ryes. When you see small tears in the surface, they're ready for the oven. A gentle press on the side of a proofed rye will just barely recover, leaving a visible indentation. **(HTBB, p 354)**

Page 708   Gliadin, Glutenin, and the types of gluten they form

These are both amino acids found in flour. When mixed with water, they join together to form the protein network called *gluten*. The technique you choose for developing (kneading) the dough favors one of these amino acids over the other.

When you use a *repeated* stretch, fold, and roll technique, the dough becomes firm and tight. It springs back more each time it is stretched. This property is called *elasticity*. The more pressure and time spent developing the dough, the more *elastic* the gluten becomes. Ultimately, the dough behaves more like a rubber band. This is the amino acid *Glutenin* at work.

When you rest dough, during an Autolyse for example, it develops an ability to stretch and then relax, retracting just slightly. This property is *extensibility*. The longer the dough rests, with *periodic* stretch and folds instead of repeated kneading, the more *extensible* the gluten becomes.

With an extensible dough, the baker can collect large air cells with irregular distribution inside the dough. This is *Gliadin* in action. **(HTBB, p 92–3)**

Appendix 2
Understanding the Formulas

See the Sample Formula on page 263.

 Salt

The Baker's Percent (BP%) of Salt in the formulas is based on the Flour used only in the Main Dough. It does not include the Flour in the Starter Culture or the Flour used in the Levain.

If this explanation suffices, you don't need to read the rest of section 1. I'll see you in the next section, **2 Mise en Place Temperatures**.

If you're still with me, here's my reasoning behind Baker's Percent of Salt based only on the Flour used to make the main dough. In the industry, bread formulas generally include ALL Flour used in the dough. That means accounting for the Flour used to feed the Culture and the Flour used to build the Levain. When all of this is taken into account, most breads average a Baker's Percent of 2% Salt in the Total Formula.

When you are managing a production shop with multiple batches of different breads, this is a useful rule of thumb. Especially when you need to adjust a formula from 200 pounds of flour to 275 pounds, for example.

That's 75 more pounds of flour. At 2%, that's one and a half pounds more Salt you'll need. Simple as that.

The Purchasing Director for the bakeshop appreciates this 2-percent rule, too. He or she knows that for every 1,000 pounds of flour that the baker orders, there needs to be 20 pounds of Salt on the requisition slip.

An interesting thing happens though, when you calculate the BP% of Salt only on the Flour in the Main Dough. Instead of 2%, you find numbers like 2.5%, 2.8%, and sometimes even 3%.

When the percents vary, as in these examples, there's an opportunity to learn something about the particular dough formula you're working with. Here are the Baker's Percents of Salt from three of the formulas in this book: *Pain au Levain, One-Build Sourdough Bread*, and *Two-Build Sourdough Bread*.

Bread	BP% Salt in Total Formula	BP% Salt in Main Dough
Pain au Levain	2%	2.5%
One-Build Sourdough Bread	2%	2.7%
Two-Build Sourdough Bread	2%	2.8%

When you look at the *Baker's Percent of Salt in the Total Formula*, these three breads are the same. At least as far as Salt is concerned. But when you look at the *BP% Salt in the Main Dough*—not including Flour from the Starter Culture or the Levain or Build—something seems to be happening that makes each dough need a different percent of Salt by the time it reaches the Mixing Phase for the Main Dough.

Now add another column and include the *BP% of Levain or Build* for each bread:

Bread	BP% Salt in Total Formula	BP% Salt in Main Dough	BP% Levain or Build
Pain au Levain	2%	2.5%	20%
One-Build Sourdough	2%	2.7%	50%
Two-Build Sourdough	2%	2.8%	80%

There's a clear relationship—the more sour Levain you use to make a main dough, the more salt you need. Seems straightforward enough.

Compare the last two columns in the table above. 20% Levain uses 2.5% Salt in the maindough. At 50% Levain, the BP% Salt increases to 2.7%. When the main dough includes 80% Levain, the BP% Salt is even higher, at 2.8%.

It's even more clear when you taste these breads in a comparative flight:

> The **Pain au Levain** has a mild sourness, the wheat flavor of the grain is pronounced.
> The main dough has 2.5% Salt.

> The **One-Build Sourdough Bread** has a moderate sourness, the taste of the grain is moderate, too.
> The main dough here has 2.7% Salt.

The ***Two-Build Sourdough Bread*** has a high sourness. The grain character of the flour is low in comparison.

The main dough has 2.8% Salt.

The more sour something is, the more salt you need to balance its basic taste profile. Chefs know this intuitively. When they reduce white wine, shallots, and vinegar to make an emulsion sauce like Beurre Blanc, they instinctively reach for more salt. Same thing when they make a vinaigrette.

This simple relationship helps demystify the concept of Baker's Percent. Maybe that's why I often get reassuring nods from students—especially chef students—when they see that bread baking is more like cooking than they first thought.

Mise en Place Temperatures

In the Mise en Place section of the Formulas, I've made a few assumptions:

> The ambient temperature of your **bakeshop is 76°F**.
> Let's say the **Flour is 74°F**. (Flour temperature is usually a few degrees cooler than the bakeshop.)

Based on these assumptions, if you:

> Temper your **Levain to 70°F** and
> Use **Water at 92°F**

Then:

> your **Main Dough** has a temperature close to **78°F** once you develop it.

Remember, the Mise en Place temperatures are based on assumptions. That means the Water Temperature can be changed. And, it often needs to be.

In summer, your flour might be much warmer. In winter, the bakeshop is usually cooler. For better results, a baker always takes the temperature of the Flour and the Bakeshop to determine what the Water Temperature needs to be.

Wild Yeast Breads have better flavor and more consistent leavening when the temperatures of the Basic Levain and the Main

Dough are on target. For Wild Yeast Breads, the main dough has a **ddt°** (desired dough temperature) of 78°F. This target temperature for the dough shouldn't be changed. Change the H20 Temp° before mixing to get the 78°F target each time.

3 Autolyse (*Auto lees*)

Nothing says *modern bread baking* more than the **Autolyse** technique. It's the brief period of rest once the flour and water from a main dough have been combined. It was first published in 1990 by Professor Raymond Calvel, a French chemist whose long nights in the lab were often supplemented with study breaks to shape, proof, and bake crusty bread loaves.

Once you wave the magic wand of *Autolyse* over the mass of flour and water, the ingredients knit together, forming strands of stretchable gluten. The dough *kneads itself,* a clumsy translation of the term.

Professor Calvel's advice is clear. Combine Flour and Water—nothing else, mind you. Especially not Salt and no Starter Culture or commercial Yeast. And give the Flour/Water mixture 20 minutes to knead itself together.

The result is a bread whose interior texture is tender yet chewy, sort of an *al dente* for bread. Compared to just about anything you could get from a machine mixer, the flavor is better, the texture superior.

Since its invention, the *autolyse* has taken its rightful place in the hierarchy of craft bread baking techniques. In the process, however, it's had to give a little to retain its spot on the leader board.

In this book for example, the main doughs combine Water, Flour, Starter Culture, and Salt. Then the dough is *autolysed.* Mostly the time period is only 15 minutes, too, instead of the originally suggested 20.

This may sound like bread heresy. Especially in light of the Professor's original prescription for good bread.

Turns out that the texture and flavor differences between a dough with a 15-minute rest period and one with a 30-minute one are small. I've done tests, though surely inconclusive.

I've enlisted the help of Certified Master Tasters™ (CMT's). There's a baseline of palate acuity that these chefs have to display before being invited for the extensive palate training required to carry the letters *CMT™* after their names. These are chefs who can detect parts per million of things.

Just for starters, an applicant to a CMT training program is given three samples of *water*. In two of them, there's Saltwater. In the third, just plain Water. The challenge is to pick the one that's different.

The trick is that there's only 4 or 5 parts per million of Salt dissolved in the Water.

To offer a visualization, that's the equivalent of a box of Kosher Salt dissolved in an Olympic swimming pool. Except for the chlorine, that's about what 4 parts per million of Salt might taste like.

Back to the *Autolyse Taste Test:*

In my experiments, there were ten to twelve CMT's per panel. I served them side-by-side samples of two different breads. One with a 15-minute autolyse, the other with 30.

In a number of tests, the CMT's found no significant difference between a bread with a 15-minute autolyse and one that was twice as long. In another round of tests, they couldn't conclusively agree on whether or not the texture of the bread was different when it was autolysed with the Salt or without it.

OK. Not enough statistical evidence to make a declaration. But enough proof for me, a baking instructor, to realize that small modifications can creep into your bread baking procedures and not noticeably change the results.

For more about the *Autolyse*, see pages 82–83.

Baker's Percent (BP%)

The Baker's Percents are based on the ingredient weights in grams. Using grams helps you see the relationship among the ingredients and reinforces your ability to think in terms of Baker's Percent. Recall that a baker divides the weight of a single ingredient by the total weight of the Flour in the formula to find its Baker's Percent.

5 Grams

In these bread formulas, the gram weights are the ones that count. These are the ones that are multiplied to give larger yields. These are the numbers you want to work with for better results and an easier time of things in the bakeshop.

For the basic yield of each formula, ingredient weights are in grams or in ounces and pounds. Ingredient weights for 8-Quart and 20-Quart mixers are given only in grams. If you have a scale that reads decimal pounds, refer to **HTBB**, Appendix 5, page 470.

6 Formula Yield

The Yield listed in the formula is approximate.

The formulas account for the loss of dough in the production process. Dough is lost to the mixer, some is lost on the bench, some on your scraper. What about the small piece you used for windowpane?

7 About Formula Yield (Number of Pieces)

Q: How many loaves of bread will I get from each formula?

A: In a professional bakeshop, the formula yield is rarely given in number of loaves. It's listed as a total weight.

The baker decides what size breads to make, not the formula. Boules, loaves, or slider rolls. Use this table when calculating the number of pieces and the size of your breads.

Q: How do I read the table?

A: For each bread, the Basic Yield appears in the shaded column of the formula table.

	Basic Yield 4 1/2 or 6 Qt	8 Qt	20 Qt
Formula Yield, approximately	1,000 g	1,800 g	5,000 g
Number of Pieces, approximately	1 @ 2#, or 2 @ 1#	2 @ 2#, or 3 @ 1# 4 oz, or 4 @ 1#	5 @ 2#, or 8 @ 1# 4 oz

A 1,000 gram batch is easy to make completely by hand, directly on the bench. It also fits a tabletop mixer with a bowl capacity of 4-1/2 to 6 quarts.

Each Basic Formula yields about 1,000 grams. That's enough dough for one 2-pound Boule or two 1-pound Loaves. But you can scale your breads at any weight, like 90-gram Slider Rolls or 4-ounce Sandwich Buns. Four ounces is 120 grams, so you'd end up with 8 Sandwich Buns from the basic 1,000-gram yield.

A rule of thumb is that 500 grams makes a 1-pound rustic loaf. That's a good size when learning how to bake hearth breads. The Basic Yield for each bread makes two of these.

500 grams is about 17-1/2 ounces. When baking a hearth bread, you can expect a 10% loss of dough weight during the bake due to water evaporation. So the 500 grams of dough that went into the oven comes out close to 450 grams. Which is darned close to one pound.

Once you start working with these formulas, your baker's instinct will kick in and you'll think intuitively about Yield and number of loaves.

8 Bowl Capacity (for Machine Mixers)

If you make these breads in a machine mixer, I assume you're working with a vertical mixer. That's a mixer on which the dough hook is aligned on a vertical axis. The KitchenAid™ Tabletop Mixer and the 20- and 30-Quart Hobarts™ found in baking classrooms are examples of vertical mixers.

It may seem that any size dough can be developed in any size machine. This is false reasoning. For the sake of dough and machine both, there is a recommended weight of dough for each type of machine. And for the capacity of each different mixing bowl that fits onto that mixer.

When there's not enough dough in the mixing bowl, a machine mixer over-develops the bread. It gets tough. When there's too much dough in the mixing bowl, the effect is reversed—it's the machine that gets overworked. Gaskets break, oil leaks down the dough hook, other mechanical problems pop up.

If you use a machine mixer, use the correct size machine for the amount of dough you are making.

9 Ounces

In the Basic Formula, the weights given in *ounces* are approximated from the *gram weights* for each ingredient.

The *ounce weights* have been rounded up or down, so things are easy to scale. One and a half ounces is quicker to weigh than one and two-fifths. It's also less likely that a scaling error will subvert your efforts when the weights are rounded.

When you total up all the *ounce weights* in a formula, it doesn't always equal the corresponding total of grams. Don't worry. The formulas have been tested using both systems.

Warning! Don't multiply the *ounce weights* to give a larger yield. What is a small variation at one loaf multiplies into a large difference as the formula is scaled up. *Always use the gram weights when increasing the yield of your formula.*

10 Levain

When making Wild Yeast Breads, it's frustrating to find yourself short about 20 grams of Levain. The formulas in this book give you a little more Levain than you'll need.

Don't assume that all the Levain from a formula is intended to be used. Always scale your fermented Levain when adding it to the main dough.

When there's a small amount of dough or Levain left over, add it to the compost bin.

11 8-Quart and 20-Quart Formulas

There are ingredient weights for 8-Quart and 20-Quart mixers. These weights yield 1,800 grams and 5,000 grams of dough, respectively. Ingredient weights are given in grams.

Sample Formula

Pain au Levain

Formula, Main Dough

| Ingredient | BP% | 4-1/2 or 6 Qt | | 8 Qt | 20 Qt |
		Ounces	Grams		
Basic Levain (from above) ⑩	20%	4 oz ⑨	120 g ⑤	240 g	500 g
Water	70%	14 oz	400 g	800 g	1,725 g
Whole Wheat Flour	20%	4 oz	120 g	240 g	500 g
Bread Flour	80%	1 #	450 g	900 g	2,000 g
Salt ①	2.5%	1/2 oz	14 g	30 g	64 g
Yields ⑥		2# 2 oz	950 g	**1,800 g**	**4,100 g**
Number of pieces		⑦	See *About Formula Yields*		

④ ⑧ ⑪

Procedure, Main Dough

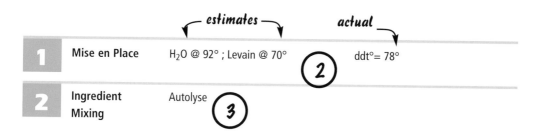

		┌ *estimates* ┐	*actual* ┐
1	Mise en Place	H₂O @ 92° ; Levain @ 70°	ddt°= 78° ②
2	Ingredient Mixing	Autolyse ③	

Appendix 3
About a Commercial Deck Oven

Baking Chart

Pain au Levain
@ 2# to 2# 2 oz

Oven	Stage I	¿Steam?	Vent @	Stage II	Duration	Int. temp°
Deck	500° (9.9.1) [3.3.1]	10 secs	8 m	435° (6.6.0) [2.2.0]	+ 8 m • • • • • • • • • check*/rotate + 8 to 10 m more	200°
Rack (w/convection + oven stone)	440°	10 secs	8 m	390°	+ 8 m • • • • • • • • • check*/rotate + 8 to 10 m more	200°

The far left column of the sample Baking Chart includes oven times and temperatures for two different types of ovens. The top row the chart labeled **Deck** refers to the ovens found in professional bakeries, restaurants, and culinary schools. Inside a deck oven there are no moveable shelves so the distance between the breads and the ceiling of the oven chamber is fixed. Depending on the manufacturer, the chamber height ranges from 7 to 10 inches. Pizza ovens, like the kind you find at most neighborhood pizzerias, are shorter versions of the deck oven with heights from 6 to 8 inches.

Deck ovens typically have burners or heating elements below the hearth (the surface of the deck) and in the ceiling above the baking area. When these burners are independently controlled, the baker can adjust the heat profile of the oven chamber. For the bottom heating element, a higher setting produces crisper pizza crusts. On the other hand, a low element setting is used for longer-baking hearth breads so the bottom crusts don't burn.

Element settings create the heat profile of a deck oven.

**500°F
(9.9.1)**

To preheat the oven for Pain au Levain the oven temperature, or set point, is 500°F. The settings (9.9.1) refer to the independent heating elements in the ceiling and in the hearth. The numbers are based on a scale of 0 (zero) to 10, 10 being maximum.

The element settings draw a picture of the oven's *heat profile*.

Typical Icon on Oven	What the Settings Mean

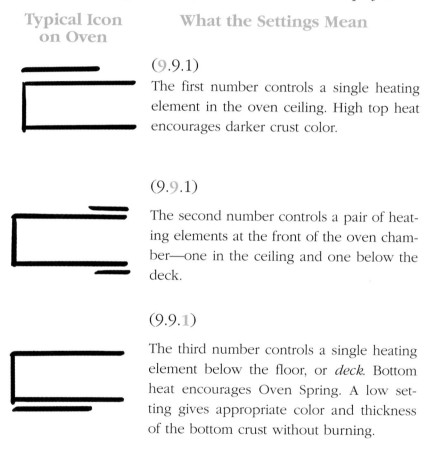

(9.9.1)

The first number controls a single heating element in the oven ceiling. High top heat encourages darker crust color.

(9.9.1)

The second number controls a pair of heating elements at the front of the oven chamber—one in the ceiling and one below the deck.

(9.9.1)

The third number controls a single heating element below the floor, or *deck*. Bottom heat encourages Oven Spring. A low setting gives appropriate color and thickness of the bottom crust without burning.

[3.3.1] Some manufacturers have element settings ranging from **0** through **4**. Zero is *Off*, 4 is *Maximum*.

Use element settings in **[brackets]** for these oven models.

In Stage II for Pain au Levain, the oven temperature and heat profile are changed.

(6.6.0)

After the oven is vented, the top and front element settings are reduced. A moderate heat intensity delivers penetrating heat to bake the interior of the bread thoroughly-- without risking a burnt top crust.

(6.6.0)

Turning the bottom element to zero prevents a burnt bottom crust, especially if the baker must extended the total baking time. Residual heat of the hearth continues to bake the bread from below.

(6.6.0)

When you assess how your bread is baking halfway through Stage II, check the color of the bottom crust. If the color is pale, you can increase the bottom heating element to 1 or 2, as necessary.

[2.2.0]
Use numbers in brackets for oven models with settings ranging from zero to 4.

In the bottom row of the baking chart, **_Rack Oven_** is the term for ovens with adjustable shelves (racks) inside the oven chamber. Most home ovens are in this category. Rack ovens, with out without convection, don't have separately controlled heating elements inside the oven chamber. The oven set point for a rack oven lists only the temperature setting. In this example, 440°F.

Appendix 4
Bibliography

For the aspiring baker looking for more information, here is a short list of books I refer to time and again. Some focus on fermentation and wild yeast, others on bread baking in general. The books about wood-fired ovens make the cut because they describe the baking process evocatively and with great detail.

There's one book that doesn't address bread baking directly. **The Third Plate** speaks instead to the state of our soil, the nurturing foundation of the foods—and especially grains—we grow and harvest as a nation.

The modern, responsible baker must consider the sustainability of our soil and the nutritional value it delivers to our wheat and other grains. That's what we ultimately transfer to our bodies through the bread we bake.

Advanced Bread and Pastry, A Professional Approach, Michel Suas, Delmar Cengage Learning, 2009

The Art of Fermentation, An In-depth Exploration of Essential Concepts and Processes from Around the World, Sandor Ellix Katz, Chelsea Green Publishing, 2012

Artisan Baking Across America, Maggie Glezer, Artisan Publishers, 2000

Bread, A Baker's Book of Techniques and Recipes, Jeffrey Hamelman, John Wiley & Sons, 2004.

The Bread Builders, Hearth Loaves and Masonry Ovens, Daniel Wing and Alan Scott, Chelsea Green publishing, 1999

From the Wood-Fired Oven, New and Traditional Techniques for Cooking and Baking with Fire, Richard Miscovich, Chelsea Green Publishing, 2013

Mastering Fermentation, Recipes for Making and Cooking with Fermented Foods, Mary Karlin, Ten Speed Press, 2013

My Bread, the Revolutionary No-work, No-knead Method, Jim Lahey, W. W. Norton & Co., 2009

Peter Reinhart's Whole Grain Breads, Ten Speed Press, 2007

Simply Ancient Grains, Maria Speck, Ten Speed Press, 2015

Tartine No. 3, Chad Robertson, Chronicle Books, 2013

The Taste of Bread, Raymond Calvel, Aspen Publishers, English translation, 2001

The Third Plate, Field Notes on the Future of Food, Dan Barber, The Penguin Press, 2014

Appendix 5
My Short List

There are many quality bakers, any list I compiled would surely overlook as many as I included. Instead, I offer a list of colleagues who've opened their bakeries and milling operations to me and shared inspiring and treasured conversations about our craft. I'm especially inspired by the consistent quality of the breads that fill their shelves, delivery trucks, or farmers' market stands.

Bakers and their Bakeries . . .

Acme Bread Corporation, Steve Sullivan, Berkeley, CA
Amy's Breads, Amy Scherber, New York, NY
Breadfarm, Scott Mangold, Bow, WA
Crossroads Bake Shop, Paul Rizzo, Doylestown, PA
Essential Baking Company, Portland, OR
Farm and Sparrow, David Bauer, Candler, NC
Grand Central Baking Company, Portland, OR and Seattle, WA
Josey Baker Breads, Josey Baker, SF, CA
Little T American Bakery, Portland, OR
Macrina Bakery, Seattle, WA
Metropolitan Bakery, James Barrett, Philadelphia, PA
Orwasher's Bakery, Keith Cohen, New York, NY
Pearl Bakery, Portland, OR
Ponsford's Place, Craig Ponsford, San Rafael, CA
Semifreddi's Bakery, Kensington, CA
Serious Pie, Seattle, WA
Sullivan Street Bakery, Jim Lahey, New York, NY
Tartine Bakery, Chad Robertson, SF, CA

Millers . . .

Anson Mills, Glenn Roberts, Columbia, SC
Castle Valley Mill, Mark and Fran Fischer, Doylestown, PA
Camas Country Mill, Eugene, OR
Central Milling, Nicky Giusto, Petaluma, CA
Lindley Mills, Joe Lindley, Graham, NC

Author's Lagniappe

It made perfect sense to me that my first book about bread should include a recipe for Bread Pudding, a comfort food classic. After all, a lot of chefs and bakers collect pieces of leftover bread in the freezer, awaiting a turkey to stuff or a reason to turn them into something else.

My editor wasn't as sure since it wouldn't fit any of the recipe categories in the book. "So we'll have a lagniappe," I said, remembering a word I'd learned from my restaurant time in New Orleans. *Lagniappe*—it means a small gift, an extra treat.

By the time this conversation had come about, the bulk of the manuscript was set and no additions were allowed. Luckily, the typesetters were still working on the indexes, so that's where the recipe ended up, tucked in near the end of the book. That's how my *Author's Lagniappe* tradition began.

In my baking classrooms, students routinely ask what they can do with the part that's discarded each time they feed their Starter Cultures. *Make pizza dough with it!* is the first thing that comes to mind.

Pizza dough made with Starter Culture is easier to shape. The dough is less elastic, so it doesn't fight you or your rolling pin. Most students can stretch it by hand on the first try.

Here's a recipe for Sourdough Pizza Dough that's quick and easy. As a double lagniappe, there's a recipe for a quick white sauce, too. Its richness balances the slight tanginess of the dough.

For shaping, saucing, and topping the pie, I'll leave that to you. That you're reading a book on wild yeast breads tells me you've likely made a pizza or two at home, or that you own one of the reliable books on the topic. If not, I recommend Tony Gemignani's *The Pizza Bible*, Jim Lahey's *My Pizza*, Peter Reinhart's *American Pie*, or if you cook with live fire, Richard Miscovich's *From the Wood-Fired Oven*. There are two formulas in my first book, along with a photo technique section for shaping.

A favorite of mine is the mushroom pie. Spread a thin layer of cream sauce over the dough before adding anything else. The cream sauce forms a moisture barrier so the crust stays crispy longer once it arrives at your table. Even if you're planning to use a tomato-based sauce or a pesto for your creation, painting a thin layer of cream sauce on the dough first brings richness to your pies.

Slice the mushrooms as thin as possible. In the classroom we use a mandoline—an adjustable, sliding board-looking tool with a razor sharp cutting edge. At home I use a Japanese *Santoku* knife to get slices 1/16th of an inch or less.

Mushrooms have a high water content and thicker slices retain more moisture. Moisture is the antagonist of a crispy crust. The thinner the mushrooms are sliced, the more of their surface area is exposed and the faster their moisture evaporates. In the oven's high heat, this effect lets a pile of mushrooms shrink to a third of its height, concentrating the earthy flavor.

As you slice the mushrooms, spread them on a baking tray or large plate that's lined with a paper towel. Let them air-dry for 10 minutes or so and then toss them with sea salt and, if you have some, fresh thyme. Heap the mushrooms over the cream sauce layer on your dough.

When your pie emerges from the oven, place it on a cooling rack for a minute or two so it sets. Extra virgin olive oil and coarse sea salt can be added at the table.

San Francisco Sourdough Pizza Dough

Ingredients

5 oz	Water
1/8 oz (half of one packet)	Dry yeast (any type)
8 oz	Starter Culture (ripe) @ ambient temp°
2 teaspoons	Honey
2 Tablespoons	Olive oil
11 oz	All-Purpose Flour
2 teaspoons	Salt
as needed to coat dough	Olive oil

Procedure

1. Warm the Water to 100°. Add Dry Yeast. Allow to hydrate thoroughly, about 5 minutes.

2. Add Starter Culture.

3. Add Honey and Oil.

4. Add Flour and Salt.

5. Stir until all flour is moistened.

6. Develop on medium speed for 3 minutes.

7. Rest 5 minutes, covered.

8. Develop on low speed for 3 minutes more.

9. Ferment dough for 30 minutes @ 80°F.

10. Divide dough into three 8-ounce rounds. Use your hands to lightly coat the dough balls with olive oil. Place on half sheet tray lined with parchment paper that's been lightly brushed with olive oil. Cover with plastic wrap.

11. Refrigerate for 30 minutes more or until needed (see *Understanding* below). Let sit 15 minutes before stretching.

Understanding

If you bake pizza the same day you make the dough, the refrigerated dough balls will hold their shape for about 2 hours. Stored longer than that, they become slack or they begin to rise. Don't stretch them at this point. You won't get a round pie.

Instead, just re-round the dough balls. Place them on the oiled parchment and cover with plastic again. After a 30-minute rest at ambient temperature, they're ready for you.

White Sauce

Ingredients

> 3 Tablespoons white wine
> 2 teaspoons white (or red) wine vinegar
> 1 clove garlic, minced
> 1/4 teaspoon salt
>
> 1 cup heavy cream (any type)
>
> Salt & fresh-ground black pepper to taste

Procedure

1. Combine wine, vinegar, garlic, and salt in a small saucepan. Boil until reduced to almost dry. Remove from heat for one minute.

2. Add cream. Return to medium heat and simmer 5 minutes, stirring occasionally.
   Remove from heat and let cool.
3. Check the thickness of the sauce (see *Understanding* below).
4. Season with pepper and add salt if needed.
5. Cover and refrigerator. Can keep up to 4 days.
   Bring to ambient temperature before using.

Understanding

This is an example of what's called a *reduction sauce*. As it simmers, water evaporates from the cream. As the volume reduces, the cream gets thicker.

The technique is simple and straightforward. Judging if the sauce is thick enough is a learned skill. After two or three times, you'll develop your eye and know just when to pull the sauce from the heat.

A cream reduction sauce thickens as it cools. When you dip a teaspoon into the sauce to test it, make sure the sauce is warm to the touch, not hot. The sauce should be thick enough to barely coat the back of the spoon when you lift it vertically from the sauce.

If it runs off the spoon and looks watery, return the sauce to the stove, cook it 2 or 3 minutes more. Cool it and test again.

When you spread the cooled sauce over the stretched dough, the sauce behaves like room temperature butter. If it's pasty, thick, or catches the dough when spread, add a little cool water to thin it.

If it's still runny, don't worry about it. Next time you'll simmer it a little longer.

Acknowledgements

Asking for an endorsement from respected authors in whose field you seek to contribute can be nerve-racking. You seek the most knowledgeable minds, and this raises the bar the value your own book needs to bring. That authors whose work I admire would find time to read my manuscript was fortune enough. For their words of praise that greet my readers on the very first page of this book, I could not be more grateful. Thank you to Mary Karlin, Nathan Myhrvold, Peter Reinhart, and Maria Speck.

To William Zinsser, my writing mentor. When discussing the shape this book would take, his advice was *trust the process*. At first I thought this overly simplistic. Once deep in writing the book, those three words became terrifying. They were literally demanding my blind faith since the book had yet to reveal a singular purpose or direction.

I pushed on in several directions, realizing that my editor would scrap a lot of the writing, delete pages, and reduce whole paragraphs to single sentences. I learned to put my trust in the process. Looking back, I realized those guiding words had been spoken by a true master. Thank you, Bill.

For sharing your bakery during the recipe development phase of this book, the warmth of your faculty and staff, and the inquisitive minds and palates of your students, I am grateful to the *Le Cordon Bleu* in San Francisco, neé the *California Culinary Academy*. Special thanks to Timothy Grable, M.Ed., Director of Education and Chef Lisa Wilson, Director of Career Services.

To Rubin Glickman, who taught me to listen. You were right, it *did* change my life!

For clarifying my questions about fermentation, I am grateful to Megan Fiskelments, Lee S. Glass MD, Sandor Ellix Katz, and Debra Wink.

For feedback about sensory science while I developed *Aroma & Flavor Notes for Bread*, thanks to Anne Noble and Leslie Norris. Developing my professional palate and learning the sensory science of the consumer product industry is a continuing benefit of my work with *Chef'sBest*. Thank you to Lisa Ligouri and Scott Thompson.

Among an army of recipe testers, two chef instructors and their students were especially helpful in troubleshooting early versions of these breads. To Leslie Eckert at the *International Culinary Schools at the Art Institute* in Tampa, FL and in Charlotte, NC and to Greg Schnorr at the *Wine Country Culinary Institute at Walla Walla Community College*, thanks for the constructive feedback. The breads are better for it.

For hands-on work in producing the book, thanks to Susie Kenyon at Sans Serif for layout and typesetting and for your patience and diligence during this project. Thank you to Kathy Brown at Sheridan Printing, Martin J. Taras for your technique photos, Nancy Walker for the author portrait, Wendy Hummel Boord for design and layout of the technical photo section and for the cover design, Clay Cleaver for turning photos into instructional sketches, and Robert Shepherd for copyright guidance.

To all the proofreaders, especially Tina Michalik and Lynne Char Bennett.

In the course of writing this book, I was fortunate to work with several authorities in wheat farming, milling, and flour analysis. Thank you to Richard S. Little, Organic Wheat Breeding Specialist, University of Nebraka-Lincoln and to Janice Cooper, Director of the California Wheat Commission.

Dr. Stephen Jones introduced me to the heirloom grains of the Pacific Northwest. His *Bread Lab* at *Washington State University* is a valuable resource for our growing awareness of these wheats and the flours made from them. To share his passion and knowledge, Steve hosts an annual educational conference. Whether your interest is farming, milling, baking, brewing, or malting, the *Grain Gathering* has cutting-edge seminars to further your knowledge and skills.

A special thank you to Tracey Chiah, bread baker and photographer. Your photo is the perfect one for my cover. Thank you for being so generous.

Supporters of *How To Bake Bread: The Five Families of Bread®*

To the generous and wise spirits who saw potential in my first book. You helped build a strong foundation on which this second book can stand.

A special thanks to Linda Carucci who supported me at the *International Culinary School at the Art Institute* in San Francisco. For bringing *HTBB* into the Art Institute's bakery curriculum, I am grateful for the support of Michael Nenes, William Tillinghast, Jonathan Gonzalez, Mark Davis, Joseph LaVilla, and David Hendricksen.

To the chef instructors and directors who brought my book into their classrooms:

Marc J-P Aguilera, Andrea Alexander, Lois Arguello, Mike Autenrieth, Christophe Bernard, Mike Buttles, Ricardo Castro, Ashley Chen, Matthieu Chamussy, Mark Facklam, Damian Fraase, Jim Gallivan, Mariela Genco, Norman Hart, Eyad Joseph, Jack Kane, Paul Kennedy, Frank Krause, Laird Livingston, Ian Mackay, Anthony Mandriota, Mark Martin, Larry Matson, Mark Mattern, Dan Mattos, Joseph O'Donnell, Phil Pinkney, Toussaint Potter, Mauro Rossi, Ken Rubin, Steven Simpson, Bill Sy, Dan Taylor, Steve Venne, Paul Vernall, Susan Wigley, Michael Zappone.

Edouard Cointreau, *Gourmand International.* By naming *HTBB* the *"Best Bread Book in the World"* at the 2010 Paris Cookbook Fair, you literally brought my book onto the world stage.

Gigi Marino, editor of the *Bucknellian* magazine. Bucknell University's Alumni Office, Kristen Stetler, Phil Kim, and Matt Hughes.

Toni Raymus and the *Great Valley Bookfest*, Manteca, CA.

Matthew Bennett, my promoter, handler, and dear friend in Denver, CO. Thanks for the Rocky Mountain welcome. David Yim, thanks for all your help.

Stephanie Swane, Publisher, *Moderniste Cuisine*, for your guidance, collegiality, and friendship.

Brianne Goodspeed at *Chelsea Green Publishing*, for guiding me through my first foreign rights contract.

Senac, São Paulo, Brazil, for *Como Assar Pães*, the lyrical translation of *HTBB* for the Brazilian culinary market.

The *American Culinary Federation* for making me a regular presenter at their national conferences. Michelle Whitfield, Gloria Wombolt, and Liz Knapke. From the *National Culinary Review*, Kaye Orde, editor-in-chief, and Wendy Hummel Boord, graphics. From *Sizzle* Magazine, Leah Craig.

Denise Michelsen, my acquisitions editor at *Craftsy*, and Jared Maher, my instructional producer. And to Julia Taylor-Brown who brought me into the fold. Special thanks to Collette Christian for introducing me to the team and for all your Crafty collegiality.

For being the first to sell, distribute, and promote *HTBB* on the national scale, I am thankful to *Partners West, Publishers Weekly, QGI Publishers*, and *Barnes & Noble*.

For their grassroots support, thank you to:

Books Inc., The West's Oldest Independent Bookseller,
San Francisco Bay Area

Celia Sack, *Omnivore Books*, SF, CA

Matt Sartwell, *Kitchen Arts & Letters*, NYC

Mariella Esposito, *Fante's Kitchen Shop*, Phila, PA

Draeger's Cooking School, San Mateo, CA

Ramekins Cooking School, Sonoma, CA

Epicurean Exchange, Orinda, CA

Judith Friedman, *The Natural Gourmet Institute*, New York, NY

Nancy Kux, *The Baker's Dozen* in SF, CA

Jody Liano, *San Francisco Cooking School,* and pastry chef Nicole Plue for inviting me to work with your talented students.

Francisco Migoya and his team of bread bakers, *Moderniste Cuisine,* Bellevue, WA

Tim Green and *WoodStone Corporation*, Bellingham, WA

Simran Sethi, special thanks for the honor of contributing to your inspiring book *Bread, Wine, Chocolate: The Slow Loss of Foods We Love*.

To Gregory Willis, thanks for your collegiality and friendship; Devon MacGregor, for the always spirited and often spiritual discussions; Shelley Handler, for helping me keep my sense of humor intact; Andrew Verna, first a student, then an apprentice, always my friend; Debbie Dunn and Jerry Geist; Michael Weller; Debbie Hohener; Butch Dutton; Jim McCloskey; Lorenzo Polegri and his *Ristorante Zeppelin* in Orvieto, Italy.

To Esther Press McManus, my first mentor in the kitchen. You opened the door to a life of culinary adventure, fitted me with a backpack of techniques, and set my compass so I would always be guided by the nurturing value of all foods. My gratitude and my love.

The biggest thanks are saved for last. And those go to my Family. The courage to travel unknown roads, to live, work, and learn in other countries amongst other cultures, is directly related to the amount of encouragement, support, and love you have on your home front. For that, my Family is the best!

Index

Fermentation for Pain au Levain,
89–91, 93
Ounces v. Grams, 260, 262
Oven
Chamber, Dimensions of, 108, 112
Cleaning, 121–3, Photo Gallery #11
Recovery Time for, 130
Reducing Settings during Baking, 126
Safety, 122, 123
Strategy for Rye Breads, 168
Temperatures for Wild Yeast
Breads, 130
Oven Spring, 124–5
Oven Stone (*see* Stone, Oven)

P

Pain au Levain
about, 5
H2O Temp° for, 73–4
Rx, 131–2, 201–4
Step by Step Procedures for, 73–130
Palate Development for Bread, 210–11,
Photo Gallery #21
Peel, Oven
Inverting Dough onto, 114–5,
Photo Gallery #13
Prepping a, 114
Peel, Transfer (*see* also Transfer Peel)
Using a, 156–7
pH, Vitamin C to lower, 18
Phases of Dough (*see* specific entries such
as Development or Baking)
Pizza, 271–75
Pizza Stone, (*see* Stone)
Plastic, (*see* Containers for Fermentation)
Porridge
Adding to Main Dough, 222–3
Creamy, How to Cook, 234
Porridge Breads
about, 219–26
Baking, 225
Cooling, 225
ddt°, 220
Ripening, 225–6
Schedule for, 226
Scoring, 224
Sensory of, 219

Shaping, 223
Step by Step, Photo Gallery #20
Stretch & Fold Technique for, 220–3
Portland, OR, 151, 153
Pre-ferments in Autolyse, 83
Proofing
Covering Dough during, 101
Longer, for White Flour Breads, 205, 208
Humidity during, 101
Phase, Step by Step, 101–3
Temperature during, 101
Testing for, 102–3, Photo Gallery #12
Uncovering Dough during, 102
Protease, 83
Provenance, 152, 153
Pumpernickel
American, 169
Baking, 171
Assessing when Done, 171
Using Steam during, 171
Coffee in, 170
Cocoa Powder in, 170
Meal, 173
Old World, 169

Q

Quick H2O Temp° Formula
for Basic Levain, 61
for Pain au Levain, 74

R

Rare-Medium-Well Test, 103
Raisin
H2O, 17–9
Golden, 176
Wild Yeast and, 17–8
Razor Blade (*see* Lame)
Recipe (*see* Formula [**Rx**])
Replenishing
Definition, 36
Wild Yeast Culture, 36
Recovery Time, Oven, 130
Reinhart, Peter, 15
Representative Bread
for Wild Yeast Breads, 71 *ff*
Rx **Pain au Levain**, 201–4
Ripe
Culture, 38, 44